Communications in Computer and Information Science 1291

Commenced Publication in 2007
Founding and Former Series Editors:
Simone Diniz Junqueira Barbosa, Phoebe Chen, Alfredo Cuzzocrea,
Xiaoyong Du, Orhun Kara, Ting Liu, Krishna M. Sivalingam,
Dominik Ślęzak, Takashi Washio, Xiaokang Yang, and Junsong Yuan

More information about this series at http://www.springer.com/series/7899

Enzo Rucci · Marcelo Naiouf ·
Franco Chichizola · Laura De Giusti (Eds.)

Cloud Computing, Big Data & Emerging Topics

8th Conference, JCC-BD&ET 2020
La Plata, Argentina, September 8–10, 2020
Proceedings

 Springer

Editors
Enzo Rucci (iD)
III-LIDI, Facultad de Informatica
Universidad Nacional de La Plata
La Plata, Argentina

Marcelo Naiouf (iD)
III-LIDI, Facultad de Informática
Universidad Nacional de La Plata
La Plata, Argentina

Franco Chichizola (iD)
III-LIDI, Facultad de Informática
Universidad Nacional de La Plata
La Plata, Argentina

Laura De Giusti (iD)
III-LIDI, Facultad de Informática
Universidad Nacional de La Plata and CIC
La Plata, Argentina

ISSN 1865-0929   ISSN 1865-0937   (electronic)
Communications in Computer and Information Science
ISBN 978-3-030-61217-7   ISBN 978-3-030-61218-4   (eBook)
https://doi.org/10.1007/978-3-030-61218-4

This Springer imprint is published by the registered company Springer Nature Switzerland AG
The registered company address is: Gewerbestrasse 11, 6330 Cham, Switzerland

Preface

Welcome to the proceedings of the 8th Conference on Cloud Computing, Big Data & Emerging Topics (JCC-BD&ET 2020), held in an interactive, live online setting due to the COVID-19 situation. JCC-BD&ET 2020 was organized by the III-LIDI and the Postgraduate Office, both from the School of Computer Science of the National University of La Plata, Argentina.

Since 2013, this event has been an annual meeting where ideas, projects, scientific results, and applications in cloud computing, big data, and other related areas are exchanged and disseminated. The conference focuses on the topics that allow interaction between academia, industry, and other interested parties.

JCC-BD&ET 2020 covered the following topics: cloud, edge, fog, accelerator, green, and mobile computing; cloud infrastructure and virtualization; data analytics, data intelligence, and data visualization; machine and deep learning; and special topics related to emerging technologies. In addition, special activities were also carried out, including one plenary lecture and one discussion panel.

In this edition, the conference received 36 submissions. All the accepted papers were peer-reviewed by at least three referees (single-blind review) and evaluated on the basis of technical quality, relevance, significance, and clarity. According to the recommendations of the reviewers, 11 of them were selected for this book (31% acceptance rate). We hope readers will find these contributions useful and inspiring for their future research.

Special thanks to all the people who contributed to the conference success: Program and Organizing Committees, reviewers, speakers, authors, and all conference attendees. Finally, we want to thank Springer for their support in publishing this book.

September 2020

Marcelo Naiouf
Franco Chichizola
Laura De Giusti
Enzo Rucci

The original version of the book was revised: Three modifications in the editors' affiliations have been made. The correction to the book is available at
https://doi.org/10.1007/978-3-030-61218-4_12

Organization

General Chair

Armando De Giusti   Universidad Nacional de La Plata and CONICET, Argentina

Program Committee Chairs

Marcelo Naiouf   Universidad Nacional de La Plata, Argentina
Franco Chichizola   Universidad Nacional de La Plata, Argentina
Laura De Giusti   Universidad Nacional de La Plata and CIC, Argentina
Enzo Rucci   Universidad Nacional de La Plata, Argentina

Program Committee

María José Abásolo   Universidad Nacional de La Plata and CIC, Argentina
José Aguilar   Universidad de Los Andes, Venezuela
Jorge Ardenghi   Universidad Nacional del Sur, Argentina
Javier Balladini   Universidad Nacional del Comahue, Argentina
Oscar Bria   Universidad Nacional de La Plata and INVAP, Argentina
Silvia Castro   Universidad Nacional del Sur, Argentina
Laura De Giusti   Universidad Nacional de La Plata and CIC, Argentina
Mónica Denham   Universidad Nacional de Río Negro and CONICET, Argentina
Javier Diaz   Universidad Nacional de La Plata, Argentina
Ramón Doallo   Universidade da Coruña, Spain
Marcelo Errecalde   Universidad Nacional de San Luis, Argentina
Elsa Estevez   Universidad Nacional del Sur and CONICET, Argentina
Aurelio Fernandez Bariviera   Universitat Rovira i Virgili, Spain
Fernando Emmanuel Frati   Universidad Nacional de Chilecito, Argentina
Carlos Garcia Garino   Universidad Nacional de Cuyo, Argentina
Adriana Angélica Gaudiani   Universidad Nacional de General Sarmiento, Argentina
Graciela Verónica Gil Costa   Universidad Nacional de San Luis and CONICET, Argentina
Roberto Guerrero   Universidad Nacional de San Luis, Argentina
Waldo Hasperué   Universidad Nacional de La Plata and CIC, Argentina
Francisco Daniel Igual Peña   Universidad Complutense de Madrid, Spain
Tomasz Janowski   Gdansk University of Technology, Poland
Laura Lanzarini   Universidad Nacional de La Plata, Argentina
Guillermo Leguizamón   Universidad Nacional de San Luis, Argentina

Edimara Luciano	Pontificia Universidade Católica do Rio Grande do Sul, Brazil
Emilio Luque Fadón	Universidad Autónoma de Barcelona, Spain
Mauricio Marín	Universidad de Santiago de Chile, Chile
Luis Marrone	Universidad Nacional de La Plata, Argentina
Katzalin Olcoz Herrero	Universidad Complutense de Madrid, Spain
José Angel Olivas Varela	Universidad de Castilla La Mancha, Spain
Xoan Pardo	Universidade da Coruña, Spain
María Fabiana Piccoli	Universidad Nacional de San Luis, Argentina
Luis Piñuel	Universidad Complutense de Madrid, Spain
Adrian Pousa	Universidad Nacional de La Plata, Argentina
Marcela Printista	Universidad Nacional de San Luis, Argentina
Dolores Isabel Rexachs del Rosario	Universidad Autónoma de Barcelona, Spain
Nelson Rodríguez	Universidad Nacional de San Juan, Argentina
Juan Carlos Saez Alcaide	Universidad Complutense de Madrid, Spain
Aurora Sánchez	Universidad Católica del Norte, Chile
Victoria Sanz	Universidad Nacional de La Plata, Argentina
Remo Suppi	Universidad Autónoma de Barcelona, Spain
Francisco Tirado Fernández	Universidad Complutense de Madrid, Spain
Juan Touriño Dominguez	Universidade da Coruña, Spain
Viale Pereira, Gabriela	Danube University Krems, Austria
Gonzalo Zarza	Globant, Argentina

Additional Reviewers

Nelson Acosta
Pedro Alvarez
Carlos Alvez
Javier Bazzocco
Cecilia Challiol
Leonardo Corbalán
Marcelo De Vicenzi
Mónica Denham
Saúl Domínguez-Isidro
Marcelo A. Falappa
Alberto Fernández
Alejandro Fernandez
María Luján Ganuza
Jorge Ierache
Martín Larrea
Xaviera Lopez Cortez

Ana Maguitman
Cristina Manresa-Yee
Diego César Martínez
Claudia F. Pons
Facundo Quiroga
Hugo Ramón
Ismael Pablo Rodríguez
Fernando Romero
Franco Ronchetti
Alejandro Rosete-Suárez
Gustavo Rossi
Cecilia Sanz
Pablo J. Thomas
Fernando G. Tinetti
Augusto Villa Monte
Álvaro Wong

Sponsors

POSTGRADO
FACULTAD DE INFORMÁTICA

CONICET

Sistema Nacional
de Computación de Alto
Desempeño

AGENCIA

Agencia Nacional de Promoción
Científica y Tecnológica

RedUNCI
Red de Universidades Nacionales
con Carreras de Informática

Contents

Cloud, Edge and High-Performance Computing

Cloud Robotics for Industry 4.0 - A Literature Review

Nancy Velásquez Villagrán[1](✉) ⓘ, Patricia Pesado[1], and Elsa Estevez[2,3]

[1] Facultad de Informática, Universidad Nacional de La Plata (UNLP), La Plata, Argentina
ngvelasquezv@gmail.com, ppesado@lidi.info.unlp.edu.ar
[2] Departamento de Ciencias e Ingeniería de la Computación, Universidad Nacional del Sur
(UNS), Bahía Blanca, Argentina
ece@cs.uns.edu.ar
[3] Instituto de Ciencias e Ingeniería de la Computación, UNS-CONICET, Bahía Blanca,
Argentina

Abstract. Robots in the industry have been used for decades, much before the so-called Fourth Industrial Revolution. They have been incorporated into industrial processes in various ways, for example, with mechanic arms, in assembly processes, welding, and painting, among others. Industrial robots are located in restricted access sites and their space is delimited by means of physical barriers and security measures. In recent years, Industry 4.0 proposes the use robots, able to collaborate with persons, known as collaborative robots or "cobots". Cobots are characterized by cooperating with human work, sharing the same workspace, and able to respond to simple human-machine interactions. In addition, given the benefits of applying cloud computing in Industry 4.0, research has been conducted in applying such technologies to robots. The approach is known as "cloud robotics" and appears as an emerging topic. The objective of this work is to carry out a systematic literature review of cloud robotics for Industry 4.0, in an attempt to present the state of the art in this field and identify opportunities for future research. From the analysis of the results, we observe an emerging interest in this area, and we identify main technologies applied, research themes, and application areas, as well as a special interest on security and safety aspects.

Keywords: Industry 4.0 · Industrial Internet of Things (IIoT) · Internet of Robotics Things (IoRT) · Cloud robotics · Big data · Machine learning · Mobile robots ←

1 Introduction

Industry 4.0 was announced by the German Government in 2011. It is also called the Fourth Industrial Revolution and is characterized for promoting the transformation of the traditional way of producing towards digitization, providing flexibility to productive value chains [1]. In such context, the concepts of smart factory and smart product emerge. In a smart factory, people and machines communicate naturally to produce

© Springer Nature Switzerland AG 2020
E. Rucci et al. (Eds.): JCC-BD&ET 2020, CCIS 1291, pp. 3–15, 2020.
https://doi.org/10.1007/978-3-030-61218-4_1

more customized products [2]. Kumar et al. explain that Industry 4.0 integrates various technologies, especially Information Technology and robotics, in the automation and control of manufacturing systems [3]. However, several authors agree that the technologies associated with Industry 4.0 are Internet of Things (IoT), Cloud Computing, Big Data Analytics, Blockchain, Cybersecurity, Augmented Reality, Automation and Industrial Robots, Additive Manufacturing, Simulation and Modeling, Cyber-Physical Systems, Semantic Technologies [4], real-time communication, advanced computing, and Information Technology (IT) in manufacturing systems [3].

Together, automation and industrial robotics are growing and multiple benefits are recognized, such as: lower defect rate, higher quality and reliability, less waste, and better use of factory space. Robots have been used in industry and their use has increased annually [5]. Industrial robots are installed in restricted spaces and their tasks are pre-programmed for specific tasks. For changes, each robot must be reprogrammed and they are limited to their own computing capacity.

Robots play an important role in Industry 4.0, and robotics will allow manufacturers to attain customized mass production. In particular, second generation industrial robots are used in Industry 4.0. They are called "collaborative robots or cobots", and present a number of advantages over their predecessors, including being more productive and flexible [6]. Cobots allow tasks between workers and machines to complement each other, they share the same workspace and can be used in different activities, such as: mobile robots for transport automation in the automotive industry, service robots for logistics in production processes [7], exoskeletons to replace the physical work of people, handling heavy loads, and automate repetitive tasks, among others [8].

Currently, the so-called "cloud robotics" enable robots to connect to the cloud to obtain computing, storage and communication capacity. Robots connected to the cloud are less expensive and more versatile than cobots. They can be programmed by accessing the cloud, communicate with other robots and share knowledge. Additionally, this robots benefit from the cloud computing infrastructure existing for Industry 4.0.

In recent years, researchers have become increasingly interested in cloud robotics. This claim is based on the increasing number of scientific publications. However, a paper on the state of the art of cloud robotics for Industry 4.0 could not be identified. Only Aissam presents a specific study on "Cloud Robotics and Industry 4.0" [10]. Some studies argue that a barrier to the implementation of Industry 4.0 is the need of a high investment [9], and thus, cloud robotics could be an approach to lower the costs. Despite these initial observations, additional studies are needed to understand the development and current trends of cloud robotics for Industry 4.0.

The aim of this article is to identify and analyze the state of the art on cloud robotics for Industry. 4.0. For this, we conducted a systematic literature review (SLR) to identify opportunities and gaps in the field, as well as to determine areas of interest for future work. Among the main contributions of this study, the IoT, IoRT, CPS, mobile cloud, as well as artificial intelligence, machine learning and neural networks were identified as the technologies applied in this field, and clearly, security aspects came up as a critical aspect as well as a priority to explore in more depth.

The rest of this paper is structured as follows, Sect. 2 presents the research methodology. In Sect. 3, we introduce the literature review; while in Sect. 4, we explain the results obtained. Finally, in Sect. 5 we discuss conclusions and outline possible research lines for future work.

2 Research Methodology

Our aim was to conduct an exploratory research to assess the state of the art of cloud robotics for Industry 4.0. We followed the approach suggested by Kitchenham [9], to identify, analyze and interpret the relevant studies. Thus, the research methodology applied comprises three phases, as shown in Fig. 1.

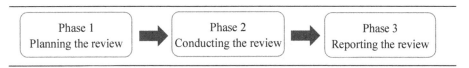

Fig. 1. Research Methodology

In phase 1, the goal was to establish a review protocol for searching and selecting papers. In phase 2, the purpose was to identify and choose the relevant studies, extract and synthesize the information. In phase 3, the results obtained are presented. To guide the research work, we formulate two research questions: Q1) What are the main technologies associated with cloud robotics for Industry 4.0 that are being investigated?; and Q2) Which are the areas of interest for researchers?

According to the research questions, we define the following keywords for conducting the searches: "cloud robotics" AND "industry 4.0". Considering that "Industry 4.0" is a "collective term" [10], we rely on the study conducted by Muhuri et al. in 2019, publishing an extensive bibliometric study of the state of the art of Industry 4.0 [11] and identified the most popular keywords for Industry 4.0. These words, enumerated in Table 1 were taken as alternative search terms. The table also shows the libraries used for the searches, i.e. Scopus and Web of Science (WoS). Both libraries were selected because they contain recognized journal publications and proceedings of academic conferences, and are well recognized in the fields of Engineering and Computer Science.

Based on the above, we used the keywords previously mentioned combined with all alternative terms, as follows - "cloud robotics" AND "industry 4.0" OR ≪alternative term≫. In addition, we define the following criteria for selecting publications.

Inclusion criteria: Articles written in English, full papers, peer reviewed, containing the keywords in their titles, abstracts or keywords.

Exclusion criteria: Non-academic papers, without references, or just presentations.

The search in Scopus found 44 papers, and the one conducted in WOS, 33. For selecting relevant and non-duplicate papers, we apply the PRISMA methodology [12] with its four phases: identification, screening, eligibility and inclusion. In total, 41 papers were selected.

Table 1. Alternative terms used for the literature review

Main terms	Alternative terms in Scopus	Alternative terms in WoS
Cloud Robotics	cloud robotics	cloud robotics
Industry 4.0	industry 4.0	industry 4.0
	industrie 4.0	industrie 4.0
	smart factory	smart factory
	smart manufacturing	smart manufacturing
	industrial internet	digital factory
	intelligent manufacturing	

To have a broader picture of the relevance of cloud robotics in Industry 4.0, we conducted searches using only the keywords "cloud robotics" in both libraries. We obtained 364 publications in Scopus, and 89 in WoS. Thus, from 453 publications in cloud robotics, 41 refer more specifically to Industry 4.0 and are of interest to this study. The systematic review of the literature was carried out with the first 41 papers.

3   Literature Review

After analyzing the literature, it was possible to find different types of studies about cloud robotics for Industry 4.0. Some of them claim that cloud robotics is an emerging and evolving field of robotics. The kind of robots applied in this field appear from the union of cloud computing and service robotics, they are characterized by obtaining the computing power, memory and storage space of the cloud, as well as, they connect to each other through the cloud to exchange information between them [13]. The use of cloud computing with the robots allows to save energy, physical space and data storage. It facilitates the utilization of big data and artificial intelligence [14].

Some of the studies describe the open source operating system for robots called Robot Operative Systems (ROS) [13], [15], OpenRAVE architecture [16] and the architecture of the global network for robots RoboEarth [17]. Santhosh et al. present a cloud robot used in industrial and manufacturing environments, it works on a ROS platform [18]. Chibani et al. present an overview of the cloud robotics concept and projects [19]. Yan et al. analyze the cloud robotics from different viewpoints, such as cloud computing, big data, applications, and the current problems and challenges [20]. Chaâri presents the potential use of cloud computing to promote cyber physical application [21]. Toquica et al. propose an open source program for the teleoperation of an industrial robot with the socket communication method [22]. Tang et al. underpin the evolution from robots to cloud robotics and presents a system architecture of cloud robotics [15]. Kehoe et al. present a survey of research on the benefits of cloud computing for robots and include a website with updated information [23]. Ronzhin et al. propose a conceptual model of a cyber physical environment for relationship among mobile robots, embedded devices, mobile client devices, stationary service equipment and cloud computing [24]. Shah proposes an energy efficient resource management system for mobile cyber physical system applications as a solution to limited battery power, high latency, and dynamic network environment [25]. Dinh et al. present a survey of Mobile cloud computing, including the definition and applications [26]. Russo el at are developing a cloud robotics architecture for deafblind people [27]. Hong et al. analyze the multi-hop cooperative communication model in robot swarms [28] and Liu, J et al. design a robot cloud platform called cloud robotics intelligent cloud platform [29].

Other studies describe the potential of the interaction of cloud computing with robotics for industry applications and explain how the improvement in the performance of robots facilitates their adoption in Industry 4.0, for example in: SLAM, grasping and navigation [30]. Hussnain et al. propose the adoption of cloud robotics in factories to improve the control and supervision of processes, he presents a scale system to carry out intelligent material handling and to support the process of handling basic products in the factory [31]. The author also analyzes the use of cloud robotics in the manufacture of personalized products, by updating the programming of the robots at runtime, without reprogramming [32]. Rahman et al. propose the optimization of the maintenance application in an oil factory. The results indicate superior performance with minimal resource consumption for industrial applications [33]. Krishna et al. present a project of a robotic cloud for supervision and security to be used in the industry. For example, it can be used to detect gas leaks. It works with ROS platform and Raspberry Pi controller, the data obtained from the robot is stored in the cloud [18].

Wan et al. introduce Context-Aware Cloud Robotics (CACR) for materials handling using the cloud for decision-making, location and mapping. CACR is aligned with industrial production requirements in the context of Industry 4.0 [34]. Lihui Wang, presents a study of a cyber physical system that connects to the cloud for remote monitoring and control of a physical robot, and for remote assembly. He argues that cloud robotics allow better energy efficiency [35].

Duran and Pobil, propose a model of a robotic system that correlates the morphology and the internal parameters of the model, uses neural networks and presents a case study. The results of this research can be used in self-configuring robots and cloud robotics for Industry 4.0 [36]. Anton et al. present a solution for accessing and controlling a manufacturing system for cloud computing research, development and training purposes, including system architecture, deployment scenarios, limitations and testing of system performance [37]. Cardarelli et al. present a cloud robotics architecture for groups of Automated Guided Vehicles (AGVs) that are used in industrial logistics processes [38].

From the point of view of mobility and autonomous vehicles, Mello et al. present a case study of cloud robotics to implement the autonomous navigation service in real time, for unmanned autonomous land vehicles. From the cloud he analyzes the download of the computing tasks on navigation. In addition, it integrates several test benches through FUTEBOL, which allows the experimentation with Industry 4.0 applications [39]. De Mello et al. also present a pilot experiment of a cloud-connected mobility assisted device, which interacts with users. For this author, robotic devices that employ small degrees of cloud computing are lighter and less expensive [40]. Okumus and Kocamaz, propose a cloud-based communication and navigation method for multiple guided autonomous vehicles, using the ROS operating system and presents the results carried out on flat surfaces obtained in the laboratory [41]. Dharmasena et al. propose an automated system to control the optimum growth of plants of a greenhouse. A cloud robotic platform controls lighting and water supply. This platform contains a robotic agent, multiple sensors, and a cloud platform using MYSQL to store all the climate data and robotic communication network [42]. Portaluri et al. propose an open testbed for Cloud robotics (Open Cloro) [43] and Do Nascimento et al. present the evolution of a software platform for experimentation of mobile robotics [44].

In addition, other studies refer to the Internet of Robotic Things (IoRT) and Industry.4.0. For instance, the research published by Nayyar et al. conduct a survey and review the IoRT architecture and technologies required for developing IoRT systems [45], Simoens et al. conduct a survey on the Internet of Robotic Things (IoRT) for the analysis of new disruptive services and technological challenges created by the fusion of IoT and robotics [46]. Harman et al. propose a framework, which aims to improve a robot´s ability to act in dynamic environments with IoT devices [47]. Horton et al. developed security best practices and a framework with an open source, for use in a secure cloud robotics infrastructure [48]. Finally, authors such as: Hussnain et al. [32], Rogue [49], Chen [50], Wang, X et al. [51] present the study of various applications and Fosch Villaronga and Millard assessed the key legal and regulatory topics about the cloud robotics [52].

In the set of publications analyzed, there was none presenting a systematic review of the literature on cloud robotics for Industry 4.0, which is why we claim that this work offers a vision of the state of the art in this field.

4   Results

The first publication on cloud robotics referring to Industry 4.0 appeared in 2015, while, 2018 and 2019 are the years with the highest number of publications. We exclude papers published on 2020, since it is ongoing and not all publications are available yet. Figure 2 shows the number of publication through the years. Results confirm the availability of studies about cloud robotics for Industry 4.0; and although scarce, the number of publications is increasing in recent years, and proves that it is an emerging topic.

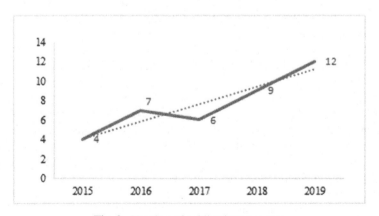

Fig. 2. Number of publications per year

The analysis of the selected publications highlights the technologies applied in the field, including big data, Internet of Things, Internet of Robotic Things, cyber-physical systems, mobile cloud, as well as artificial intelligence (AI), machine learning, neural networks and even open source technologies. The identified technologies are shown in Table 2.

Table 2. Technologies and studies in cloud robotics for Industry 4.0

Technology	References
Big Data	Kehoe et al. [23], Nayyar et al. [45], Tang et al. [15], Wan et al. [34], Duran and Pobil [36], Chaâri et al. [21], Aissam [13]
Internet of Things	Nayyar et al. [45], Dharmasena et al. [42], Portaluri et al. [43], Simoens et al. [46], Tang et al. [15], Wan et al. [34], Chaâri [21], Harman et al. [47]
Internet of Robotic Things	Nayyar et al. [45], Simoens et al. [46], Harman et al. [47]
Cyber Physical Systems	Nayyar et al. [45], Simoens et al. [46], Wan et al. [34], De Mello et al. [40], Hussnain et al. [31], Okumus and Kocamaz [41], Wang [35], Ronzhin et al. [24], Chaâri et al. [21]
Mobile Cloud	Shah [25], Dinh et al. [26]
Artificial Intelligence	Nayyar et al. [45], Aissam et al. [13]
Machine Learning	Nayyar et al. [45], Dharmasena et al. [42], Wan et al. [34], Duran and Pobil [36], Aissam et al. [13]
Neural Network	Nayyar et al. [45], Duran and Pobil [36]
Open Source	Kehoe et al. [23], Portaluri et al. [43], Tang et al. [15], Wan et al. [30], Okumus [41], Yan et al. [20], Aissam et al. [13], Toquica et al. [22]

Through our analysis, we identified major research themes of cloud robotics for Industry 4.0. As summarized in Table 3, they include autonomous robots, ambient intelligence, Automatic Guided Vehicle (AGV), Context Aware Cloud Robotics, mobile robots, localization and mapping, service robots and robot swarms. In addition, some of the application areas, e.g. industrial processes, manufacturing systems, agriculture and oil, gas industries (see Table 4).

Table 3. Research themes of cloud robotics for Industry 4.0

Research themes	References
Autonomous robots/systems	Dharmasena et al. [42], Nayyar et al. [45], Simoens et al. [46], Diankov and Kuffner [16], Aissam et al. [13]
Ambient intelligence	Chibani et al. [19], Harman et al. [47]

(continued)

Table 3. (*continued*)

Research themes	References
Automatic guided vehicle	Okumus and Kocamaz [41], Cardarelli et al. [38]
Context-Aware Cloud Robotics	Wan et al. [34]
Mobile robots	Nayyar et al. [45], Simoens et al. [46], Ronzhin et al. [24], Harman et al. [47], Mello et al. [39], Yan et al. [20], Rahman et al. [33], Aissam et al. [13], Toquica et al. [22], Do Nascimento et al. [44]
Localization and mapping	Yan et al. [20], Wan et al. [34]
Service robots	Liu et al. [29], Russo et al. [27], Chaâri et al. [21], Fosch-Villaronga and Millard [52]
Robot swarms	Hong et al. [28]

Table 4. Application areas of cloud robotics for Industry 4.0

Application Areas	References
Industrial processes	Hussnain et al. [31], Okumus et al. [41], Cardarelli et al. [38], Yan et al. [20], Chaâri et al. [21], Anton et al. [37], Rahman et al. [33], Krishna et al. [18], Fosch-Villaronga and Millard [52], Aissam et al. [13], Toquica et al. [22]
Manufacturing systems/applications	Anton et al. [37], Krishna et al. [18], Aissam et al. [13], Toquica et al. [22]
Oil factories	Rahman et al. [33]
Gas industry	Krishna et al. [18]
Agriculture	Dharmasena et al. [42], Simoens et al. [46]

Finally, we identified that a major aspect investigated in the field refers to safety and security. Table 5 identifies the papers addressing such topics.

Table 5. Publications analyzing safety and security aspects

Aspect	References
Safety	Nayyar et al. [45], De Mello et al. [40], Chibani et al. [19], Cardarelli et al. [38], Mello et al. [39], Chaâri et al. [21], Anton et al. [37], Fosch Villaronga and Millard [52], Wang et al. [51]
Security	Nayyar et al. [45], Kehoe et al. [23], Wan et al. [34], Tang et al. [15], Wan et al. [34], Wang et al. [51], Chibani et al. [19], Do Nascimento et al. [44], Yan et al. [20], Chaâri et al. [21], Dinh et al. [26], Toquica et al. [22], Anton et al. [37], Krishna et al. [18], Fosch Villaronga and Millard [52], Aissam et al. [13], Horton et al. [48], Liu et al. [29], Mello et al. [39]

5   Discussion, Conclusions and Future Work

In this paper, we presented a systematic literature review aiming at analyzing the state of the art of cloud robotics for Industry 4.0. Cloud computing and robots are enabling technologies for Industry 4.0 [53], and their combination, cloud robotics, leverages their potential by taking computing, storage and communication resources from the cloud. Such feature avoids the obsolescence of robots.

Results show that the first publication appeared in 2015 and since then, the number of publications is slowly increasing, hinting that is an emerging field. Through the assessment of the state of the art, we were able to identify major technologies applied in the field, including Internet of Things, Big Data, Cyber Physical Systems [21], Internet of Robotics Things, mobile cloud, as well as artificial intelligence, machine learning and neural networks [45]. There are even authors who are working with open source technologies. We also classified main themes being investigated in relation to cloud robotics for Industry 4.0 including: autonomous robots/systems, ambient intelligence, automatic guided vehicles, mobile robots, localization and mapping, service robots and robot swarms. Similarly, we identified some application areas of cloud robotics for Industry 4.0, including industrial processes, manufacturing systems, agriculture, oil factories and gas industry.

As shown by the work of many authors, two areas of interest refer to security and safety. Even more, considering that connecting to a cyberspace requires greater protection [54], cloud robotics, for its nature based in the cloud, is vulnerable to threats of cloud computing, e.g. a hacker attacks could interrupt the provided services and damage to customers or industrial information stored in the cloud and more risky, the attacks could change the orders that the robots execute

In general, the available publications show that there is interest of the scientific community in broadening the application of cloud robotics for Industry 4.0. In this line, future work can be considered in the Internet of Robotic Things and security aspects. Another important research line to explore is the use of cloud robotics for Industry 4.0 to support production processes in the digital factory.

Finally, a line yet not fully explored is the use of cloud robotics in SMEs [55] and security [20]. Cloud robotics could help more industries to implement Industry 4.0 at lower costs compared to currently existing robots. SMEs are characterized by contributing to the local economy and being job generators. They generally react more quickly to changes in market demand, have a greater diversity of products and are closer to customers. Thus, robots contributing to SMEs should be versatile, inexpensive, learn from experience, and relate their work to human workers. With this lens and in this line, we plan to continue our future work.

The limitation of this study is that the literature revised on cloud robotics for Industry 4.0 comprises scientific publications available in Scopus and WoS databases. Thus, we do not claim that the review was complete.

References

1. Kagermann, H., Anderl, R., Gausemeier, J., Schuh, G., Wahlster, W.: Industry 4.0 in a Global Context: Strategies for Cooperating with International Partners (Acatech Study), Munich: Herbert Utz Verlag (2016)
2. Henning, K., Wahlster, W., Helbig, J.: Recommendations for implementing the strategic initiative INDUSTRIE 4.0. Final Report of the Industrie 4.0 Working Group, Frankfurt (2013)
3. Kumar, S., Suhaib, M., Asjad, M.: Industry 4.0: complex, disruptive, but inevitable. Manag. Prod. Eng. Rev. **11**, 43–51 (2020). https://doi.org/10.24425/mper.2020.132942
4. Ghobakhloo, M.: The future of manufacturing industry: a strategic roadmap toward Industry 40. J. Manuf. Technol. Manag. **29**, 910–936 (2018). https://doi.org/10.1108/JMTM-02-2018-0057
5. Karabegović, I., Karabegović, E., Mahmić, M., Husak, E.: Implementation of industry 4.0 and industrial robots in the manufacturing processes. In: Karabegović, I. (ed.) NT 2019. LNNS, vol. 76, pp. 3–14. Springer, Cham (2020). https://doi.org/10.1007/978-3-030-18072-0_1
6. Ferraguti, F., Pertosa, A., Secchi, C., Fantuzzi, C., Bonfè, M.: A methodology for comparative analysis of collaborative robots for Industry 4.0. In: Proceedings of the 2019 Design, Automation and Test in Europe Conference and Exhibition, DATE 2019, pp. 1070–1075 (2019)
7. Poschmann, H., Brüggemann, H., Goldmann, D.: Disassembly 4.0: a review on using robotics in disassembly tasks as a way of automation. Chem.-Ing.-Tech. **92**, 1–20 (2020). https://doi.org/10.1002/cite.201900107
8. Bragança, S., Costa, E., Castellucci, I., Arezes, P.M.: A brief overview of the use of collaborative robots in industry 4.0: Human role and safety. Stud. Syst. Decis. Control. **202**, 641–650 (2019). https://doi.org/10.1007/978-3-030-14730-3_68
9. Tebes, G., Peppino, D., Becker, P., Olsina, L.: Especificación del modelo de proceso para una revisión sistemática de literatura. In: XXII Ibero-American Conference on Software Engineering, CIbSE 2019 (2019)
10. Abraham, A., et al.: Industry 4.0: Quo Vadis? Eng. Appl. Artif. Intell. **87** (2020). https://doi.org/10.1016/j.engappai.2019.103324
11. Muhuri, P.K., Shukla, A.K., Abraham, A.: Industry 4.0: a bibliometric analysis and detailed overview. Eng. Appl. Artif. Intell. **78**, 218–235 (2019). https://doi.org/10.1016/j.engappai.2018.11.007
12. Moher, D., Liberati, A., Etzlaff, J., Altman, D.: Preferred reporting items for systematic reviews and meta-analyses: the PRISMA statement. PLoS Med. **6**, 1–2 (2009). https://doi.org/10.1371/journal.pmed1000097
13. Aissam, M., Benbrahim, M., Kabbaj, M.N.: Cloud robotic: opening a new road to the industry 4.0. Stud. Syst. Decis. Control. **175**, 1–20 (2019). https://doi.org/10.1007/978-981-13-2212-9_1
14. Civera, J., Ciocarlie, M., Aydemir, A., Bekris, K., Sarma, S.: Guest editorial special issue on cloud robotics and automation. IEEE Trans. Autom. Sci. Eng. **12**, 396–397 (2015). https://doi.org/10.1109/TASE.2015.2409511
15. Tang, S., Wan, J., Cai, H., Chen, F.: Cloud robotics: Insight and outlook. ICST Inst. Comput. Sci. Soc. Telecommun. Eng. **173**, 94–103 (2016). https://doi.org/10.1007/978-3-319-44350-8_10
16. Diankov, R., Kuffner, J.: OpenRAVE: a planning architecture for autonomous robotics. Robotics 1–15 (2008). https://doi.org/CMU-RI-TR-08-34
17. Waibel, M., et al.: Robo earth - a word wide web for robots. IEEE Robot. Autom. Mag. **18**, 69–82 (2011). https://doi.org/10.1109/MRA.2011.941632

18. Santhosh Krishna, B. V., Oviya, J., Gowri, S., Varshini, M.: Cloud robotics in industry using Raspberry Pi. In: 2016 2nd International Conference on Science Technology Engineering and Management, ICONSTEM 2016. pp. 543–547 (2016)
19. Chibani, A., Amirat, Y., Mohammed, S., Matson, E., Hagita, N., Barreto, M.: Ubiquitous robotics: recent challenges and future trends. Rob. Auton. Syst. **61**, 1162–1172 (2013). https://doi.org/10.1016/j.robot.2013.04.003
20. Yan, H., Hua, Q., Wang, Y., Wei, W., Imran, M.: Cloud robotics in smart manufacturing environments: challenges and countermeasures. Comput. Electr. Eng. **63**, 56–65 (2017). https://doi.org/10.1016/j.compeleceng.2017.05.024
21. Chaâri, R., et al.: Cyber-physical systems clouds: a survey. Comput. Networks. **108**, 1–63 (2016). https://doi.org/10.1016/j.comnet.2016.08.017
22. Toquica, J.S., Benavides, D., Motta, J.M.S.T.: Web compliant open architecture for teleoperation of industrial robots. In: IEEE 15th International Conference on Automation Science and Engineering (CASE), pp. 1408–1414 (2019)
23. Kehoe, B., Patil, S., Abbeel, P., Goldberg, K.: A survey of research on cloud robotics and automation. IEEE Trans. Autom. Sci. Eng. **12**, 398–409 (2015). https://doi.org/10.1109/TASE.2014.2376492
24. Ronzhin, A., Saveliev, A., Basov, O., Solyonyj, S.: Conceptual model of cyberphysical environment based on collaborative work of distributed means and mobile robots. In: Ronzhin, A., Rigoll, G., Meshcheryakov, R. (eds.) ICR 2016. LNCS (LNAI), vol. 9812, pp. 32–39. Springer, Cham (2016). https://doi.org/10.1007/978-3-319-43955-6_5
25. Shah, S.C.: An energy-efficient resource management system for a mobile Ad Hoc Cloud. IEEE Access. **6**, 62898–62914 (2018). https://doi.org/10.1109/ACCESS.2018.2876600
26. Dinh, H.T., Lee, C., Niyato, D., Ping, W.: A survey of mobile cloud computing: architecture, applications, and approaches. Wirel. Commun. Mob. Comput. **13**, 1587–1611 (2011)
27. Russo, L.O., Airò Farulla, G., Geraci, C.: A cloud robotics platform to enable remote communication for deafblind people. In: Miesenberger, K., Kouroupetroglou, G. (eds.) ICCHP 2018. LNCS, vol. 10896, pp. 203–206. Springer, Cham (2018). https://doi.org/10.1007/978-3-319-94277-3_33
28. Hong, Z., Huang, H., Guo, S., Chen, W., Zheng, Z.: QoS-aware cooperative computation offloading for robot swarms in cloud robotics. IEEE Trans. Veh. Technol. **68**, 4027–4041 (2019). https://doi.org/10.1109/TVT.2019.2901761
29. Liu, J., Zhou, F., Yin, L., Wang, Y.: A novel cloud platform for service robots. IEEE Access. **7**, 182951–182961 (2019). https://doi.org/10.1109/ACCESS.2019.2927743
30. Wan, J., Tang, S., Yan, H., Li, D., Wang, S., Vasilakos, A.V.: Cloud robotics: current status and open issues. IEEE Access. **4**, 2797–2807 (2016). https://doi.org/10.1109/ACCESS.2016.2574979
31. Hussnain, A., Ferrer, B.R., Lastra, J.L.M.: Towards the deployment of cloud robotics at factory shop floors: a prototype for smart material handling. In: Proceedings - 2018 IEEE Industrial Cyber-Physical Systems, ICPS 2018, pp. 44–50 (2018)
32. Hussnain, A., Ferrer, B.R., Martinez Lastra, J.L.: An application of cloud robotics for enhancing the flexibility of robotic cells at factory shop floors. In: Proceedings: IECON 2018 - 44th Annual Conference of the IEEE Industrial Electronics Society, pp. 2963–2970. IEEE (2018)
33. Rahman, A., Jin, J., Cricenti, A.L., Rahman, A., Kulkarni, A.: Communication-aware cloud robotic task offloading with on-demand mobility for smart factory maintenance. IEEE Trans. Ind. Inform. 1–12 (2018). https://doi.org/10.1109/tii.2018.2874693
34. Wan, J., Tang, S., Hua, Q., Li, D., Liu, C., Lloret, J.: Context-aware cloud robotics for material handling in cognitive industrial Internet of Things. IEEE Internet Things J. (2017). https://doi.org/10.1109/JIOT.2017.2728722
35. Wang, L.: An overview of internet-enabled cloud-based cyber manufacturing. Trans. Inst. Meas. Control. **39**, 388–397 (2017). https://doi.org/10.1177/0142331216687817

36. Duran, A.J., del Pobil, A.P.: Predicting the internal model of a robotic system from its morphology. Rob. Auton. Syst. (2018). https://doi.org/10.1016/j.robot.2018.08.014
37. Anton, F., Borangiu, T., Răileanu, S., Anton, S., Ivănescu, N., Iacob, I.: Secure sharing of robot and manufacturing resources in the cloud for research and development. In: Berns, K., Görges, D. (eds.) RAAD 2019. AISC, vol. 980, pp. 535–543. Springer, Cham (2020). https://doi.org/10.1007/978-3-030-19648-6_61
38. Cardarelli, E., Digani, V., Sabattini, L., Secchi, C., Fantuzzi, C.: Cooperative cloud robotics architecture for the coordination of multi-AGV systems in industrial warehouses. Mechatronics **45**, 1–13 (2017). https://doi.org/10.1016/j.mechatronics.2017.04.005
39. Mello, R., Sierra, S., Múnera, M., Cifuentes, C., Ribeiro, M., Frizera - Neto, A.: Cloud robotics experimentation tesbeds: a cloud based navigation case study. In: 2019 IEEE 4th Colombian Conference on Automatic Control (CCAC). IEEE, Medellin (2019)
40. De Mello, R.C., Jimenez, M.F., Ribeiro, M.R.N., Laiola Guimarães, R., Frizera-Neto, A.: On human-in-the-loop CPS in healthcare: a cloud-enabled mobility assistance service. Robotica **37**, 1477–1493 (2019). https://doi.org/10.1017/s0263574719000079
41. Okumus, F., Kocamaz, A.F.: Cloud based indoor navigation for ros-enabled automated guided vehicles. In: 2019 International Conference on Artificial Intelligence and Data Processing Symposium, IDAP 2019. IEEE (2019)
42. Dharmasena, T., De Silva, R., Abhayasingha, N., Abeygunawardhana, P.: Autonomous cloud robotic system for smart agriculture. In: MERCon 2019 - Proceedings, 5th International Multidisciplinary Moratuwa Engineering Research Conference, pp. 388–393. IEEE (2019)
43. Portaluri, G., Ojo, M., Giordano, S., Tamburello, M., Caruso, G.: Open CLORO: an open testbed for cloud robotics. In: IEEE International Workshop on Computer Aided Modeling and Design of Communication Links and Networks, CAMAD. IEEE (2019)
44. do Nascimento Jr, A., Cardozo, E., Souza, R.S., Guimarães, E.G.: A platform for cloud robotics. In: IFAC-PapersOnLine, pp. 48–53 (2016)
45. Nayyar, A., Batth, R.S., Nagpal, A.: Internet of robotic things: driving intelligent robotics of future - concept, architecture, applications and technologies. In: Proceedings - 4th International Conference on Computing Sciences, ICCS 2018, pp. 151–160. IEEE (2018)
46. Simoens, P., Dragone, M., Saffiotti, A.: The Internet of Robotic Things: a review of concept, added value and applications. Int. J. Adv. Robot. Syst. **15**, 1–11 (2018). https://doi.org/10.1177/1729881418759424
47. Harman, H., Chintamani, K., Simoens, P.: Robot assistance in dynamic smart environments—a hierarchical continual planning in the now framework. Sensors (Switzerland) **19**, 2–33 (2019). https://doi.org/10.3390/s19224856
48. Horton, M., Samanta, B., Reid, C., Chen, L., Kadlec, C.: Development of a secure, heterogeneous cloud robotics infrastructure: implementing a mesh VPN and robotic file system security practices. In: Conference Proceedings - IEEE SOUTHEASTCON. IEEE (2018)
49. Rogue, R.: Cloud robotics: a review of technologies, developments and applications. Ind. Robot Int. J. 44 (2017). https://doi.org/10.1108/ir-10-2016-0265
50. Chen, B., Wan, J., Shu, L., Li, P., Mukherjee, M., Yin, B.: Smart factory of Industry 4.0: key technologies, application case, and challenges. IEEE Access. **6**, 6505–6519 (2018). https://doi.org/10.1109/ACCESS.2017.2783682
51. Wang, X.V., Wang, L., Mohammed, A., Givehchi, M.: Ubiquitous manufacturing system based on cloud: a robotics application. Robot. Comput. Integr. Manuf. (2016). https://doi.org/10.1016/j.rcim.2016.01.007
52. Fosch-Villaronga, E., Millard, C.: Cloud robotics law and regulation: challenges in the governance of complex and dynamic cyber–physical ecosystems. Rob. Auton. Syst. **119**, 77–91 (2019). https://doi.org/10.1016/j.robot.2019.06.003
53. Bahrin, M.A.K., Othman, M.F., Azli, N.H.N., Talib, M.F.: Industry 4.0: a review on industrial. Autom. Robotic. **78**, 137–143 (2016)

54. Lezzi, M., Lazoi, M., Corallo, A.: Cybersecurity for Industry 4.0 in the current literature: a reference framework. Comput. Ind. **103**, 97–110 (2018). https://doi.org/10.1016/j.compind. 2018.09.004
55. Perzylo, A., et al.: SMErobotics: smart robots for flexible manufacturing. IEEE Robot. Autom. Mag. **26**, 78–90 (2019). https://doi.org/10.1109/MRA.2018.2879747

An Edge Focused Distributed Shared Memory

Matías Teragni[1]([✉]) [iD], Ricardo Moran[1,2] [iD], and Gonzalo Zabala[1] [iD]

[1] Universidad Abierta Interamericana, San Juan 983, Buenos Aires, Argentina
{matias.teragni,ricardo.moran,gonzalo.zabala}@uai.edu.ar
[2] Comisón de Investigaciones Científicas de la Provincia de Buenos Aires, Calle 526 e/10 y 11,
La Plata, Buenos Aires, Argentina

Abstract. Edge computing proposes access to largely unused computational resources without the added cost of the latency between the user and the Cloud. To take advantage of it we designed and implemented an abstraction layer compatible with standard JavaScript that builds a distributed shared memory on top of any existing web browser, like the ones present in smartphones or tablets, and a cloud server, enabling developers to use existing application code and enhance it by enabling collaboration between those devices. The synchronization mechanism supports mixed consistency, preferring eventual consistency but providing a stronger serializability when required, allowing the developers to tune it to their specific needs.

Keywords: Distributed shared memory · Edge computing · Eventually consistent

1 Introduction

Cloud computing changed the world by providing a seemingly infinite amount of processing power and available memory on demand. But the transmission latencies caused by the centralized architecture that cloud computing imposes cannot be escaped. Edge computing is a rising field of interest where the storage and processor usage is moved to the "edge" of the network, to the devices closest to the user and the data sources [1]. The implementation of systems that make use of the edge devices is hindered by the inherent complexity of using heterogeneous devices over untrusted networks. In order to deal with these issues, we propose the design and construction of an abstraction layer compatible with the devices available at the edge of the network, that handles the synchronization of state between the devices, hiding in the process the geographical distribution, and simplifying the process of developing these kinds of systems.

A distributed system can be defined as a set of different pieces of software and hardware that work in unison in a way that, from at least a specific point of view, can be perceived as a single unit. To implement a distributed system, it results essential then to have an abstraction that hides the physical distribution of the execution. That abstraction not only enables the developer to concentrate on the business logic from the requirements, but it also enables the system to tolerate partitions, resist failures and use redundancy to balance an excessive workload.

E. Rucci et al. (Eds.): JCC-BD&ET 2020, CCIS 1291, pp. 16–29, 2020.
https://doi.org/10.1007/978-3-030-61218-4_2

The two main paradigms used to provide that abstraction are: the idea of (1) synchronization via message passing [2], where the different sub processes communicate with each other explicitly and the abstraction is provided in the means of how we find the receiver of a specific message, for example by using a naming system instead of a physical address; and the concept of a (2) distributed shared memory [3], where different sub processes can access some shared state by using virtual addresses, either replicating the shared state or by acquiring it on demand, avoiding the need of communicating with each other.

In both cases, the application code to be executed is not tied explicitly to a specific execution environment, which allows it to be deployed to multiple nodes and to be relocated when a node fails. Each paradigm can be built on top of the other [4], and the performance penalty of the distribution is not a consequence of which abstraction is used but is usually related to cost of accessing remote data.

There are valid arguments to prefer any of these approaches, but as [5] demonstrated, programming with shared data is a well understood problem, and since most of the top used programming languages expose this idea, we believe it has a comprehension advantage to the application developer.

Despite the rapid growth of the Internet of Things (IoT) gadgets, most of the devices present at the edges of the internet are user-facing like laptops, wearables and smartphones, all of which are used to browse the web. Given that every browser available today contains a JavaScript VM, the web can be used not only to distribute content but to deliver application code to be executed. In this context, providing the possibility to build a distributed system on the edge of the network on top of a standard JavaScript VM enables taking advantage of a largely untapped processing power available today, without incurring in the extra cost of deploying a network of devices.

This paper is structured as follows. In Sect. 2 we discuss the specific requirements that must be fulfilled by the synchronization layer to be deployable into the target platforms. In Sect. 3 we define the internal data structure of the distributed shared memory and its properties. In Sect. 4 we go into how the synchronization operations are integrated into a standard JavaScript execution. In Sect. 5 we show some functionalities of the working prototype, and in Sect. 6 we address the limitations of the current proposal, how others have addressed similar issues, and the next steps of this project.

2 Requirements

In order to access the proposed devices, the abstraction layer that handles the synchronization of the shared state must work on top of the standard JavaScript defined in the ECMA specification [6], since any change to that would require a specialized browser or plugin to be installed on the device, effectively narrowing the possible participants of the distributed system.

On top of that, it should be compliant with JavaScript's existing idioms and tools, making it compatible with existing JavaScript code and easing the development process. We have a flexible definition of what is compatible, we aim to ensure that synchronized code behaves as a non-synchronized one would, just as an experienced developer could expect when reading the program. For example, if an existing JavaScript object that resides on the shared memory is mutated, that mutation must be visible to every node without explicitly executing extra code to observe the mutations. If an operation of the abstraction layer is not completed synchronously, it should return a JavaScript Promise like every other asynchronous operation in the language. Every existing JavaScript code that can execute on a single node should, in theory, be allowed to run on the shared environment.

In this way, the provided platform should work as a library, allowing it to extend any project with its capabilities, instead of a framework that restricts the possible actions that both the developer and the code can take.

Since the network connecting the devices and the cloud is not reliable, partitions must be tolerated and offline operation has to be supported, and even though the efficiency of this proposal is not our main concern, it should work well enough to prove the concept, leaving possible optimizations as future work.

3   Synchronization Mechanism

In order to maximize the data locality, improving performance, and ensuring partition tolerance, the proposed system imposes an overly optimistic replication [7], allowing the users to access the shared data in any replica at any time. It is based on the optimistic presumption that conflicting updates are rare, and that the contents are consistent enough with those on another replica. The developer can choose what gets shared by explicitly sharing it, triggering an asynchronous process that saves the complete object subgraph that is reachable from that instance into the shared memory, and from that point on that state will be replicated in every connected node. This implies that the data corresponding to those objects will always be available in any node that has connected after that moment, and, therefore, the consistency of that data must be relaxed.

Since the application state of a JavaScript program is composed of the alive objects in the memory heap, and execution specific information (such as instruction pointers, parameters, return addresses and values, etc.) [6], where each device has its own independent execution, the only thing needed to be synchronized is the state of the objects present in the heap. But synchronizing every object in the memory of every device increases severely the costs (bandwidth consumption, memory required, etc.), without providing any benefits because in most cases what needs to be shared is just a small set of objects. Additionally, and for most applications there is nothing to gain by synchronizing state related to, for example, the user interface, like mouse event handlers. For these reasons, the synchronization will only take place on a subset of the object graph (the complete set of alive objects and their relations) explicitly defined by the programmer, allowing the developers to fit the synchronization layer to their specific needs. The proposed architecture is composed of two types of nodes:

A set of client or processor nodes, consisting of a standard web browser (running on a computer, mobile phone, etc.), where the desired behavior of the system takes place on the edge of the network by executing JavaScript or web assembly [8] code.

A series of memory nodes, consisting of eventually consistent [9], possibly distributed, cloud database each containing either a shard or the complete shared memory.

When a processor accesses the corresponding webpage, it executes its program (JS), initializing the synchronization layer and loading into the local memory the shared state of the application from the memory node. Every time that the local state is mutated it queues a notification to be sent asynchronously in the background by the synchronization layer, propagating the state mutation to the corresponding memory nodes, where an operation order is established, and from there to the other processor nodes that will update their local replicas, and resolve any conflict by treating the memory as a series of last-write-win records.

Internally, the distributed shared memory will be composed exclusively of Conflict-free Replicated data types (CRDTs) [10], data structures that by definition or construction provide eventual consistency by guaranteeing that the operations performed on them are commutative, and in consequence as long as every update reach every replica, then the state of the whole distributed system will converge. Usually CRDTs are categorized as either state based [11], where the update notification carries information about the new state of the data structure, or operation based [12], where the notification carries the information required to replicate the operation. The latter tends to be more efficient but requires knowledge of the specific semantics of the possible operations to design the CRDT, and since we aim to allow any arbitrary mutation must be discarded.

There has been work to build a CRDT [13] that can represent a JSON file, that is a serialization of an object graph in the literal object notation provided by the JavaScript language, handling complex problems like nested conflicts without losing any data, nor requiring user input. However, that hierarchical tree structure fails to represent the possible cycles that can take place on an alive object graph, and as such does not have enough expressiveness to represent correctly in-memory objects. To address these specific issues, we serialize the object graph in a specially designed tree-like structure where it is flattened into a list with identifiers, and any reference between objects is represented using these identifiers, removing in the process the existence of nested conflicts.

The shared structure is composed by combining the following 4 elements:

3.1 Slot

A slot is defined as a register that contains a tuple with a value, and its associated metadata like the type information, working in a similar way than a memory cell. The slot can be internally constructed by using a Last-Write-Win Register [10], a standard CRDT where the eventual convergence holds the last value written to it. The extra metadata added to the register is used on the clients to correctly rebuild the object graph in their local memory.

We identify 3 different subtypes of Slots. Those that contain a literal value (like a string, a number, a Boolean, etc.) that, when encountered on a client, are converted into the internal values. Those that contain an object, where the value of the slot is a unique identifier associated with one specific instance in the shared heap and are converted into a JavaScript object with the corresponding keys and values in the client's local memory. And those that contain an Array, where the value is a unique identifier associated with one specific ordered collection present in the shared heap.

3.2 Array

With array we refer to a sparse representation of an ordered list that uses unsigned integers as its keys, and a slot as its value. Each array gets converted into a JavaScript array in the local memory of the clients, and has a unique identifier associated with it in the object dictionary. This element can be created using a Replicated Growable Array as described in [14].

3.3 Object

An object works as an associative set that uses strings as its keys, and slots as its values. Each object in the data structure gets converted into a JavaScript object in the local memory of the clients, and has a unique identifier associated with it in the object dictionary. Internally this can be implemented with the set described in [10], or the structure used in [13].

3.4 ObjectDictionary

The previous data structures are used as components in the shared memory object dictionary, a representation of the complete synchronized heap. This structure is defined as an associative set that uses unique identifiers as keys, and one of the listed components as values.

The objects in the shared heap can be either explicitly added by a user, or implicitly added by the synchronization layer because they are reachable from an explicitly added object. This distinction is important because those explicitly added objects can be requested by other users and can operate as roots in a garbage collection process, that deletes all the objects that are non-reachable from the roots.

The root objects could be identified simply as an array of unique identifiers, but for usability's sake a user defined name will be associated with those identifiers. This allows the user's code to request instances from the shared memory using human-readable identifiers.

This means that the object graph can be constructed using two associative sets, one that assigns the identifiers to each slot in the shared heap, and a second one that defines the identifier associated with the root names defined by the programmer.

For example, the following object, described in JavaScript Object Notation can be serialized into the tree displayed in Fig. 1.

```
{
  foo:{
    bar:"baz"},
  qux:[3, 5, 7],
  zort: false
}
```

From this, the memory node can be implemented specifically for this purpose, or be replaced by any open source, or private no-sql database that provides eventual consistency as long as they have a record-like structure, and a public API that can be accessed

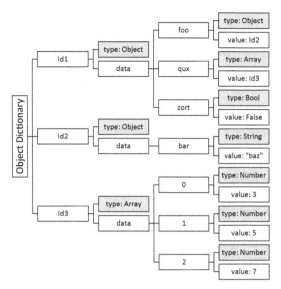

Fig. 1. Object tree serialization example

from the clients (web browser). In any case the abstraction layer present in the clients will have to interact with the memory node and, if required, an adapter will have to be built between them.

3.5 Consistency Guarantee

The PACELC theorem [15] describes the possible behaviors of a replicated data system, where in the case of a partition the system can either be available or consistent, but not both, and during the normal operations it can either privilege latency or consistency. In fact, availability can be seen as a function of the latency, where the lack of availability equals an infinite latency.

Since performance is greatly impacted by data locality, and the network partitions are unavoidable in the target context, we decided to embrace the inconsistency, prioritizing latency and availability over consistency. This means that, by default the access to the shared memory will be highly available, and with low latency, since the complete synchronized heap is copied into the local memory of each client, at the cost of relaxing the consistency of the data.

With an intelligent design of the internal structure of the synchronized data conflicts can be avoided, having the access speed of the relaxed consistency without any of the pitfalls, but that design requires an experienced developer and an application domain that can be modeled in a conflict-free way, which is rarely the case. In order to allow any kind of application to be built on top of the synchronization layer proposed, we designed it to have a mixed consistency level, meaning that in most scenarios it will work with a relaxed consistency, allowing the existence ôf execution anomalies, but if required explicitly by the developer, it will operate with a stronger sequential consistency.

Several programming languages have followed a similar strategy to solve this issue in the scenario of a multiprocessor computer. In Java, for example, any code executed in parallel that access the same variables can, and probably will, create anomalies, but using the keyword "volatile" on a variable declaration or "synchronized" before a block will cause the compiler to generate locks and fences that ensure the correct propagation of the data.

In a similar way we provide a specific function, called lock, that receives a shared object and a function to be executed, and asynchronously performs a compare-and-set operation into the memory node, executing the provided code if and when the lock can be guaranteed. To provide this functionality the memory node has to perform an atomic conditional operation, we used the HTTP conditional requests [16], in particular the If-Match header stating that the requested operation can only succeed if the provided entity tag (ETag) represents the current version of the resource on the server, and failing in any other case. When a lock is requested a Get operation is performed to the memory node querying about the existing locks for an object identifier, the result carries the current version of that resource. If no lock is active on that object then a second operation is emitted that carries the received version, trying to create a lock for that specific identifier. If the server implements the HTTP standard, then the operation can either succeed, meaning that the data we had when we requested the lock was still valid, or fail because between our operations another node had created a lock for the same identifier. In the latter case the abstraction layer retries the operation after some time and will eventually have access to the lock if the node holding it releases it.

The final implementation of this process includes some extra logic to handle the cases of nested locks, even if they are reentrant, and for clarity's sake we encourage the reader to inspect the implementation if more details are needed.

4 Integration to JavaScript

Much effort has been devoted to formalizing the behavior of JavaScript [17, 18], and since we have not changed either the semantics nor the syntax of the language in order to ensure our compatibility with the existing standard browsers, our synchronization engine can be built on top of this formalization. Additionally, we added some formalization as a part of this work because the existing formalization does not represent the current version of JavaScript, excluding some useful features that are available in modern browsers.

The synchronization mechanism aims to be as transparent as possible to the programmer, requiring only the explicit addition of an instance to the shared memory to ensure the synchronization of that complete subgraph. This implies that, if an object is shared before being used, any existing JavaScript code should work on the shared instance.

4.1 The Issue of Synchronizing Behavior

JavaScript imposes several restrictions that conditioned the design of this project. First of all, it lacks a reflection mechanism capable of inspecting the variables captured in a closure. This means that any function created in runtime cannot be safely synchronized because there is no way of ensuring the correct synchronization of the object subgraph related to that function, and since the runtime created function are indistinguishable from the statically created ones, the safest approach is to avoid synchronizing functions. In consequence, only object state will be shared, not their behavior.

4.2 The Blocking Code Issue

Another peculiarity of JavaScript is that the code executes on a single thread, in a specific order imposed by an event loop. This means that the code that performs the synchronization cannot be blocking, because it would stop the user's code, and if the user's code is blocking it might stop the synchronization. For example, the following code would prevent the synchronization process while continually mutating some shared state (obj.x) only for the local user.

```
let obj={x:1}
while(true)
{
  obj.x+=1;
}
```

To cope with this issue, instead of building a looping function in the background that handles the synchronization (as proposed in [7]) the only possible alternative that does not involve a modification of the virtual machine (VM) is to use a feature added to ES6 called Proxies [6, 19]. The idea of this functionality is to create a wrapper of an object that can intercept certain kinds of operations performed on the wrapped instance, in a similar way to the decorator pattern. Since it is integrated into the execution environment, it can intercept operations by their kind without requiring previous knowledge of the operation's name or parameters.

When an object is explicitly added or read from the shared memory, a proxy to it is returned. This proxy can then intercept the calls to the getters and setters of the object, triggering the functions that synchronize the mutations as required. In this way, any existing code can be used on top of the proxies, since no special call needs to be made, and any blocking code will still have a chance to synchronize.

Since [20] targets ES3, it does not formalize this feature so we propose a formalization to it that fit our needs, the definition of the semantics of JavaScript's Proxies presented in Eqs. 1 through 5 is intentionally incomplete in this article because the synchronization process only requires to intercept two of the possible operations, and it results trivial to formalize the rest on top of our definition.

$$\frac{(l, \{str_1 : v_1 \cdots str_n : v_n\}) \in H}{Proxy(l, h) \hookrightarrow \{\text{"\_\_proto\_\_"} : Proxy.prototype, \text{"target"} : l, \text{"handler"} : h\}} \tag{1}$$

$$\frac{h = \{\cdots \text{"get"} : f \cdots\} \quad f = \textbf{func}\ (target\ property)\{\textbf{return}\ e\} \quad (l, \{str_1 : v_1 \cdots str_n : v_n\}) \in H}{\{\text{"\_\_proto\_\_"} : Proxy.prototype, \text{"target"} : l, \text{"handler"} : h\}[str_x] \hookrightarrow f((\textbf{deref}\ l)\ str_x)} \tag{2}$$

$$\frac{h = \{str'_1 : v'_1 \cdots str'_n : v'_n\} \quad \text{"get"} \notin (str'_1 \cdots str'_n) \quad (l, \{str_1 : v_1 \cdots str_n : v_n\}) \in H}{\{\text{"\_\_proto\_\_"} : Proxy.prototype, \text{"target"} : l, \text{"handler"} : h\}[str_x] \hookrightarrow (\textbf{deref}\ l)[str_x]} \tag{3}$$

$$\frac{h=\{\cdots"set":f\cdots\}\quad f=\textbf{func}\ (target\ property\ value)\{\ \textbf{return}\ e\}\quad (l,\{str_1:v_1\cdots str_n:v_n\})\in H}{\{"\_\_proto\_\_":Proxy.prototype,\ "target":l,"handler":h\ \}[str_x]=v\hookrightarrow f((\textbf{deref}\ l)\ str_x\ v)} \quad (4)$$

$$\frac{h=\{str_1':v'_1\cdots str_n':v_n'\}\quad "set"\notin(str_1'\cdots str_n')\quad (l,\{str_1:v_1\cdots str_n:v_n\})\in H}{\{"\_\_proto\_\_":Proxy.prototype\,,\ "target":l\,,"handler":h\ \}[str_x]=v\hookrightarrow(\textbf{deref}\ l)[str_x]=v} \quad (5)$$

From this, if the mutations to the objects are performed via the returned proxy, every mutation will be correctly propagated. In Eq. 6 we specify a global function (share) that creates a proxy pointing to a provided object executing a function pull, to acquire any new data from the corresponding memory node before returning the intercepted get operations, and calling push to propagate one specific mutation to the memory node after performing any set operation. Then, since the getting and setting are intercepted creating a window to synchronize, the case of an infinite loop created by the user's code no longer presents a limitation. This can be easily included in existing code by modifying the instance creation, either by explicitly calling the share function, or by using a Factory or some kind of creation pattern.

$$\frac{(l,\{str_1:v_1\cdots str_n:v_n\})\in H \\ g=(\textbf{func}(target\ prop)\{\textbf{return}\ pull(\ );target[prop]\}) \\ s=(\textbf{func}(target\ prop\ value)\{\textbf{return}\ target[prop]=value;push((l,target))\})}{\text{share}(\{str_1:v_1\cdots str_n:v_n\})\hookrightarrow Proxy(l,\{"get":g,"set":s\})} \quad (6)$$

By using the share function, the code example presented at the top of this section can be extended with a call to the share function:

```
let obj=share({x:1})
while(true){ obj.x+=1; }
```

Where obj now will point into a proxy wrapping the real instance, and thus the code is equivalent to the following one, where the proxy is removed and the get and set operations are expanded.

```
let obj = {x:1};
while(true)
{
  pull();
  obj[x]=obj[x]+1;
  push((ref(obj), obj));
}
```

From the expanded code it is clear that the user written code gives the opportunity to receive new information before accessing any data, and to inform any modification after it happens.

5 Implementation

The ideas exposed so far have been implemented into a single JavaScript library of less than 1000 LoC [21], that can be added and used in any modern web browser.

Experiences have been built and tested on different operating systems and devices, including notebooks, smartphones, and cloud hosted virtual machines.

As a memory node, from the plethora of options available today, like CouchDB [22], MariaDB [23], or Cloudant [24], we chose to use Google's Firebase [25] because of two main reasons. First of all, at the time it was the only platform that could inform changes via Web Sockets [26], a technology that increases the propagation speed, reducing the latency of our distributed system. The second reason was because for our needs, the free tier was more than enough, saving us the need to procure the cloud servers needed to build the memory nodes.

Although the current implementation is designed to work with Firebase, there is no reason it could not work with another database system as long as it provides the functionalities exposed in the previous sections.

5.1 Promises, Continuations, and Locks

Every asynchronous operation performed by the synchronization library returns a JavaScript Promise that can be used to build continuations. The main example of these operations is the previously discussed Lock, that returns a Promise that can be used to execute code after the requested operation was executed and lock has been released. In the following code, for example, one client tries to acquire a lock over a shared instance obj, generating a mutex with any other node attempting to do the same, if and when the lock is acquired, the first message is logged into the console, and after it has been released the second one appears.

```
hive.lock(obj,()=>{  console.log("Lock Acquired");
}).then(()=>{console.log("Lock Released");})
```

The final implementation of the locking process also includes a validation of what locks are assigned to the current node, allowing to execute reentrant locks instantly and avoiding the performance penalty of performing extra interactions with the memory node. In the following example the first lock interacts with the memory node to ensure the mutual exclusion, but the second one is executed immediately.

```
hive.lock(obj,()=>{  console.log("Lock Acquired");
   hive.lock(obj,()=>{    console.log("Reentrant Lock");
    })}).then(()=>{console.log("Lock Released");})
```

Since the code to be executed once the lock is obtained is completely arbitrary, the developer can require another lock. The semantics of the synchronization layer for nested locks aim to preserve the intent of the programmer. In the case of a nested lock, no locks are released until any sub-lock is released. In the following example three shared objects are used, referenced by the variables A, B and C. The client that executes this code tries to obtain a lock on A, once it has achieved a mutual exclusion over that resource, tries to obtain a lock on B, and after that one on C. The code states clearly that the lock on B depends on also having one on A, and the one on C depends on the other two. The order of acquisition then becomes A, then B, then C, and nothing gets released until the innermost code finishes, releasing the three objects in inverse order (first C, then B, then A) in a single commit to the memory node.

```
hive.lock(A,()=>{
  console.log("Got A");
  hive.lock(B,()=>{
    console.log("Got B");
    hive.lock(C,()=>{console.log("Got C");})
        .then(()=>{console.log("Released C");});
  }).then(()=>{console.log("Released B");});
}).then(()=>{console.log("Released A");});
```

5.2 Work Queues

The synchronization library includes some extra functionalities built upon the previously exposed synchronized object graph and mixed consistency. One of the needs we encountered more often was to solve a producer-consumer kind of problem, where some nodes of the distributed system created some data that other nodes required to process. To simplify the work needed to solve that kind of problems, we added to the object graph the concept of work queues, where a node can enqueue some specific data into a named queue (by calling the function "request") and will receive a Promise representing that process. The nodes can also try to process work pending on any named queue (by calling the function "process" and providing the function to be applied to the requested data), this second method also returns a Promise.

Once the desired operation is completed, its result is injected into both promises involved in that process, giving to both, the producer and the consumer, the possibility of doing something with that data. In the following code a node adds into a work queue named "queue" an object with a long string, and a character to count in it. Once that task is performed, it logs the result into the console.

```
hive.request("queue",  {count:"a",in:"Lorem ipsum dolor
sit amet, elit, sed..." }).then((r)=>console.log(r))
```

Any node can execute the following code that tries to obtain an entry from the same queue and performs a not particularly efficient count of the occurrences of the required character into the provided long string.

```
hive.process("queue",(data)=>{
  return data.in.split(data.count).length-1;})
```

There is no guarantee that given any moment in time both roles will be connected, so this whole process is asynchronous. When a node tries to process a value present in a queue before something has been put into it, it will wait until there is data available. On the other hand, if data is put into the queue, and there is no one to process it the producer will wait until someone process the data.

5.3 Initial Benchmark Results

A simple test was built to measure the latency of the synchronization platform, and therefore the size of the inconsistency window, by using two different nodes to perform a ping-like operation by mutating a set of two variables with values of a given size. While using the relaxed consistency mode the first node mutates the first variable and starts a stopwatch, when the second node receives that information it mutates the second one, finally when the first node receives the mutation generated by the second node it takes note of the elapsed time of the roundtrip. It is important to remark that this process is implemented as user code on top of the synchronization library, reflecting the complete cost of the synchronization, not just the network propagation. This test was performed 10 k times for two different setups, two computers on the same local area network, and two computers located several kilometers apart.

Since in both cases the nodes only connect to a cloud server (working as memory node) the measures of both tests are consistent, and as can be seen in the Fig. 2, even considering there are a lot of possible optimizations lacking from the prototype in over 80% of the cases the nodes achieved convergence under 300 ms.

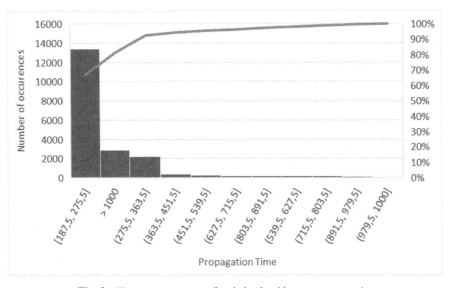

Fig. 2. Time to propagate a fixed size load between two nodes

6 Conclusion and Future Work

We have proposed, implemented and exposed a synchronization layer that enables to build a distributed shared memory on top of standard JavaScript to take advantage of Edge devices like smartphones and tablets, allowing the construction of a new kind of massively parallel distributed system that is less impacted by the implicit latency present in the classical client-server architecture present in Cloud Computing.

This project provides similar benefits to those that GEMs [27] does, without imposing the restriction of using only NodeJS, a server-side JavaScript environment, the need of a special Virtual Machine (VM) called GraalJS, and allowing the use of client-side execution. In this way [28–30] aim to enable the use of the same network nodes, but those frameworks only enable the distribution of a functional map-reduce like program effectively restricting what the programmer can express, while our engine allows any kind of JavaScript code to be distributed, including the map-reduce style if desired. Currently the biggest limitation of the present work comes from the inability to inspect the memory from inside JavaScript, making it risky to synchronize functions since they can access any variable from their scope and there is no way to traverse that graph without modifying the execution engine. In the future, if the ECMA standard provides a way to inspect those variables, then this issue can be fixed. The working implementation is to be regarded as a prototype because there is large room for optimization including building a distributed garbage collection, improving the memory footprint of the synchronization layer, and avoiding unnecessary traffic. Despite this, our initial tests and demos have shown that this mechanism works well in certain kind of applications, and is appealing to developers, that without incurring in extra costs can build complex systems on top of existing technology.

References

1. Shi, W., Cao, J., Zhang, Q., Li, Y., Xu, L.: Edge computing: vision and challenges. IEEE Internet Things J. **3**(5), 637–646 (2016)
2. Soneoka, T., Ibaraki, T.: Logically instantaneous message passing in asynchronous distributed systems. IEEE Trans. Comput. **43**(5), 513–527 (1994)
3. Protic, J., Tomasevic, M., Milutinovic, V.: Distributed shared memory: concepts and systems. IEEE Parallel Distrib. Technol.: Syst. Appl. **4**(2), 63–71 (1996)
4. Nitzberg, B., Lo, V.: Distributed shared memory: a survey of issues and algorithms. IEEE Comput. **24**(8), 52–60 (1991)
5. Vasava, H.D., Rathod, J.M.: A survey of software based Distributed Shared Memory (DSM) implementation methodologies for multiprocessor environments. Int. J. Innov. Res. Sci. Eng. Technol. **2**(7), 3055–3060 (2013)
6. Standard ECMA-262, ECMAScript Language Specification. http://www.ecma-international. org/publications/standards/Ecma-262.htm. Accessed 11 Nov 2019
7. Saito, Y., Shapiro, M.: Replication: Optimistic Approaches. HP Labs Technical Reports (2002)
8. Haas, A., et al.: Bringing the web up to speed with WebAssembly. In: Proceedings of the 38th ACM SIGPLAN Conference on Programming Language Design and Implementation, vol. 52, no. 6, pp. 185–200 (2017)
9. Bailis, P., Ghodsi, A.: Eventual consistency today: limitations, extensions, and beyond. Queue **11**(3), 20 (2013)
10. Shapiro, M., Preguiça, N., Baquero, C., Zawirski, M.: A Comprehensive Study of Convergent and Commutative (2011)
11. Almeida, P.S., Shoker, A., Baquero, C.: Efficient state-based CRDTs by delta-mutation. In: Bouajjani, A., Fauconnier, H. (eds.) NETYS 2015. LNCS, vol. 9466, pp. 62–76. Springer, Cham (2015). https://doi.org/10.1007/978-3-319-26850-7_5
12. Baquero, C., Almeida, P.S., Shoker, A.: Making operation-based CRDTs operation-based. In: Magoutis, K., Pietzuch, P. (eds.) DAIS 2014. LNCS, vol. 8460, pp. 126–140. Springer, Heidelberg (2014). https://doi.org/10.1007/978-3-662-43352-2_11

13. Kleppmann, M., Beresford, A.R.: A conflict-free replicated JSON datatype. IEEE Trans. Parallel Distrib. Syst. **28**(10), 2733–2746 (2017)
14. Roh, H.-G., Jeon, M., Kim, J.-S., Lee, J.: Replicated abstract data types: building blocks for collaborative applications. J. Parallel Distrib. Comput. **71**(3), 354–368 (2011)
15. Patinge, O., Karkhanis, V., Barapatre, A.: Inadequacies of CAP theorem. Int. J. Comput. Appl. **151**(10), 18–20 (2016)
16. Fielding, R., Reschke, J.: Hypertext Transfer Protocol (HTTP/1.1): Conditional Requests, RFC 7232, June, 2014
17. S5: A Semantics for Today's JavaScript, 11 November 2011. http://blog.brownplt.org/2011/11/11/s5-javascript-semantics.html. Accessed 5 Feb 2020
18. Loring, M.C., Marron, M., Leijen, D.: Semantics of asynchronous JavaScript. SIGPLAN Not. **52**(11), 51–62 (2017)
19. Zakas, N.C.: Understanding ECMAScript 6: The Definitive Guide for JavaScript Developers (2016). https://amazon.com/understanding-ecmascript-definitive-javascript-developers/dp/1593277571. Accessed 5 Nov 2019
20. Guha, A., Saftoiu, C., Krishnamurthi, S.: The Essence of JavaScript, pp. 126–150. arXiv: Programming Languages (2010)
21. Teragni, M.: Hive project's Github Repository. https://github.com/HiveProject/hiveproject.github.io/tree/master/Firebase. Accessed 25 Mar 2020
22. Bhardwaj, N.D.: Comparative study of CouchDB and MongoDB – NoSQL document oriented databases. Int. J. Comput. Appl. **136**(3), 24–26 (2016)
23. MariaDB 10.0.0 Release Notes. https://mariadb.com/kb/en/mariadb/mariadb-1000-release-notes/. Accessed 25 Mar 2020
24. IBM: Cloudant – Overview. https://www.ibm.com/cloud/cloudant. Accessed 25 Mar 2020
25. Google: Firebase. https://firebase.google.com/. Accessed 25 Mar 2020
26. Soewito, B., Christian, Gunawan, F.E., Diana, Kusuma, I.G.P.: Websocket to support real time smart home applications. Proc. Comput. Sci. **157**, 560–566 (2019)
27. Bonetta, D., Salucci, L., Marr, S., Binder, W.: GEMs: shared-memory parallel programming for Node.js. In: ACM SIGPLAN International Conference on Object-Oriented Programming, Systems, Languages, and Applications (2019)
28. Ryza, S., Wall, T.: MRJS: A JavaScript MapReduce Framework for Web Browsers (2010)
29. Constela, J.: "joseconstela/acio-js," 5 November 2019. https://github.com/joseconstela/acio-js
30. Lavoie, E., Hendren, L., Desprez, F., Miguel, C.: Pando: Personal Volunteer Computing in Browsers. arXiv (2019)

Towards a Malleable Tensorflow Implementation

Leandro Ariel Libutti[1]([⊠]) [iD], Francisco D. Igual[2] [iD], Luis Piñuel[2] [iD],
Laura De Giusti[1] [iD], and Marcelo Naiouf[1] [iD]

[1] Instituto de Investigación en Informática LIDI (III-LIDI) Facultad de Informática,
UNLP-CIC, La Plata, Argentina
{llibutti,ldgiusti,mnaiouf}@lidi.info.unlp.edu.ar
[2] Departamento de Arquitectura de Computadores y Automática, Universidad
Complutense de Madrid, Madrid, Spain
{figual,lpinuel}@ucm.es

Abstract. The TensorFlow framework was designed since its inception
to provide multi-thread capabilities, extended with hardware accelerator
support to leverage the potential of modern architectures. The amount
of parallelism in current versions of the framework can be selected at
multiple levels (*intra- and inter-paralellism*) under demand. However,
this selection is fixed, and cannot vary during the execution of train-
ing/inference sessions. This heavily restricts the flexibility and elasticity
of the framework, especially in scenarios in which multiple TensorFlow
instances co-exist in a parallel architecture. In this work, we propose the
necessary modifications within TensorFlow to support dynamic selection
of threads, in order to provide transparent malleability to the infrastructure. Experimental results show that this approach is effective in the
variation of parallelism, and paves the road towards future co-scheduling
techniques for multi-TensorFlow scenarios.

Keywords: TensorFlow · Malleability · Containers · Resource
management · Co-scheduling

1 Introdution and Motivation

The exponential growth in the interest of Machine Learning in the last decade is
directly related to three fundamental advances, namely: *(i)* the development of
better algorithms with direct applications in many fields of science and engineering; *(ii)* the availability of massive amounts of data and the feasibility of efficiently storing and analyzing it; and *(iii)* the appearance of novel hardware architectures, typically parallel and/or homogeneous, that allow a proper exploitation
of both new algorithms on large datasets in an affordable time.

Actually, the application of High Performance Computing techniques and
architectures has renewed the interest on the application of Machine Learning
on a plethora of problems, including applications to image recognition, segmentation, speech recognition, natural language processing or language translation,

© Springer Nature Switzerland AG 2020
E. Rucci et al. (Eds.): JCC-BD&ET 2020, CCIS 1291, pp. 30–40, 2020.
https://doi.org/10.1007/978-3-030-61218-4_3

among many others. Together with new computing architectures, the evolution of specific-purpose software frameworks has also contributed to the democratization of Machine Learning, hiding many of the underlying details in order to attain high-performance implementations. Many of these frameworks consider parallelism in general, and heterogeneity exploitation in particular, as a nuclear feature. Tensorflow [1], Caffe [2], Keras [3] or PyTorch [4], to name a few, offer optimized versions targeting specific hardware architectures, hiding many of the details to the final user while keeping performance for both training and inference near the peak of the underlying systems.

Tensorflow is, currently, one of the most extended frameworks targeting both training and inference. Its design is based on a dataflow-like execution model, in which users build an execution graph in which nodes represent operations (typically mathematical transformations), and edges between them denote dataflow between operations in terms of multi-dimensional arrays (that is, *tensors*). The amount of concurrency among operations is dictated by data dependences, while internally, each operation can be further parallelized in order to boost performance. Regarding parallelism, Tensorflow allows a static, a priori selection of two different levels of parallelism, namely: *inter-node parallelism*, denoting the amount of operations that can be executed in parallel at a given execution point respecting data dependences; and *intra-node parallelism*, that determine the amount of internal parallelism per operation. This double degree of parallelism is, however, static and must be selected by the user or the runtime software prior to the launch of a graph session; in other words, the parallelism in Tensorflow is *rigid* and cannot be reconfigured while an operation is running, opposed to a *malleable* nature other software packages.

Experiments have been carried out on the *intra-node parallelism* and *inter-node parallelism* parameters, seeking the definition of the most optimal values for certain Machine Learning algorithms, running in cpu backend [5]. The quest of *malleability* has been previously explored in other fields, mainly in the linear algebra arena [6–8], with promising results in terms of flexibility, resource usage and performance. Applied to Machine Learning in general, and Tensorflow in particular, a fully malleable TensorFlow implementation would allow a dynamic reconfiguration of the amount and nature of the effective parallelism while a training session (for example) is on the fly.

This static selection in the degree and type of parallelism allows a proper exploitation of the underlying hardware by deciding appropriate values for each parameter depending on the available resources and operation types. However it is merely static. In scenarios in which multiple TensorFlow instances arise at any temporal point (e.g. multiple training sessions sharing a common platform), a flexible and dynamic resource management scheme becomes mandatory; that is, considering a graph in which inter-parallelism is decided a priori, for example, the emergence of a second training session needs a re-configuration of the degree of parallelism in order to properly divide the underlying computing resources. This feature is, as of today, not possible within TensorFlow.

Our final target is a common scenario in which individual TensorFlow instances are confined inside a container, which is a typical setup on common cloud services [9]; on shared-resources scenarios, reducing the amount of cores per container would encompass oversubscription situations provided the Tensor-Flow instance within is not informed consequently. Our goal, hence, is to inform the internal TensorFlow instance to reduce/increase the amount of parallelism according to the reduce/increased amount of resources assigned to the container.

In this paper, we provide the necessary mechanisms and modifications in TensorFlow to allow *malleability*, that is, dynamic variation of the number of threads at any point of the execution. Our approach is general enough to reduce or expand the level of inter- and intra-parallelism within the framework from an external entity (e.g. a co-scheduler system software) with no impact for the user. As of our knowledge, this is the first effort to introduce thread malleability in the framework, and paves the road towards the development of co-scheduling schemes that allow an efficient sharing of computing resources in architectures shared by multiple TensorFlow instances. As far as we are aware, this is the first effort towards malleability integration within TensorFlow.

The rest of the paper is structured as follows. Section 2 describes the internal infrastucture of TensorFlow in terms of multithreading support, with special interest in the deployment of threadpools and queues to support this functionality. Section 3 introduces and deeply describes the necessary modifications within the framework to support malleability. Section 4 reports execution traces for the modified malleable TensorFlow implementation. Finally, Sect. 5 closes the paper with a number of conclusions and future research lines opened by this fundamental modification in the framework.

2   Threading Model in Tensorflow

2.1   Execution Components

The computation within Tensorflow is defined by means of a graph composed by an arbitrary number of *compute nodes*. Each compute node features zero or more inputs and outputs, and represents an instance of a kernel operation defined in the framework, such as a general matrix-matrix multiplication (MATMUL). The values that flow across nodes (input and output values) are called *tensors*, data structures of arbitrary dimensions, where the element type is specified at graph construction time. Additionally, nodes can present dependences that must be satisfied before the execution of the next node.

Tensorflow defines a client who is responsible for communicating with one or more workers. Each worker controls a set of devices identified by type and name. Each device is responsible for handling the execution of *ready nodes*, that is, compute nodes whose input dependences have been satisfied.

Hence, the compute nodes of the graph are executed in an order dictated by their input dependences, following a so-called *dataflow* execution model. Once they are fulfilled, the node becomes eligible for execution and it is added to a *ready node queue* belonging to a worker, from which it is extracted, scheduled and finally executed. Upon finishing its execution, the number of dependencies of the nodes that are linked to it is decreased by one. The ready node queue is scheduled in an unspecified order, delegating each node to an available computing *worker* for execution (itself or another worker).

To handle the execution of the graph nodes, the Tensorflow framework defines an *executor* entity in charge of planning and dispatching elements in the task queues of each *thread* of a deployed *threadpool*. Therefore, multiple threads may be scheduling the tasks of the ready node queue within the executor. Each thread analyzes whether it can run the nodes by checking various decision criteria. If they are met, it pushes the node in its own Q_{inline}, which contains all the nodes that thread can execute. Otherwise, if one of the decision criteria is not met, it delegates the node to be executed in another thread.

2.2   Thread Behavior

Each thread in the thread pool features two main procedures to *(i)* schedule and *(ii)* execute the nodes of the graph. Specificaly, each thread in the pool features two different task queues, namely Q_{ready}, containing nodes ready to be scheduled, and Q_{inline}, containing nodes ready to be executed.

Node Scheduling Stage. The scheduling of ready nodes is performed by means of the following steps:

(STEP 1) Check if Q_{ready} is not empty. If it is not empty, proceed to the following step. Otherwise, finish scheduling.
(STEP 2) Get the next node N_{next} in Q_{ready}.
(STEP 3) If N_{next} is not an *expensive task* (that is, expected execution time is small) queue in Q_{inline} for its execution. Back to step 1.
(STEP 4) If N_{next} is expensive and the current thread already has a node of the same type ready, assign the node execution to another thread. Back to step 1.

Figure 1 illustrates the per-thread *scheduling* process.

Node Execution Stage. Second, the node execution procedure proceeds as follows:

(STEP 1) Check if Q_{inline} is not empty. If it is not empty, perform node planning. Otherwise, it waits for new nodes to be sent to it or for graph execution to finish.
(STEP 2) Get the next node N_{next} in Q_{inline}.
(STEP 3) Verify that it meets the conditions for execution.
(STEP 4) Run the node using the required kernel implementation.
(STEP 5) Decrement the dependencies of the nodes that depend on the execution of the current node.
(STEP 6) Check for new nodes to schedule. In case it is fulfilled, call the scheduling procedure.
(STEP 7) Back to step 1.

Figure 2 shows the node *execution* procedure.

2.3 Multi-level Parallelism: Intra- and Inter-parallelism

Tensorflow exposes and exploits two independent levels of parallelism, namely *intra-* and *inter-*parallelism. Both can be exploited in conjunction and under user request.

Intra-parallelism controls the number of threads to be used for the execution of a kernel operation (MATMUL, CONCAT, etc.). Obviously, the underlying implementation of the kernel –task– must support parallelization to leverage different degrees of intra-parallelism. On the contrary, inter-parallelism controls the amount of independent kernel operations that can be concurrently executed, leveraging the strategies depicted in the previous section.

Intra- and inter-parallelism, hence, can exploit per-task and per-graph parallelism, provided it is available. The framework provides simple mechanisms to determine each level of parallelism through its high-level API; the selected values, however, are valid across the complete task graph, which make Tensorflow a *rigid* piece of software from the threading control perspective.

Regarding implementation details, Tensorflow delegates the handling of inter-parallelism (also referred as *non-blocking* parallelism in the literature) to the implementation of the *ThreadPool* in the Eigen library [10] leveraging its flexibility and efficiency.

Each thread in the *threadpool* features a third queue of tasks (Q_{eigen}) that ultimately includes tasks to be executed by the corresponding thread; under situations without assigned tasks, work stealing between Q_{eigen} queues is inplace to improve thread occupancy. Under situations in which there are no available tasks in Q_{eigen}, the thread spins, and in case of being the only thread awake without tasks, stalls for a certain time waiting for the arrival of new jobs; after that time the thread falls asleep waiting for another thread to wake it up for work.

3 Malleability Integration in Tensorflow

The integration of malleability in the threadpool associated with non-blocking tasks (that is, inter-parallelism), requires a number of modifications both in the Tensorflow core and the management of the internal threadpool in the Eigen framework.

3.1 Required Modifications in the Eigen Threadpool

The Eigen library responsible for managing the threadpool does not allow a dynamic control of the number of active threads at any arbitrary moment. Therefore, extra information including *status* information is required on a per-thread basis in order to activate/deactivate the normal behavior of the thread exposed in the previous section, effectively stopping the processing of Q_{eigen}.

In addition, the *wait* operation performed by the threads also requires modifications. In our modified version, each thread begins the process of waiting

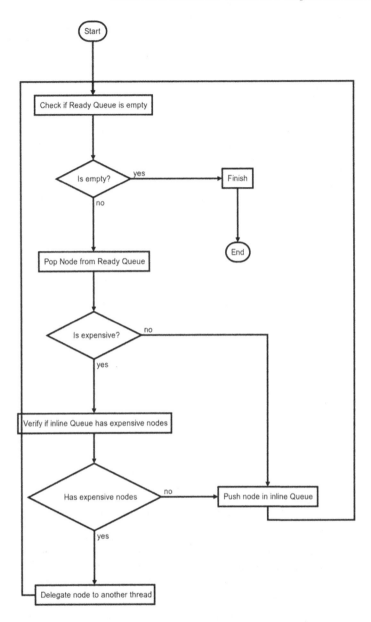

Fig. 1. Thread task scheduler.

for work by evaluating whether it should remain active or not depending on its current *state* (which can be modified externally in an asynchronous fashion).

In case the state is active, the corresponding thread analyzes if it is possible to continue executing nodes that are in its Q_{eigen} or in the queue of another thread. If the thread is inactive, it analyzes if it should wake up to another

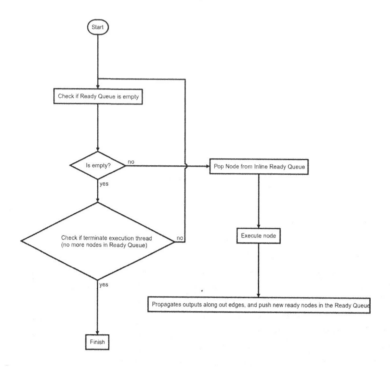

Fig. 2. Execution task procedure.

thread (in case the queue of another thread is not empty and the other threads are asleep) and if it should not fall asleep because it is the only active thread. Finally, if tasks are not available (in a proprietary or alien queue), it waits for another thread to submit work.

3.2 Required Modifications in the Tensorflow Core

The *executor* entity defined in the core of Tensorflow is in charge of scheduling and execution of the graph, as stated in the previous Section, and therefore, it also requires modifications in order to support malleability.

So far, the thread status of the threadpool cannot be controlled from the executor. Actually, the only possible communication allows delegating the execution nodes to another thread. To add this type of extra control, the executor receives information from the thread pool of non-blocking tasks with the possibility of consulting the status of the threads and modifying the number of active threads.

In our modified TensorFlow version, if the executor receives a change in the number of active non-blocking threads from an external entity, it invokes a method of the threadpool so that the number of active threads is increased or decreased (executing nodes).

In addition, each thread keeps information regarding its activation state (*active* or *inactive* thread). This allows checking whether the thread can run or delegate new nodes to another thread. All these changes are made in the node queue scheduling procedure explained in the previous section. Figure 3 depicts the main steps performed by the new thread task scheduler.

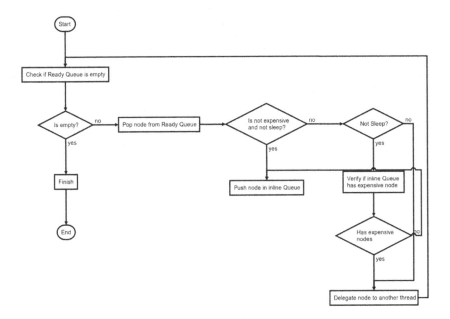

Fig. 3. New thread task scheduler.

4   Experimental Results

Figure 4 report some experimental results obtained on a real malleable TensorFlow implementation modified to integrate the modifications described in Sect. 3. These results were extracted on a system based on an Intel Core i7-8750H processor featuring 6 physical cores (12 logical cores via HyperThreading technology), running at 2.2 GHz of nominal frequency. The system features 32 GBytes of DDR4 RAM memory. From the software perspective, TensorFlow version 2.0.0 was used as our baseline implementation, running on an Ubuntu 18.04 OS.

The traces report execution timelines (one horizontal line per worker thread) for a RESNET56 model defined through Keras, trained through 5 epochs, with 20 steps per epoch. Input dataset images were defined for a dimension 32 × 32 and 3 channels. The number of classes is fixed to 10, with a batch size 128.

We report three different scenarios for the aforementioned training process, namely:

– Figure 4a is a typical TensorFlow implementation with 12 worker threads from the beginning to the end of the execution.
– Figure 4b corresponds to a modified, malleable TensorFlow implementation in which two different thread count changes are performed: the first one limits the number of threads to 6 (reducing from the original 12 worker threads), at the point marked with a vertical red line. Afterwards, worker threads are again restored to 12, at the point marked with a vertical green line. It is observed that before the red line, only two threads run. This occurs because the threads they are running do not delegate operations to others. Operations are delegated when it is expensive and there are other light operations to execute. After the green line, thread number 10 does not execute operations as explained above. It is observed that between the green and red lines, thread 1 becomes inactive and thread 9 begins to run. This is because thread 1 had no more nodes to run and competes with the other threads to get a new one. In this case, thread 9 got new nodes, leaving thread 1 idle.
– Figure 4c shows a similar situation, but reducing the number of active threads to 2 instead of 6, and restoring to full parallelism afterwards. After the green line, threads 3 and 6 are not activated as explained in the previous trace.

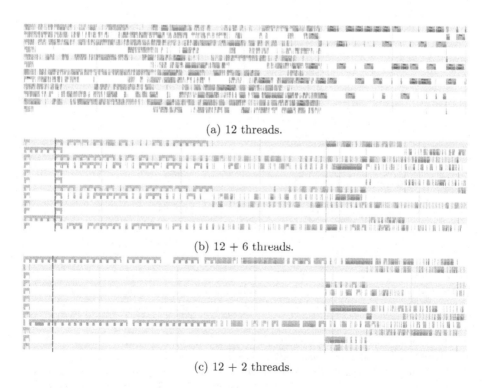

(a) 12 threads.

(b) 12 + 6 threads.

(c) 12 + 2 threads.

Fig. 4. Execution traces for three different threading scenarios. (Color figure online)

Although still general, these results demonstrate the ability of our modified TensorFlow version to seamlessly achieve malleability, and paves the road towards the integration or this malleable version with an application co-scheduler that orchestrates, under demand, the assigned resources to independent Tensor-Flow implementations.

5   Conclusions and Future Work

In this paper, we have introduced and described the main modifications that are required to transform a fixed-parallelism TensorFlow implementation into a *malleable* implementation, in which the degree of parallelism can be dynamically selected and varied (reduced or increased) while the application is running.

This functionality is not present nowadays in the default TensorFlow distribution, and can pave the road towards flexibility and elasticity in shared-resources scenarios (e.g. cloud servers running multiple TensorFlow instances).

Our work, however, is still a fundamental step towards more advanced functionality proposed as future work, among which we can name:

1. *Integration with a co-scheduler.* A malleable library/framework infrastructure only makes real sense when combined with a higher-level resource manager (or co-scheduler), that leverages malleability of the underlying malleability (in this case within TensorFlow) and dynamically modifies the amount of resources assigned to them in a co-ordinated fashion. We are working in this type of resource orchestrator to support efficient co-existence of TensorFlow instances in the same machine.
2. *Creation of a malleability API.* As of today, the malleability is internally selected on specific execution points as proof of concepts. Its management, however, must be transparent and externally selectable, on demand. For that to happen, an ad-hoc API to select the number of active/inactive threads will become mandatory, together with an infrastructure to support thread variation by means of OS signal reception. Both functionalities are in our roadmap.
3. *Management through containers.* Containers allow a dynamic reduction of resources in terms of number of cores, amount of memory and external devices, among others. However, externally reducing the number of assigned cores without a proper reduction of internal software threads derives in a non-acceptable oversubscription effect. As TensorFlow training/inference processes are usually confined within Docker containers, it is mandatory to support malleability in the framework. The interaction between per-container resource management and mallebility in TensorFlow is thus a primary goal of our research.
4. *Intra-task malleability.* The introduced techniques only affect *inter-* parallelism. Malleability within nodes/tasks (*intra-*) is also of interest for us to create a completely malleable parallelism. For that to happen, malleable underlying libraries are mandatory (e.g. malleable BLIS [7] for BLAS tasks –e.g. MATMUL for fully connected layers–).

5. *Heterogeneity support (use of GPUs)*. The integration of worker threads associated with hardware accelerators –mainly GPUs–, and its dynamic activation/deactivation is also in our roadmap, so that graphics processors can also be assigned or unassigned to existing TensorFlow instances at runtime.
6. *Test with real-world problems*. Obviously, the evaluation of the overhead and benefits introduced by malleable TensorFlow implementations on real models and workloads is mandatory and will be of interest in the near future.

References

1. Abadi, M., et al.: TensorFlow: large-scale machine learning on heterogeneous systems (2015). Software available from tensorflow.org
2. Jia, Y., et al.: Caffe: convolutional architecture for fast feature embedding. In: Proceedings of the 22Nd ACM International Conference on Multimedia, MM 2014, New York, NY, USA, 2014, pp. 675–678. ACM (2014)
3. François Chollet et al. Keras (2015). https://keras.io
4. Paszke, A., et al.: Pytorch: an imperative style, high-performance deep learning library. In: Wallach, H., Larochelle, H., Beygelzimer, A., Alché-Buc, F., Fox, E., Garnett, R. (eds.) Advances in Neural Information Processing Systems 32, pp. 8024–8035. Curran Associates Inc. (2019)
5. Hasabnis, N.: Auto-tuning tensorflow threading model for CPU backend. In: 2018 IEEE/ACM Machine Learning in HPC Environments (MLHPC), pp. 14–25. IEEE (2018)
6. Catalán, S., Herrero, J.R., Quintana-Ortí, E.S., Rodríguez-Sánchez, R., van de Geijn, R.A.: A case for malleable thread-level linear algebra libraries: the LU factorization with partial pivoting. IEEE Access **7**, 17617–17633 (2019)
7. Rodríguez-Sánchez, R., Igual, F., Quintana-Orti, E.S.: Integration and exploitation of intra-routine malleability in blis. J. Supercomput. 11 (2019)
8. Rey, A., Igual, F.D., Prieto-Matías, M.: Variable intra-task threading for power-constrained performance and energy optimization in DAG scheduling. J. Supercompu. **75**(3), 1717–1731 (2019). https://doi.org/10.1007/s11227-019-02760-6
9. Xu, P., Shi, S., Chu, X.: Performance evaluation of deep learning tools in docker containers. In: 3rd International Conference on Big Data Computing and Communications, BIGCOM 2017, Chengdu, China, August 10–11, 2017, pp. 395–403. IEEE Computer Society (2017)
10. Guennebaud, G., Jacob, B., et al.: Eigen v3 (2010). http://eigen.tuxfamily.org

Viral Diseases Propagation Analysis in Short Time

Maximiliano Lucero, Natalia Miranda, and Fabiana Piccoli(✉)

LIDIC, Universidad Nacional de San Luis, San Luis, Argentina
{mlucero,ncmiran,mpiccoli}@unsl.edu.ar

Abstract. Studying potentially harmful infectious agents for some population and trying to explain and predicts how the disease evolves in the time are difficult because many factors interactions. An solution is to analyse real systems by mean of simulations models. In these cases, Cellular Automata have been used with success, they can recreate a virtual world take account problem main features and their correlations. We developed an efficient and portable cellular automata model in Graphic Processing Units to simulate viral diseases propagation. The achieved efficiency allows us estimate in a short time the viral disease behaviour when it is known or not, as well as its associated uncertainty. Besides, it is suitable to test effects of different measures that tending towards stop the spread. We describe the solution and evaluate it for two viral diseases: Seasonal Influenza and COVID-19.

1 Introduction

Making decisions is not simple, even more so when systems are complex, they have many interrelated factors. A good solution is to analyse them through simulation techniques.

Permanently, the viral disease diffusion is a great humanity concern. There were cases where a disease caused entire populations extinction and important demographic changes (the plague Europe, yellow fever in Buenos Aires, among others) [14]. On this day, the situation persists, there are many monitored diseases as: malaria, Influenza A, AIDS, and other new as COVID-19. It is important and priority their study and control. One way to address the problem is analysing how each of them is spread in a particular population. The study and analyses of complex real systems like these can be done through some simulation models.

Modeling epidemics by means mathematical tools, we would allow to explain and predict the behavior of infectious agents to human or animal. In 1927 Kermack and McKendrick proposed a SIR (*S*usceptible-*I*nfected-*R*ecovered) model that became the basis for modern epidemic modeling [9]. It considers a hypothetical scenario, a disease develops over time and each involved individuals is in one of three state: Susceptible, Infected and Removed. The SIR model has positively impacted the epidemic area modelling and control by its simplicity, applicability to real data and extensively to other diffusion problems, with more complex

© Springer Nature Switzerland AG 2020
E. Rucci et al. (Eds.): JCC-BD&ET 2020, CCIS 1291, pp. 41–57, 2020.
https://doi.org/10.1007/978-3-030-61218-4_4

mechanisms. From these states and dynamic of each system, different models can arise, some of them are: SI (Susceptible-Infected), SIS (Susceptible-Infected-Susceptible), SEIR (Susceptible-Exposed-Infected-Recovered), and other variants (SIRS, SEIRS, SEIQR, etc.).

When system is simple, the SIR model (or its variants) and differential equations allow predict how is disease behaviour in a population. This can not true to more complex systems (their specifications include many characteristics as environment, population, interactions, evolution, etc.). For this case, it is recommended to use simulations. The simulation allows observing the system evolution over time, understanding their behaviour and, perhaps, being able to predict future events. These systems, generally, use generated data from sensors or mobile devices, and recreate the reality in a time period. Their results allow to define, for examples, evacuation strategies (in case forest fires or floods), massive vaccination or quarantine (to mitigate infectious diseases impact), among others [2,4,19]. Cellular automata is a good election.

Since its popularization in 1970, when Conway defined *Game of Live* [3], the cellular automata (CA) has been successfully used in simulation of diffusion process and, it is a valid alternative when we work with discrete dynamic systems which have complex behaviours from a simple set of evolution rules. In this way, it is possible to model complex dynamic systems from local specification. CA behaviour can display graphically the system evolution, allowing an easy comprehension of studied dynamics. Besides, it is appropriate to apply high performance computing techniques (HPC): each cell can be calculated simultaneously, i.e. in parallel, to others [12,18]. Particularly, we focus in parallel computing over Graphic Process Unit (GPU) [6,7].

This work presents parallel simulator of viral diseases propagation using CA and SEIR model to different GPU. Two diseases are considered: seasonal flu and COVID-19. The solutions allows to study, in short time, how spread each diseases in different environments and conditions, considering type of population, its distribution and other characteristics. From their results, we can take decisions in health, education, economy, etc.

The paper is organized as follows: the next section describes all the previous concepts. Sections 3 and 4 sketch our parallel proposal and their empirical performance. Finally, the conclusions and future works are exposed.

2   Background

In this section, we explain the main concepts to develop this work.

2.1   Cellular Automata

A CA is a mathematical system with discrete values in space, time and state. John Von Neumann and Stanislaw Ulam were the first in formulate it, but Conway proposed the *game of life*, the most known CA. Among CA characteristics, *auto-replication*, universal computation capabilities and *auto-organisation* effects are important [8,20]. CA have been used to simulate different phenomena as chemical reactions, diffusion processes, hydrodynamic, mechanic, filtration, chaos theory and others [13].

A CA is defined as a 4-tuple $M = <A, Q, \delta, N>$ where:

- A is a D-dimensional array, each component (cell) has associated a *finite automata*.
- Q is a finite set of cell states.
- N is the neighbourhood, $N \equiv \{c_i\} \cup N_{c_i}$ such that N_{c_i} are c_i adjacent cells.
- Let $\sigma \equiv Q^n$ where $n = |N_{c_i}|$. The *states transition function*, $\delta : Q \times \sigma \to Q$, is a mapping such that if $q_i \in Q$ is c_i state in the time t and $q_{i+1}, q_{i+2}, ..., q_{i+n} \in \sigma$ are adjacent cells state to c_i, and $\delta(q_i, q_{i+1}, q_{i+2}, ..., q_{i+n}) = q'_i$, is the new state of c_i at the time $t + 1$.

In some cases, it is possible to specify probabilistic transition rules, where an arbitrary probability p can be associated to a transition rule.

2.2   SIR Model and Derivated

If some propagation phenomenon is studied, we have to take into account several considerations, some important are infectious agents (they are responsible of disease transmitting and the states that an individual goes through) and transmission modes (person-to-person, the environment: air, water, etc., food, some vectors such as insects or agents, or among animals of the same or different species). In consequence, as a disease involves many factors, it is impossible to study them of same way. A good start point is to classify states in that an diseased individual can be. A possible states set is:

- S: Healthy individuals and *Susceptible* to be infected.
- E: *Exposed* individual to disease, infected but not infect others (i.e., the disease is latent).
- I: *Infected* individual who contaminates others.
- R: *Recovered* individuals to diseases (normally, it happens after that a person recovers from illness or vaccinates).

In a same time, an individual can be in a single disease stage, therefore for a population of N persons, if we consider the above set of state, the following equation must be satisfied:

$$S + E + I + R = N$$

SIR model consists of three stages: *Susceptible*, *Infected* and *Recovered*. It is easily written using ordinary differential equations (ODEs), this implies a deterministic continuous model. It assumes relationship among infected (I) and susceptible (S) individuals at a rate proportional to their population. These analytical techniques are good to address basic problems, but to epidemics (or pandemics) study, the whole system is more complex, it is necessary realistic solutions and major detail level during the process.

In next paragraphs, we describe the two viral diseases referenced in this work: Seasonal Flu and COVID-19. Their main characteristics are:

– *Seasonal Flu*: There are three types of seasonal influenza: A, B and C. The influenza virus A and B are the most common, they are classified into subtypes according to the combination of two proteins in virus surface (H and N). Influenza affects, primarily, the humans respiratory tract. Usually it accompanied by other symptoms such as sore throat, weakness, dry cough, fever, and muscle aches, of stomach and head. In some cases, it may be complicated and derive in fatal pneumonia. This can occur in two age groups: young children and elderlies.

Virus transmission is done person-to-person, mainly through particles ejected when a sick person coughs, sneezes or talks. Also, it can be transmitted by means blood or contact with surfaces or objects contaminated. Besides, flu virus is resistant to dry and cold environment, this property allows its rapid spread mainly in autumn and winter, seasons when it becomes epidemic. The virus can keep its infections level about one week, however, there are patients that require 15 days. Most people recover without medical treatment.

An infected person with the flu virus goes through an incubation period (approximately from two to four days). The contagious period begins one day before that person has symptoms (this person could be spreading the influenza without knowing that is sick). After a week, the transmission power is reduced, even it disappears. The Fig. 1 summarizes how the disease evolves in a person, from he/she is susceptible until his/her recovering or, in the worst case, death.

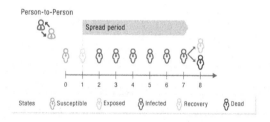

Fig. 1. Influenza progression in people

The most effective way to prevent the flu and its consequences is vaccination. In healthy adults, it can provide reasonable protection, while in elderlies can reduce its severity, the incidence of complications and deaths. There are vaccines for three influenza types, but the vaccination effectiveness depends of the match between the vaccine virus and surrounding virus. Moreover, a vaccine made one year may not be effective to the next by two reasons: the virus mutates rapidly, and its strains have variable dominance [15].

- *COVID-19*: Coronaviruses are a large family of viruses which may cause illness in animals or humans. In humans, several coronaviruses are known to cause respiratory infections ranging from the common cold to more severe diseases. The most recently discovered virus, December 2019, causes COVID-19. It is an infectious disease, its the most common symptoms are fever, tiredness, and dry cough. Some patients may have aches and pains, nasal congestion, runny nose, sore throat or diarrhea. These symptoms are usually mild and begin gradually. Some people become infected but do not develop symptoms. Most people (about 80%) recover from the disease without needing special treatment. Around 1 in 6 people who get COVID-19 becomes seriously ill and develops difficulty breathing. Older people and who with underlying medical problems like high blood pressure, heart problems or diabetes, are more likely to develop it serious.

Virus transmission is done person-to-person, mainly through small particles from nose or mouth which are spread when an infected person coughs, breathes or exhales. These particles land on objects and surfaces, then other people touch them, pass their hands by eyes, nose or mouth and catch COVID-19.

An infected person with the COVID-19 goes through an incubation period (approximately from five to six days). The contagious period starts a few days before the incubation period ends (this person could be spreading it without knowing that is sick). After fourteen days from exposure to the virus, the transmission power is reduced, even it disappears. The Fig. 2 summarizes how the disease evolves in a person, from he/she is susceptible until his/her recovering or, in the worst case, death. From the current world situation, the virus is weather resistant and spreads rapidly any season.

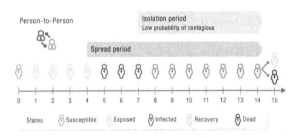

Fig. 2. COVID-19 progression in people

Actually, there are not vaccines or any drugs to prevent it. The only effective measures are identify infected patients, isolate and optimized care them early. Daily, new researches and news are communicated, mainly, by WHO [16].

The both diseases behaviour is similar, the main differences are development period, treatment and prevention measures.

2.3   GPGPU Programming

Mapping general-purpose computation onto GPU implies to use the graphics hardware to solve any applications, not necessarily of graphic nature. This is called GPGPU (General-Purpose GPU), GPU computational power is used to solve general-purpose problems [11,17].

The parallel programming over GPUs has many differences from parallel programming in typical parallel computer, the most relevant are: *The number of processing units, CPU-GPU memory structure* and *Multi-threads programming model.* This is the natural form to generate work on GPU: a single CPU process launches hundreds of threads on GPU. All of them share the same space memory, and they are able to execute independently and at the same time. The traditional multi-threading is used to do time-slicing or take advantage of idle time, i.e. while a thread waits, another could execute.

When the GPU is used as a parallel computer, it necessary taken into account its own characteristics: processing units, memory structure and programming model. Today, there are two mainly frameworks: CUDA y OpenCL, and three GPU makers: NVidia, AMD and Intel.

CUDA was developed by NVidia to own GPU. It provides an essential high-Level development environment with standard high level programming language. It defines the GPU architecture and its programming model: parallel-concurrent threads and the memory hierarchy. Instead, OpenCL is, by definition, an open multi-platform standard, i.e. you can use the most hardware (CPU, GPU, FPGA, among others) to execute your OpenCL program. This program is portable.

NVidia and OpenCL have different approach, but they are actually solving the same problem: how to use the GPU as a general purpose computer. In this work, we present a simulation system for viral diseases transmission using CA, SEIR as models and parallel programming techniques on GPU. We consider different GPU technologies to software and hardware.

3   Parallel Simulation of Viral Diseases

CA have been used with success in simple and complex systems simulations of different scientific areas, such as chemistry, biochemistry, economy, physics, etc. [1,5,10]. In this work, we use it to specify and implement a simulation model that allows to investigate behavioural dynamics for two viral diseases: Seasonal Flu and COVID-19. Our model applies SEIR epidemiological approach and GPGPU techniques. Some experimental results about performance and diseases behaviour are showed.

3.1 Diseases Propagation Model

To simulate diseases propagation, we develop $D - CA$. It has a cellular space defined by a finite two-dimensional lattice. Each CA cell is a place busy by only one person. The cellular space represents a social space, two adjacent occupied cells represent two individual or neighbours in touch. To perform the simulation, it is necessary to establish the following considerations:

- **Neighborhood**: We consider the Moore neighborhood: eight cells surrounding the central cell define it. Every individual interacts with at most 8 people by once [13].
- **Cell State**: A cell is in one Q state, $Q = \{F, S, E_E, E_S, I_A, I_I, I_W, R, D\}$ where:

  - F: Free Cell, there is not any person and it can be selected to occupy.
  - S: The person is susceptible to contract Influenza or COVID-19.
  - E_E: When the person is in incubation period but not spread.
  - E_S: The individual is in incubation period and spreads.
  - I_A: The individual is asymptomatic: he/she is without symptoms but infected and spreads.
  - I_I: The person is infected and spreads the Influenza or COVID-19.
  - I_W: The person is infected but does not spread (She/he has low or zero probability to spread it). The isolated persons can be this case.
  - R: When the person is recovered.
  - D: Dead person. Generally, the deaths can be by any complication.

The transition through each of the states is shown in Fig. 1 and 2. For Seasonal Flu, I_A and I_W not are valid states, they are used for COVID-19.

- **Initial Configuration**: Before simulation begins, it is necessary to set relevant information such as surface size, population, its distribution, the infected population percentage and their ages.
- **Virtual Clock**: Time is discrete, at the simulation beginning, a time interval is set. During this interval, a person can relate with his/her neighborhood and moves to free cell. This movement follows some probabilistic pattern.
- **Model Evolution Rules**: There are two kinds of rules which are: those related to diseases propagation and the persons movement inside CA. Each one of rules are:

1. **Diffusion and Spread Rules**: Influenza A and COVID-19 are two different viral diseases, in consequence they have nonidentical diffusion and spread rules. A cell occupied by a person in time t, also could be occupied in time $t + 1$. It changes its state according to:
   - Seasonal Flu
     - If at time t, the central cell is susceptible (S) and some of its adjacent cells are infected (I). It will be incubating the influenza (E_E) at time $t + 1$. The state change probability is proportional to number of adjacent cells I_I ($S \rightarrow E_E$).

- If the cell is incubating flu (E_E) and t is the end of the asymptomatic period, at time $t+1$ the cell will be in infected state I_I $(E_E \rightarrow I_I)$.
- After 7 days, an infected cell (I_I) in time t will pass to state infected without spread (I_W) at time $t+1$ $(I_I \rightarrow I_W)$.
- In time t, an infected cell $(I_I$ or $I_W)$ could become recovered (R) or dead (D) state (time $t+1$). The selection between two stages depends of a probability function $(\{I_I, I_W\} \rightarrow \{R, D\})$.

- COVID-19
  - If at time t, the central cell is susceptible (S) and, some of its adjacent cells are in some of these three state: E_S, I_A or I_I, the central cell will change its state to E_E (incubating without spread) at time $t+1$, $(S \rightarrow E_E)$. The probability of state change is proportional to contagious adjacent cells number, disease power and the person susceptibility (central cell).
  - At time t, if a cell was 4 days in state E_E, it will pass to state E_S at time $t+1$, $(E_E \rightarrow E_S)$. It begins to spread.
  - If the cell is incubating COVID-19 (E_S) and it is end of incubation period (5 days from it was infected, at time $t+1$, the cell will be in one of two states: I_I or I_A $(E_S \rightarrow I_I/I_A)$.
  - At any time, an asymptomatic cell (I_A) can start to have symptoms $(I_A \rightarrow I_I)$.
  - After 2 days, at time t, a cell infected with symptoms (I_I) has a high probability to be isolate at time $t+1$. From that moment, the person has medical cares and a new state: I_W. The isolation would prevent to continue with propagation $(I_I \rightarrow I_W)$.
  - At time t, a cell infected $(I_A, I_I$ or $I_W)$ could become recovered (R) or dead (D) state (time $t+1$). The new state will be determined by many factors, among them are disease mortality degree, age and comorbidity $(I_A/I_I/I_W \rightarrow \{R, D\})$.

2. **Rules of Person Motion**: A person can move to a neighbour cell if it is free (state F). All free neighbour cells have the same probability to be occupied (uniform distribution). This assumption simplifies the problem. The model represents the people interrelation, a movement in the surface is an abstraction, it can mean that a person moves to speak with other (for example an work-mate) or, he/she goes to a business and relates with a vendor. A neighbourhood change implies at least two virtual clock periods. The movement is not physical, it models the interaction between a person and its neighbourhood.

Whit this specification, the implementation is easier.

3.2 GPGPU Solution

Every GPGPU solution has many basic steps, first the input data transfers to the graphics card. Once data are in place, many threads/work-items can start with little overhead (In this text, we use CUDA and OpenCL terminology because the solution is suitable to both). Each thread/work-item works over its data and, at the computation end, the results should be copied back to the host main memory. Algorithm 1 presents the deceases spread simulation core, which performs a complete simulation on particular environment.

Algorithm 1. CPU-GPU D-CA Main

1: Init environment
2: Set Simulator Parameters
3: Show (Env-Stat-Perf)
4: **while** time or cell in $\{E_E, I_A, I_I, I_W\}$ **do**
5:      GPU-Parallel threads/work-items calculate
6:          New Cell State
7:          Cell Movement Intention
8:      GPU-Parallel threads/work-items: Solve
9:          Movement Conflict
10:     Update Environment
11:     Collect statistics
12:     Show (Env-Stat-Perf)
13: **end while**

At lines 1 and 2, input simulator parameters are initialized, they are environment, population size, its distribution, each persons characteristic and random seed (we work with a stochastic system, many variables/states are set random). Then, lines 4–12, the deceases are propagated. First a GPU threads/work-items set (CUDA Grid or OpenCL Index Space) is launched to calculate each new cell state and its movement intention according its neighborhood. Once all these are done for every cell, other GPU threads/work-items set is launched, in this case each one solves movement conflicts and sets the new position of its cell. A thread/work-item is in charge only one cell. Finally, the new situation is established (line 10), partial results for statistics are collected (line 11) and some them are showed, they are:

- *Env*: CA and the state of every cells. It is possible select how often is displayed: each 5 periods, one of day, etc.
- *Stat*: Values to calculate statistics: number of illness, dead, healthy, etc.
- *Perf*: Simulation times. This values are printing only at the simulation end.

Two steps are necessary on GPU, in the first, if cell is not free and person lives, each thread/work-item computes own next state and decides if he/she has intention to move. To determine the next state, the CA rules are applied. Once established it, the cell can choose to move to one of its free neighbours cells (When there are two o more, one is random selected). The thread/work-item adds its cell to the movement intentions list of selected free cell. When this step finishes, the new CA is obtained and each free cell has an intention list to be occupied by one of its neighbour.

The second step resolves movement conflicts, only those threads/work-items work whose cell is free. They take into account its intentions list of its cell and select randomly one of candidates to move there. Selected cell is moved and its old position is marked free. In the worst case, the list of intentions will have a maximum of eight candidates to move (Moore neighbourhood).

These two steps are two different kernels and are executed in strict sequence. Both launch the same quantity threads/work-items (cells number), but work over disjointed subset of cells: lives or free, respectively.

The simulation can end when one of these two conditions is achieved: maximum simulation time or some stable state, whichever first occurs. Maximum simulation time can be modified and set. The second condition is possible when the last sick person is cured or dies, nobody in the current population could get it. This situation can be occur in small populations or with strict health measures or high demographic distribution.

The next section some experimental results of this GPGPU D-CA are displayed.

4   Experimental Results

In this section, we show and analyse the experimental results to D-CA. Each reported value is the average of many executions of the corresponding algorithm. For each simulation, we consider different social scenarios. All of them have in common the maximum time of simulation: 120 days, and the virtual clock: a timestep is equivalent to 1 h.

The analysis was made for three GPU, whose characteristics are:,

	Architecture	Global memory	Cores	Clock rate
GTX1070	Pascal	8 GB	1920 CUDA cores	1683 MHz
AMD R7 M260	Topaz	2 GB	384 stream processors	980 MHz
Iris graphics 6100	Generation 8.0	1.5 GB	384 shading processors	1100 MHz
CPU	Intel i7-7700K	16 GB	4	4.20 GHz

Each social scenarios is defined by a next parameters combination:

- Environment
  - Population: 10%, 25%, 50% and 90% of cells of lattice. We consider a stationary type of population pyramid, each individual has an age between 1 to 90 years and there are three groups of person: *Children* (Up to 18 years old), *Young-Adult* (19 to 60 years) and *Elder* (Greater than 61 years). The degree susceptibility to infection and the mortality rate is determined according of individual age [15,16] and other pre-existing diseases.
  - Lattice Size: 100, 200, 1500, 5500 and 8500 by side. These lattice size we can compare with real urban center.
- Disease

	Seasonal Flu	COVID-19
Disease power	0.6	2.7
Mortality index	0.01	0.057
Initial infected population	0.02%, 2%, 10%	5, 35 and 75 persons
Risk group	Children and elder	Elder or person with comorbidity
Isolation probability	None	85%

We divide the tests in two groups: Performance and Diseases behaviour. For the first case, we evaluate if our GPGPU proposals work well and their performance are better than sequential solution. The Fig. 3(a) shows the time (in seconds) reached for different simulation scenarios in different technologies: software (CUDA and OpenCL), and GPU architectures (NVidia, AMD and Intel). There are some cases that hardware resources are not enough to solve the problem.

The Fig. 3(b) graphs the achieved time for three population scenarios. In all case, the best performance is reached to NVidia GPU and CUDA. Even more, if we compare between the CUDA-solution and OpenCL-solution over the same GPU, the lowest time is reached by CUDA-solution. The difference is small, but you have to evaluate what do you want: portability or performance. In this sense, the Fig. 4 shows the spent time for the same surface dimension and different population amount. The time is similar in most GPUs, although it is observed influence of population size or disease spread degree, mainly in GPU with few resources.

Lattice Size		100x100	200x200	1500x1500	5500x5500	8000x8000
Cells Number (KB)		10	40	2250	30250	64000
CPU: Intel I7 7700k		3,44	13,86	807,72	13.429,73	-
CUDA	Nvidia GTX1070	0,25	0,36	10,44	146,62	344,59
OpenCL	Nvidia GTX1070	0,27	0,45	11,55	150,77	-
	AMD R7 M260	2,06	5,56	228,30	-	-
	Iris Graphics 6100	3,22	5,69	132,31	-	-

(a)

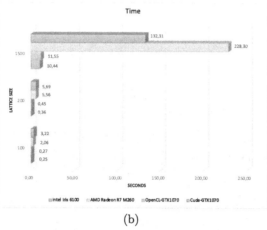

(b)

Fig. 3. Time of GPGPU D-CA for 50% population and the lowest initial infection.

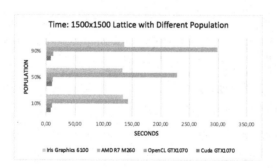

Fig. 4. Time of GPGPU D-CA for 1500 × 1500 lattice and different population

The second tests group is related to diseases behaviour analysis. GPGPU D-CA would allow us, in a short time, to study how act each disease for different environments and parameters, for example we can analyse:

- How many active and total case for a population and different number of initial infected persons. The Fig. 5 shows the Influenza and COVID-19 behaviour for 8500 lattice, 50% population and two size of initial infections.
- The daily amount of recovered, deaths and active sick persons, see Fig.6.
- Disease behaviour according to population density. In Fig. 7, we show the same population amount distributed different surface sizes, and in Fig. 8 the same space with different population densities.

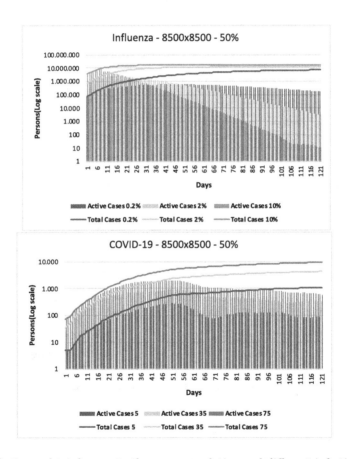

Fig. 5. Active and total cases to the same population and different infection initial

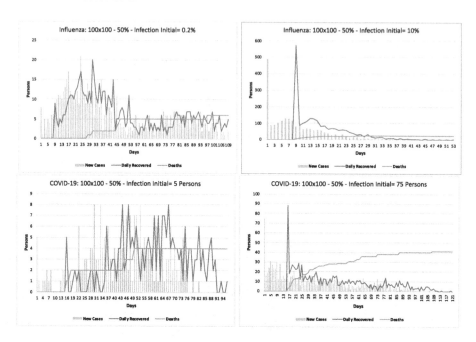

Fig. 6. Number of deaths, recovered and new cases for different scenarios

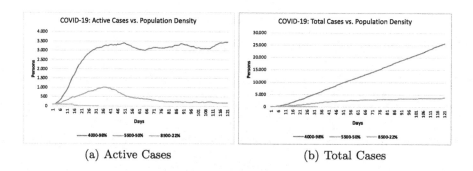

(a) Active Cases   (b) Total Cases

Fig. 7. Same Population for different densities and initial infection (75 persons)

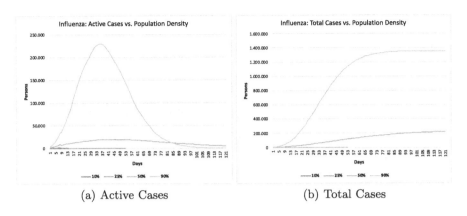

(a) Active Cases　　　　　　　　　　(b) Total Cases

Fig. 8. Same space and initial infection (0.2%), but different densities

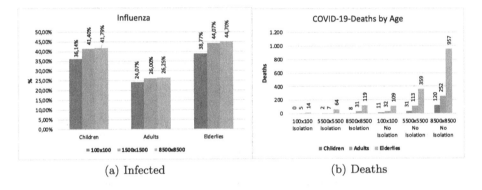

(a) Infected　　　　　　　　　　(b) Deaths

Fig. 9. Disease effects by each age group for different surfaces with 50% population

– How each illness affects each age group, for example percentage of Influenza Infected (Fig. 9(a)), and deaths number by COVID-19 with or without isolation (Fig. 9(b)).
– If health measures have benefits or not. The Fig. 10 displays total and actives cases of COVID-19 with and without quarantine.

All results, both performance and diseases behaviour, show that GPGPU D-CA enables, in a short time, to analyse effects of viral diseases propagation. Their behaviours were checked against the reported by WHO.

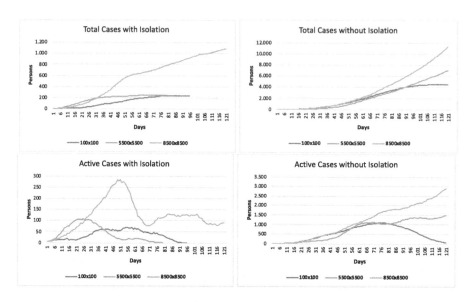

Fig. 10. Effects of isolation measure for 50% population and initial infection (5 persons)

5   Conclusions and Future Work

In this work, we have developed an application to viral diseases propagation simulation using a CA and HPC techniques to GPU. We accomplish with two goals: study viral diseases behaviour from different view points, and implement an efficient solution: D-CA. The proposal model uses the CA and SEIR concepts to analyse the effects of Seasonal Flu and COVID-19 for populations with a territorial distribution and interactions among people.

All performance and disease behaviour results show that GPGPU D-CA is a good analysis tools. In short time, it could help us to better understand the diseases spread mechanisms for different population or regions. Beside it is portable and has good scalability, mainly to problem size.

The next step will be to solve the limitations derived from GPU resources, mainly memory size. In this direction, there are two alternatives, one is considering data partition and many GPU steps, and the other is multi-GPU environments.

Another open lines are, related to improve performance: studying the application memory use in order to reduce memory latencies as well as to enhance memory bandwidth usage; or with the simulator: including a visualization tool for diseases propagation in OpenGL and a graphic interface to set dynamically diseases environments and some parameters related with, for examples health measures: vaccines or comorbidity diseases characteristics.

References

1. Beauchemin, C., Samuel, J., Tuszynski, J.: A simple cellular automaton model for influenza a viral infections. J. Theor. Biol. **232**(2), 223–234 (2005)
2. Casares, F., Tissera, P., Piccoli, F.: A parallel proposal for seir model using cellular automata. In: XXII Congreso Argentino de Ciencias de la Computación (CACIC 2016), pp. 208–219 (2016)
3. Gardner, M.: Mathematical games. Sci. Am. **222**(1), 124–127 (1970)
4. Gaudiani, A., Luque, E., Garcia, P., Naiouf, M., De Giusti, A.: Optimización y computación paralela aplicados a mejorar la predicción de un simulador de cauce de ríos. In: XXII Congreso Argentino de Ciencias de la Computación (CACIC 2016), pp. 179–188 (2016)
5. Gu, Y., Ding, J.: Research on rumors spread based on cellular automata. In: Yang, Y., Ma, M. (eds.) Proceedings of the 2nd International Conference on Green Communications and Networks 2012 (GCN 2012): Volume 1. Lecture Notes in Electrical Engineering, vol. 223. Springer, Heidelberg (2013). https://doi.org/10.1007/978-3-642-35419-9_28
6. Han, J., Sharma, B.: Learn CUDA Programming: A Beginner's Guide to GPU Programming and Parallel Computing with CUDA 10.x and C/C++. Packt Publishing, Birmingham (2019)
7. Kaeli, D.R., Mistry, P., Schaa, D., Zhang, D.P.: Heterogeneous Computing with OpenCL 2.0. Elsevier, Amsterdam (2015)
8. Kauffman, S.: Emergent properties in random complex automata. Phys. D: Nonlinear Phenom. **10**(1), 145–156 (1984)
9. Kermack, W., McKendrick, A., Walker, G.: A contribution to the mathematical theory of epidemics. Proc. R. Soc. Lond. Ser. A Contain. Pap. Math. Phys. Character **115**(772), 700–721 (1927)
10. Kier, L.B., Seybold, P.G., Cheng, C.K.: Modeling Chemical Systems Using Cellular Automata. Springer, Heidelberg (2005). https://doi.org/10.1007/1-4020-3690-6
11. Kirk, D., Hwu, W.: Programming Massively Parallel Processors, Λ Hands on Approach. Morgan Kaufmann, Elsevier, Burlington (2010)
12. Kurgalin, S., Borzunov, S.: Implementation of parallel algorithms. A Practical Approach to High-Performance Computing, pp. 93–115. Springer, Cham (2019). https://doi.org/10.1007/978-3-030-27558-7_6
13. Li, X., Wu, J., Li, X.: Concluding remarks—looking to the future. Theory of Practical Cellular Automaton, pp. 323–352. Springer, Singapore (2018). https://doi.org/10.1007/978-981-10-7497-4_9
14. McMillen, C.W.: Pandemics: A Very Short Introduction. Very Short Introductions. Oxford University Press, Oxford (2016)
15. World Health Organization: Influenza (seasonal) (2018). Fact sheet
16. World Health Organization: Coronavirus disease (covid-19) (2020). Situation Report 116
17. Owens, J., Houston, M., Luebke, D., Green, S., Stone, J., Phillips, J.: GPU computing. IEEE **96**, 879–899 (2008)
18. Pacheco, P.: An Introduction to Parallel Programming. Elsevier, Amsterdam (2011)
19. Tissera, P., Castro, A., Printista, A., Luque, E.: Simulating behaviours to face up an emergency evacuation. CoRR arxiv:1401.5209 (2014)
20. Wolfram, S.: Universality and complexity in cellular automata. Phys. D: Nonlinear Phenom. **10**(1), 1–35 (1984)

Architectural Design Criteria for Evolvable Data-Intensive Machine Learning Platforms

Gonzalo Zarza$^{(\boxtimes)}$ (ID) and Juan José López Murphy (ID)

Data and Analytics, and Artificial Intelligence Studios,
Globant, Buenos Aires, Argentina
{gonzalo.zarza,juanjose.lopez}@globant.com

Abstract. Recent advances in Artificial Intelligence (AI) have fostered a widespread adoption of Machine Learning (ML) capabilities within many products and services. However, most organizations are not well suited to fully exploit the strategic advantages of AI. Implementing ML solutions is still a complex endeavor due to the fast-pace evolution and the intrinsic exploratory nature of state-of-the-art ML techniques. In many respects, the evolution of data platforms through highly parallel or high performance technologies have focused on the capacity to massively process the elements consumed by these ML models. This separate consideration renders reference architectures to be either suited for analytics consumption, or for raw storage. There is no joint consideration for the complete cycle of data management, models development, and serving with feedback and human-in-the-loop requirements. This paper introduces design criteria conceived to help organizations to architect and implement data platforms to effectively exploit their ML capabilities. The main objective of this work is to expedite the development of data platforms for ML by avoiding common implementation mistakes. The proposed guideline constitutes the methodical articulation of the empirical knowledge acquired over the last years designing, developing, evolving and maintaining a broad spectrum of relevant industry-oriented Data and AI solutions. We have focused on evaluating our proposal by assessing the functionality and usability of the architectures and implementations originated from our design criteria.

Keywords: Data platform · Design criteria · Deep learning · Big data

1 Introduction

Artificial Intelligence (AI) plays a major role in a growing number of services and products we use and consume everyday, ranging from navigation apps (Waze, Google Maps) and recommendations systems (Netflix, Amazon, Elsevier) up to more critical health-support systems including automatic cancer detection and classification [8,21], and even helping to fasten the diagnosis of patients infected by the novel *COVID-19* [22].

© Springer Nature Switzerland AG 2020
E. Rucci et al. (Eds.): JCC-BD&ET 2020, CCIS 1291, pp. 58–77, 2020.
https://doi.org/10.1007/978-3-030-61218-4_5

There is a general consensus that such developments have been enabled by major improvements made in the fields of Machine Learning (ML), and particularly in Deep Learning (DL), over the last few years. This trend implies that ML and its applications have become a major actor in our day to day routine and will have a non-stopping and ever-growing impact on our lives in the near future. ML applications are mostly characterized by being intensive in terms of both data and computing processing, thus requiring the best of both worlds to be useful for the users and at the end to the society as a whole: High-Performance Computing (HPC) to support the ever-growing demand for on-line calculations; and Big Data to enable the extraction of valuable knowledge from both structured and unstructured massive data sources.

Despite sharing common origins in the research community, conjugating the best of both spaces to cope with the blended data and computing needs of ML applications is not an easy task, mainly due to the underlying subtle discrepancies in the solution approach taken by each field of knowledge. On one hand, Big Data solutions are currently oriented towards providing highly efficient streaming or Near Real-Time (NRT) data processing features and effective knowledge extraction, while delegating most of the fine-grain computing efficiency technicalities on hardware providers –and to some extent, on the major cloud service providers. On the other hand, HPC solutions are well-known by excelling in computing performance and paying great attention to efficient software-hardware cohesion and complement. However, given the large-scale and long-haul nature of computing tasks that run on supercomputers, most HPC systems are highly optimized to ensure the completion of job executions by providing the necessary mechanisms to this end (such as fault tolerance and disaster recovery) rather than on providing support to handling and exploiting data generated from real-time user interaction and feedback. For instance, most HPC applications have not being designed to react *on-line* to data streams being generated in real-time by end-users, as it happens in large-scale applications based on Participatory Sensing Systems (PSSs) [5,18] such as Waze or Google Maps.

This paper describes our effort to shorten the aforementioned gap, leveraging the knowledge from both fields to enable efficient interactive data-intensive ML applications. To address this challenge, we have focused on defining design criteria to guide the development of efficient yet evolvable system architectures. The proposed guideline constitutes the methodical articulation of the empirical knowledge acquired over the last years designing, developing, evolving and maintaining a broad spectrum of relevant industry-oriented Data and AI solutions for business verticals such as Operations Research Optimization, Industrial Automation, Investment Banking and Health Care, among others. The design criteria we present in this paper has two main purposes. First, to facilitate and expedite the development of effective data platforms to handle the complete life cycle of ML applications. Second, to help avoid common –and not that common– mistakes when implementing evolvable data-intensive platforms. The proposed design criteria have been validated through the successful rapid implementation and deploy of data-intensive ML platforms for different verticals and industries, as well as being used as the main AI platform on Globant's R&D initiatives. In our evaluation, we explore scenarios and real cases where the tenets of the present guidelines are applied to showcase their usage.

This paper is organized as follows. First, a deep discussion about the motivation of our proposal, together with the review of the most relevant related work in the literature, are presented in Sect. 2. Then, the proposed design criteria is described in detail in Sect. 3; and the resulting experiences and observations are introduced in Sect. 4. Finally, the conclusions are drawn in Sect. 5.

2 Motivation

Large scale AI developments, once a latent research line leveraged almost exclusively by companies such as Google or Facebook, are nowadays available and strategic for most modern organizations, regardless of their size and budget. This broader use base has fueled an explosion of interest in this area of knowledge given that not being well suited for AI implies a major strategic disadvantage for most industries. Notwithstanding, implementing AI solutions is still a complex endeavor mainly because of the fast-pace evolution and the intrinsic exploratory nature of state of the art ML techniques [17]. This complexity also extends to the platforms that support and serve those developments given that, in general, ML projects consist of a vast array of separate elements that need to be integrated with current systems, and also linked with a clear vision on how that adds value to users, whether internal or external.

The first step to deal with the above-mentioned complexity is to identify the predominant characteristics that drive ML applications. Identifying their dominant attributes creates a significant opportunity to define a common set of building blocks that can be used to design systems and platforms capable of effectively handling such complexities. We try to seize that opportunity by defining the design criteria for evolvable data-intensive platforms based on this analysis, as discussed in Sect. 3. A study of popular ML applications suggests that there are shared dominant features to most of them:

- **Heterogeneous computing.** Given the compute-intensive nature of training DL models, there is a prominent trend towards hardware specialization to improve performance, given raise to specific processing unit architectures such as GPUs, TPUs, or the Intel's Nervana and Habana neural network processor families. Even though the problem of dealing with computing heterogeneity has been widely addressed –and solved– for HPC systems, it is not very common to be addressed outside the academic and super-computing spheres. In fact, it still poses huge challenges for small and medium size companies and organizations that do not rely on extensive experience on high-performance solutions, and have limited budget compared with large corporations or research institutions.
- **Non-uniform use of resources.** The use of resources in ML applications depends on the stage of their development life-cycle and presents different

characteristics, e.g. modeling, training and serving that make them intensive on the use of different resources. For instance, most ML applications, and specially DL solutions, are often made of very deep neural networks which implies that training them for inference takes up a lot of computer power. A similar bridge can be found between the use and serving of DL models and data-intensive access patterns. In addition, the access to share resources (mainly computing) pose new challenges given that the modeling and training phases of ML developments are characterized by being predominantly interactive or even based on *try-and-failure*, while the serving phase responds to a more traditional access pattern.

- **Deployment and versioning dependencies.** A lot of research work has been devoted in recent years to advance the frontiers of ML, particularly in DL, fostering the continuous evolution of models due to data changes, new methods, new training strategies, etc. This situation gives raise to a whole new set of challenges in terms of efficient identification, checkpointing and serving of ML models because they need to be updated more frequently than other types of software applications. It is not uncommon to host a model that relies on different set of parameters to serve several clients. Or even having the same client accessing different sets of parameters for the same solution, e.g. financial services from multinational banks targeting different markets or countries (thus requiring different network parameters). This dynamism presents new challenges to the linear branching approach of current versioning systems.

The aforementioned features pose a narrow solution space for creating manageable and cost effective platforms for ML. Several academic and industrial organizations made significant investments to develop custom solutions. Some of the most relevant are the following: Facebook's AI backbone, *FBLearner Flow* [7], optimized to ease the reuse of algorithms and leveraging their own infrastructure, akin to cloud-based ML services such as Microsoft's Azure Machine Learning; Uber's ML platform, *Michelangelo* [13], enables internal teams to cover the end-to-end ML workflow, from building to training, up to deploy and monitor thousands of models in production across the company; *MLflow*, the open-source ML platform from Databricks [24], designed to automate the life cycle of ML solutions with an open interface to most ML libraries; Google's platform for deploying production ML pipelines, *TensorFlow Extended* (TFX) [4], providing production-grade support to their ML pipelines with a focus on TensorFlow; and the Stanford *Data Analytics for What's Next* (DAWN) research project [3], intended to make tools for AI and data product development more efficient and accessible by working on several research lines, including new interfaces to ML, end-to-end ML systems, and new substrates for ML.

These solutions emerged in the context of specific angles of the problematic, with a sizable number of configurations remaining that still pose challenges as of this writing. There are three main regions or groups of solutions, according to their scale: Proof of Concepts (POCs), not meant to be productive nor part of the critical path of most businesses; really massive applications supported by well-funded companies such as Google, Amazon or Uber, with a set of specific requirements addressed by custom-made and highly-scalable solutions, often open-sourced as in the case of the Hadoop implementation [2,20] based on the Google's MapReduce [6] and Google File System (GFS) [11] developments; and the wide span between the previous two groups, which are not covered by any existing solution to the best of our knowledge, regardless of representing most of current and future ML endeavors. Within this group we will find applications such as Elsevier's ScienceDirect, medical devices augmented by AI, and even real-time systems used for security purposes such as automatic license plate recognition at nerve centers of neuralgic cities such as Buenos Aires.

This wide range of applications laying in the middle of the spectrum, share common functional requirements and patterns including complex management, an increased hardware footprint, and data and processing duplication. Currently, those needs are addressed on an on-demand or ad-hoc manner, but whose solution has the potential of being standardized. To overcome these issues and provide more flexibility for future demands, we have first identified and characterized those requirements by leveraging the experience gained over the last years implementing Data and AI solutions. An effort to incorporate that learning requires the formulation of design criteria to guide the development of data-intensive platforms for the wide-range of ML applications that are not properly covered at this moment. This is the ultimate goal of this work and will be introduced in detail in the following section.

3   Architectural Design Criteria

Some of the most predominant and difficult problems found on ML installations have to do with the variety of data, use cases, users, and environments the underlying platform must support through the different stages of the ML life cycle. Such problems tend to be the least glamorous to address but are also among the most important since they may fundamentally limit the usefulness of the system as a whole [12]. The typical life cycle of a ML application covers not only the model development but also the stages of training, inference and serving. Each stage imposes different requirements to the underlying platform and demands solutions to address common problems such as neural network modeling, feature management, data provenance and storage, low-latency serving, etc. This situation emphasizes the need of unifying design principles and systems architected to address those requirements.

In the following paragraphs, we introduce and describe in detail the results of our effort to overcome this situation, leveraging the knowledge from HPC and Big Data to enable the design and development of efficient data-intensive ML platforms. First, we elaborate and present the principles of the proposed architectural design criteria for evolvable ML platforms. Then, we articulate and describe in detail each unit. We start by analyzing the characteristics of the data to be handled and maintained in Sect. 3.1. In Sect. 3.2, we focus on the modules needed to support the most critical functionalities of ML platforms.

A technology-agnostic reference platform architecture is introduced in Sect. 3.3. Relevant examples of custom implementations based on the reference architecture are described in Sect. 3.4.

Our design criteria have been built from the ground up to aid on designing and developing efficient data-intensive ML platforms, taking into account the issues discussed above. We realize the need of characterizing the dominant attributes of effective data platforms as the first step in defining useful guidelines for the specific needs of ML [14]. Based on our experience implementing data platforms for many industries, we have identified the following dominant attributes:

1. **Agnosticism.** The prevalent uninterrupted evolution of tools and frameworks –together with their vertiginous blossom and obsolescence– highlights the importance of designing systems that are independent of specific technologies. Being technology-agnostic became almost mandatory for modern platform architectures. An agnostic approach will prevent being held captive of technology life cycles and feature prioritization, thus avoiding unnecessary architecture constraints given by the applicability –or incompatibility– of particular tools and frameworks, as in some examples in Sect. 2.

2. **Evolvability.** As stated by Ford et al. [9], changes in software projects are usually driven by a reevaluation of functionality and/or scope. Therefore, given the ever-evolving nature of ML systems, where users constantly experiment with new datasets, models, software libraries, parameters, etc., it is imperative to carefully design platforms to cope with such changes. This has turned evolvability into a critical feature for effective ML platforms.

3. **Modularity.** The separation and isolation provided by modular architectures are key to ensure that one component (typically a module) does not interfere with the behavior of others [1]. Consequently, the design of a proper modular architecture –to the largest possible extent– will leave room for further expansions of the platform by enabling seamless updates, upgrades and replacements of modules. In addition, relying on a modular architectural design is paramount to achieve effective evolvability.

4. **Data-savviness.** Undoubtedly, handling data and user data flows efficiently is the most challenging and valuable operation to be performed on any modern ML platform. It is of utmost importance because data is the raw material that fuels ML and AI initiatives in a broad sense [19]. Many data flows are generated throughout the life cycle of ML applications, however, correctly handling them entails significant data challenges for many reasons. First, the high-throughput and low-latency data reads and writes required in ML. Second, their specific processing requirements that often go beyond aggregation and join operations on the data. Third, the need to combine data –frequently unstructured or semi-structured– from disparate storage systems and heterogeneous sources.

We now turn to describing how the above mentioned building blocks are materialized in an architecture proposal by following an incremental development approach, starting from the analysis of the data and storage needs up to implementation blueprints for different reference solutions. Many of these concepts are not new, but rather viewed through a new lens in which these attributes enable platforms to effectively cope with the prevailing ML application challenges (introduced in Sect. 2): heterogeneous computing, non-uniform use of resources, and deployment and versioning dependencies. This is where much of our effort was devoted, and what makes the proposed criteria a useful guideline for designing data-intensive ML platforms.

3.1   Data-Savviness: Analysis of Data Needs

Nowadays, it is almost a no-brainer noticing the criticality of data to ML. The theory is solid, but in practice, things became challenging when dealing simultaneously with vast amounts of structured, semi-structured and unstructured data from heterogeneous sources, specially for NRT multi-tenant applications. Under these circumstances, usual in ML developments, it is imperative to thoroughly and deeply identify and evaluate each data flow and the specific data operation requirements for the ML solutions to support. It is possible to identify a number of relevant data categories by analyzing the operation modes a ML platform needs to provide support to over its life cycle. The most meaningful groups are:

1. **Checkpoints.** Commonly large binary files (dozens and even hundreds of GBs) that maintain a fixed size given a certain model. The file may evolve into a different file (different hash) if the model parameters change, which does not imply a variation in size but in content of the file.
2. **Training datasets.** There are several major groups of datasets currently being used by ML models, including text and multimedia inputs such as images, audio, video, etc. The type of data to be stored, and the corresponding requirements, will strictly depend on the use case. The access pattern of these inputs will be sporadic, however, their retrieve pattern will stress the storage system since the media will be access as a whole (ideally in parallel) to generate a specific checkpoint.
3. **Metadata.** The majority of files stored in the platform will be paired with their corresponding metadata. Such information will be used as the main search criteria for datasets. It will be represented by dictionaries with different hash codes indicating where to look for the specific data in a stored file and also which tags are associated with it.
4. **Model feedback.** Feedback formats will depend on the use case and the support the models count with to provide it. Frequently, it will be represented by a simple Yes/No, Agree/Disagree or a reasonably sized JSON object specifying more details. In other scenarios, users might provide the correct solution to the original data (e.g. painting the zone of the image which presents what should have been detected), increasing the feedback size significantly.
5. **Model resolution.** Resolution formats will depend on the specific model. To avoid unnecessary overheads, when dealing with multimedia data, it is important to design the model –if possible– to provide resolutions based

on text files to enhance the media (such as JSONs) instead of re-sending the resolved media over the network. This is particularly important when working with audio and video files that tend to be large. However, there will be some cases in which the same input media data needs to be returned to the client (as in style transferring models), thus the data pipelines need to be designed accordingly.

6. **Execution feedback.** It represents the entire set of data –and information– obtained during the execution of the platform components, such as message brokers, APIs, ML models, etc.

The data corresponding to each group can be grouped around relevant data characteristics, as summarized in Table 1. The data framed on each category interacts with –and is originated from– diverse data flows that may pose specific requirements for segregated storage paths due to several reasons, such as:

- **Security.** Data platforms often handle proprietary data (e.g. industrial, commercial or trade secret data) that should not be accessed nor available to other clients or entities. For this reason, it may be necessary to set up and provide segregated access to such assets.
- **Confidentiality.** Some subset of data, regardless of its category, may be subject to specific regulations and thus, it will be necessary to either segregate and restrict access to that data, or even provide a completely isolated (and potentially replicated) storage.
- **Efficiency.** Data consumption and use patterns convey highly different requirements on data storage and retrieval, thus enabling (or demanding) different storage solutions, locations, and technologies. For instance, efficiently accessing and retrieving non-structured data greatly differs from fetching binary data.

Additional data topics to be considered are: encryption; replication and fault tolerance; certified data destruction policies (e.g. medical records); and unique data identification (crucial to have an effective destruction policy), among others.

3.2   Modularity: Analysis of Requirements

There is no doubt that ML is all about data and that the amount of effort and rigor it takes to discover, source, manage, and version data is inherently more complex and different than doing the same with software code [1]. Therefore, the first step to design a data platform for ML is to accurately identify those components that can be grouped together and operate as independent parts with standard interfaces between them. The analysis previously introduced constitutes a solid starting point for the identification of predominant features and common reusable components to most data platforms.

The main idea underlying modular design is to organize complex systems as a set of distinct components that can be developed independently and then plugged together to operate as a cohesive entity [10]. This concept, materialized as modular architectures, has become essential to reduce the impact and hassle of software and technology obsolescence in modern data platforms caused mainly by the fast-pace evolution of ML models, tools and frameworks. The main modules are illustrated in Fig. 1(a). Similarly, Fig. 1(b) shows the key functionalities encapsulated within each module.

Starting from the analysis of data needs, it is possible to identify the need of two data-focused modules: persistence and exploitation. The **data persistence** module is responsible for providing a common abstract layer to persist each data type to its corresponding storage solution, based on the categories detailed in Table 1, decoupling the business logic of the platform entities from the underlying storage technologies. In addition, the data persistence module typically includes automated data integration tools to perform basic data transformation to incoming data flows. The **data exploitation** module groups together the tools and frameworks that operate on the system data. It is usually composed of tools for data visualization, filtering, full-text search and processing.

Taking into account the data handling operations required in ML platforms, it is evident the need for a third module that would be responsible for securing and protecting the access and transit, not only of data but also to the entire platform, together with the administration of users, groups and operation permissions. The **security** module groups functionalities compassing the overall security of the platform, including data governance and access control. At a minimum, this component should have three sub-modules: data encryption, user management, and access control (crucial for APIs). Data encryption capabilities are required to secure and protect data in transit and in storage within the platform. User management comprises user authentication and authorization tools, and support for permissions, roles and groups management. The access control sub-module

Table 1. Summary of data from the major groups.

Category	Write freq.	Read freq.	Size	Type	Queryable	Main stages
Checkpoints	Low	Low to medium	Large, single files	Binary	No	Training, serving
Training datasets	Low[a]	Medium	Variable, many files	Text & multimedia	No[b]	Training, serving
Metadata	Low	High	Small, many records	Text	Yes	Training
Model feedback	Medium to high	Low	Small, many records	Primarily text	Yes	Serving
Model resolution	Medium to high[c]	Low	Variable, many files	Text & multimedia	No[b]	Serving
Execution feedback	Low to medium	Low	Small, many records	Text, logs	Yes	N/A

[a] The write frequency could be higher when applying data transformation models.
[b] Querying capabilities on text files may be required.
[c] Note that resolutions will probably be stored for further analysis.

is in charge of securing the external access to critical system interfaces, and to validate the clearance level required to perform each predefined set of actions within the platform.

In addition, given the event-based nature of modern data and ML frameworks and tools, it is necessary to rely on a shared core utilities module that includes features and mechanisms for event handling. This gives rise to the **core utilities** module, intended to standardize the development tools and centralize common features among all components, including the infrastructure scripts.

The complex and ever-growing nature of modern platforms are not easy to manage and handling. For this reason, it is crucial to provide platforms with efficient management and monitoring capabilities based on analytics from the platform, users and products. The **management** module comprises two main sub-modules: analytics and monitoring. The analytics sub-module is responsible for enabling real-time analytics and monitoring on current traffic, topology status and APIs activities. It provides usage information for every user and across users. Usually, it offers users their own analytics as a separate product. The goal of the monitoring sub-module is to provide services to: prevent incidents, proactive alerts 24/7, evaluate SLA, prevent service loss or degradation, etc. It should provide two types of metrics: internal to the platform, and related to the external usage of the system.

The aforementioned modules are embodied into a technology-agnostic reference architecture in Sect. 3.3, while specific design blueprints are presented in Sect. 3.4.

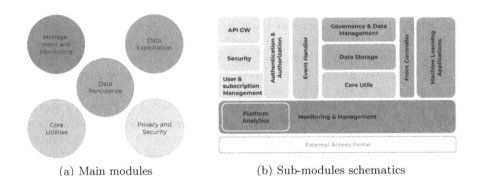

(a) Main modules   (b) Sub-modules schematics

Fig. 1. Details of common modules of ML data platforms.

3.3   Agnosticism: Technology-Agnostic Reference Architecture

In the process of designing, implementing and maintaining large-scale data platforms for different business verticals we have gained a lot of useful experience and learned many lessons. The most important lesson was to keep the architecture designs as clean and simple as possible. One of our main objectives is to enable systems to keep resources and operational cost low since platforms are expected to store and process an ever-increasing amount of data and provide services to myriads of users.

The architecture illustrated in Fig. 2 depicts the key components of the proposed reference architecture, aimed on providing the general design details which should be then easily portable to any cloud provider and to on-premise solutions as well. We have put special attention on avoiding any constraint or dependence on specific technologies during the design of the reference architecture. Conversely, production-ready platform architectures, together with technology alternatives for each component, are presented in Sect. 3.4.

In order to describe and clarify the purpose of each component shown in Fig. 2, we will introduce a practical data-flow example. The data platform flow begins when the user or client app pushes data or feedbacks (analog to the datasets and model feedback detailed in Sect. 3.1) into the platform. This data enters the system through a gateway, which will manage authentication, authorization and data compression, among other features, and is then stored in the corresponding queuing module topic. An extra pre-processing layer could be optionally included in between to transform input raw data in real-time before storing it into topics.

Real-time data flow and processing are commonly based on queue management systems, comprised of topics which are also split into partitions. Whenever pushing a new message, a partition key should be specified to increase the system performance and ease consumption on later stages, being able to process a specific client data as an ordered sequence of events. Most data platforms will typically need three main topics: 1) data topics that will handle raw or pre-processed input data; 2) model resolution topics, storing the outputs generated by the corresponding ML applications; and 3) optional feedback or interaction topics which will handle whenever the user wants/needs to provide some feedback such as "the answer was not correct" (e.g., specifying a person presence within an image where there are just some dogs). In addition, it is possible to set up a segregated group of topics to provided clients with isolated access to their own specific model resolutions.

In order to persist the different groups of data detailed in Table 1, a storage layer must be included. This layer should allow at least structured and unstructured data and expose an API to consume its content. A versioning strategy must also be implemented to deal with different versions of datasets, checkpoints, etc. There are several sources of user and application data to be persisted (temporarily or permanently), identified and numbered in Fig. 2. Since persisted data may come from different clients, which will probably demand privacy politics, authentication and authorization are also requirements for this layer. Whenever possible, compression should also be taken into account to reduce the huge amount of data that will be handled. Once the above described flow is completed for an input, it is necessary to provide clients with asynchronous access to the corresponding model results (e.g., a car image with its license plate highlighted). Note that external users should not have access to the data stored in this layer. Instead, they should only be able to connect to their own resolutions topics/streams.

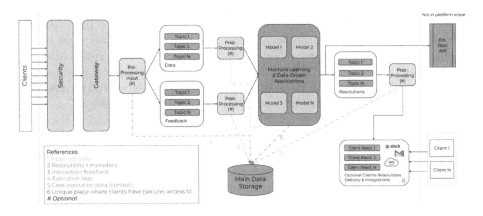

Fig. 2. High-level agnostic architecture for ML data platforms.

3.4   Evolvability: Design Blueprints for Custom Implementations

Agnosticism was the main driver for the definition of the reference architecture outlined in the previous section. Here, we introduce the blueprints of tailored architectures designed for production-ready environments and large-scale data processing needs. Given that a plethora of organizations have transitioned and migrated their mission critical operations technology infrastructure to cloud-based environments, we have favored cloud-based architectures and we share the implementation details for the most relevant cloud platforms below[1].

We introduce two examples of system architecture blueprints in this section based on the reference architecture outlined in Fig. 2, with some slight implementation differences. On one hand, the cloud-based architecture design shown in Fig. 3, built with the cloud computing solutions from Amazon Web Services (AWS). On the other hand, the container[2]-based alternative shown in Fig. 4, designed to be set-up on-premise or on scalable virtualized environments such as Amazon EC2, Google Compute Engine or Microsoft Container Instances, among others. This architecture has been designed to be independent of the underlying hardware configurations (or virtualized environments).

There are three leading services in the Amazon-based implementation of Fig. 3: AWS Lambda, Amazon Kinesis, and Amazon S3. AWS Lambda is a server-less computing service that has been used to execute specific code in response to

---

[1] The tools and frameworks specified on the blueprints constitute, to the best of our knowledge, the most mature state-of-the-art alternatives as of this writing.

[2] A standard unit of software that packages up code and all its dependencies so the application runs quickly and reliably from one computing environment to another.

events/triggers such as gateway calls, data pre and post processing, etc. Kinesis, Amazon's data streaming solution, has been used as a temporary data storage solution and to decouple data flow management and computation. Amazon S3 (Simple Storage Service) has been used to implement the mid and long term storage system due to it's security, flexibility and simplicity to interact with Amazon's data transfer and compute services. The approach used to design the Amazon-based architecture has been tailored to create the architectures corresponding to the other two main cloud computing providers, Microsoft Azure and Google Cloud Platform (GCP). For comparison purposes, Table 2 summarizes the correspondence between the components of the reference architecture and the equivalent service for the three main cloud computing providers.

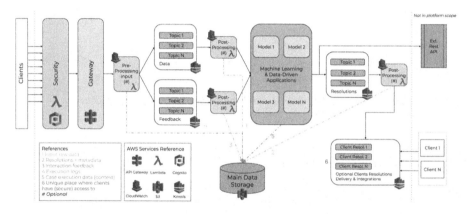

Fig. 3. Cloud-based architecture diagram - AWS implementation.

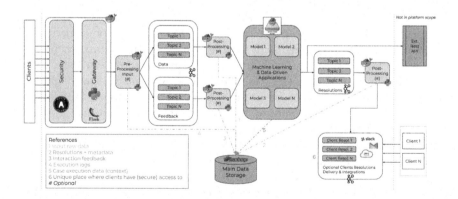

Fig. 4. Container-based architecture diagram - on-premise implementation.

Table 2. Components of reference architecture implementations.

Deployment	Gateway	Message broker	Light processing	Persistence
AWS	API gateway	Kinesis	Lambda	S3
Azure	Azure functions	Event hubs	Azure functions	Blob storage
GCP	Cloud endpoints	Cloud pub/sub	Cloud functions	Cloud storage
On-premise	OAuth	Apache Kafka	Python, flask	HDFS

4   Results

In this section, we describe the evaluations that have been carried out to validate our work. We have focused on evaluating our proposals by assessing the functionality and usability of the architectures and implementations originated from our design criteria. We have chosen not to pursue a direct raw-performance measurement in this work since the results of such assessment would not contribute significantly to evaluate the suitability of the proposed design criteria. Conversely, due to the large number of uncontrolled variables impacting the evaluation (characteristics of instances, replicas, regions, storage solutions, processing units, etc.), the results would expose the capabilities of each cloud computing provider and available hardware installations rather than the benefits offered by the proposed design criteria and the resulting architectures. Notwithstanding, we are constantly monitoring alternatives to expand the assessment of our proposal, including the many efforts being devoted to design and evolve ML benchmarks for different types of processing architectures, as in the preliminary works made public by Wang et al. [23], Mattson et atl. [15] and Reddi et al. [16].

4.1   Functional Evaluation

In order to assess the capabilities of the guidelines presented above, in this section we cover how it applies to varying scenarios across three relevant dimensions, enabling us to examine how the architecture lends itself to adaptation to the combinations between them.

The first dimension is related to the type of data that AI models can handle, not to the specific algorithm, as the relevant dimension considers how the data type needs to flow through the architecture, which includes the following types:

- **Binary data.** While images represent the most common type for binary data, other usual cases are video, audio, protocol buffers and common formats such as PDF files. The specific process applied to this data –including serialization– is encapsulated in the application, decoupled from the flow of the data in the architecture. Use cases like computer vision models can leverage queue optimization in order to take advantage of GPU architectures through complex batches.

- **Sequence data.** Commonly text data, ranging from simple strings up to complex documents in a JSON-like representation. Typically smaller than binary data, the size of the message can grow as to require custom handling, e.g. genome sequences. Applications of information retrieval like *multi-hop inference*, specially in *distractor*-like settings, require long spans of text to be applied meaningfully.
- **Structured data.** Any tabular-form input that can be handled by traditional databases is serializable in standard ways, though for most use cases, structured data would be a final endpoint to register metadata associated with a combination of the previous types of data, a version of a process, and more.

These modes can interact, e.g. a binary file (PDF) is processed through OCR on its image components, the resulting text piped into another algorithm, and its output registered as structured metadata on a database. The combination of file-driven storage for binary data, together with document-driven storage for sequence data, and relational-driven storage for structure data completes the use case for any AI model.

The second dimension relates to the deployment requirements in terms of the capacity to access, scale, and control of the architecture deployment, with the following considerations:

- **Cloud agnostic.** The highest level of elastic scaling is realized through a cloud infrastructure, considering usage restrictions depending on the region that will be served, reliability of network components, or fixed/variable cost structures. The capacity to transition from, or integrate into, several providers while maintaining a unique code based requires a set of cloud agnostic components to be deployed, orchestrated or called upon by other systems with a high level of abstraction.
- **On premise.** There are arguments to be made about leveraging existing hardware, particularly compute clusters and GPUs, for an already existing workflow, like deploying a closed-off version of a given ML model that is going to process private data that cannot be exposed to external networks. Given the agnosticism of the proposed design criteria, designing different architectures based on the deployment constraints is unnecessary and inefficient.
- **Portable.** There are many instances where access to significant hardware components or network infrastructure can be severely limited, whereas on remote locations like cruises, events on highly securitized areas, traveling displays, etc. In such cases, being able to deploy a specific instance of the same architecture (as the ones based on the reference architecture from Fig. 2) means that the decision of architecture deployment is not a prerequisite of the specific instance of the design, enabling even utilization of low power or mobile devices as compute options.

The third dimension considers the computing architectures for model execution: GPU/TPU, CPU, low power/embedded compute solutions and the adaptation of the required model components. E.g. when serving events in securitized areas, where given the limitation of network access and hardware deployment, most compute needs to occur in low power devices, demand will be erratic but concentrated in rapid bursts, and connective failures are expected. Also in the development of a service within the company that leverages open-source data and components, alongside proprietary data that cannot be processed outside the on-premise hardware facilities. Storage components, versioning strategies, tenancy and other aspects can be solved following a cloud-oriented approach (as the one exemplified in Sect. 3.4), while the compute and internal calls will require to be served through on-premise hardware.

4.2   Real-World Use Cases

In order to demonstrate the adaptability and evolvability of our proposal, this section analyzes the implementation of custom large scale ML platforms for real-world use cases. These architectures have been designed following the criteria detailed along this paper and are currently in-production in a wide range of business domains such as health care, banking and energy. It is worth noting that some architecture details have been omitted in order to comply with the corresponding confidentiality and Non-Disclosure Agreements (NDA).

The fundamentally flexible and customizable design provided by the reference architecture introduced in Sect. 3.3 makes it possible to materialize many different implementations. We have taken advantage of that flexibility to overcome a variety of issues –operational and technical– in the process of building and deploying the ML platforms for the above mentioned business verticals.

– **Global-scale Health Care Institution.** This project was intended to develop a smart assistant tool to aid medical practitioners on real-time evaluation of a specific pathology. It required a delicate balance between enhancing the work-flow of the physicians, avoiding straight-out diagnosis while guiding the professional in producing them, handling private and sensitive data, and working in environments where a very low latency was required without special guarantees of network bandwidth or mobile device power. The ML algorithms were composed of a Directed Acyclic Graph (DAG) of semantic segmentation Computer Vision (CV) algorithms, with a multi-task classification model ensemble outputting a score to inform the diagnosis, while exposing the outputs of each separate algorithm. The physician can accept or correct the output from the system. When a patient provides clearance, the final physician-submitted result is used as a validated new data point, maintaining the human-in-the-loop, enabling continuing the training of the algorithms, with the capacity of using different reliability scores on results accepted "as is" and modified ones. The platform architecture needed to be flexible to be migrated to different cloud providers, given the world-wide scope of the project, as each region where the application was meant to be used could require different privacy regulations (GDPR, SOC 2, HIPAA, etc.), even when defaulting to the most stringent ones by design. The platform enabled the on-premise execution of the ML applications to comply with the sensitive medical data protection regulations.

- **Multinational Investment Bank.** A complete re-engineering of the bank's international trading systems due to performance and technology obsolesce problems, the new platform replacing the trading production systems that fed investment systems on different geographical regions in a phase manner. The solution consisted on an enhanced version of the on-premise architecture designed to improve the overall system performance by processing data in batches rather than following the default step-by-step data stream processing. This enhancement was crucial to reduce the overhead introduced by strict real-time stream processing given that the nature of high-trading operations enabled micro-batch processing without incurring performance penalties. The resulting architecture, together with the tools and frameworks implemented on-premises, are depicted in Fig. 5.
- **Energy company.** A project to reduce the security clearance time to access corporate facilities through ML-powered facial recognition. Guests are registered as they accept invitations to events, meetings, etc., and once in the company facilities, they are recognized by the security system that authorizes their entry. The ML algorithms needed to account for a large drift in detection scope, while minimizing full re-trainings, resulting in a moving target in the recall objective that needs to be updated in real-time, whether on inclusion or deletion, and a need for NRT responsiveness for effective access management. A full cloud-based ML platform has been designed based on the architecture from Fig. 3 but implemented on Microsoft Azure instead of AWS, with a tool set similar to the one summarized in Table 2. In addition, it was necessary to orchestrate on-demand asynchronous interactions with external devices, sensors and other actuators in other to grant physical access to each type of facility (corporate buildings, physical industrial plants, etc.), following an approach analog to the API call depicted in the upper part of Fig. 2.

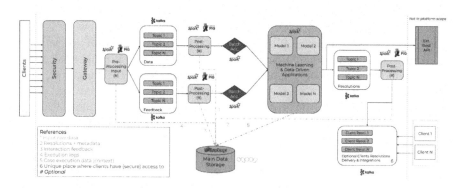

Fig. 5. Schematics of the enhanced on-premise architecture for the financial vertical.

5   Conclusions

In this paper, we propose design criteria for architecting evolvable data-intensive ML platforms. Our work aims to bridge the gap between existing state-of-the-art ML, HPC and Big Data technologies to efficiently develop interactive data-intensive ML platforms for complex real-world use cases.

The strongest point and main contribution of our proposal is that it facilitates and expedites the development of comprehensive platforms that cover the entire life cycle of ML solutions for a wide spectrum of often insufficiently served business verticals. To this end, we have embedded in our proposal the knowledge and practical learning gathered from an incremental three-stages analysis of the ML ecosystem. The first stage corresponds to the characterization of dominant attributes of effective data platforms for ML: agnosticism, evolvability, modularity and data-savviness. The second level of analysis is centered on the prevalent features of typical ML applications: heterogeneous computing, non-uniform use of resources, deployment and versioning dependencies. The third stage of analysis covered the most critical asset of ML solutions: data and its characterization.

We have evaluated the functionality of the proposed architecture guideline through the rapid implementation and deploy of data-intensive ML platforms for different verticals and industries. In addition, the flexibility of the resulting architectures have been hard-proved (and stressed to the limit) serving as the Globant's main R&D AI platform concurrently running multiple applications and supporting random user distribution and operation behavior.

With regard to the open lines, there are a number of directions that we would like to pursue in the future. The strengthening and evolution of standardized data security and testing solutions for ML platforms constitutes a particularly interesting example of a constantly growing –and relatively uncovered– research topic. In addition, the challenges of adapting the ideas behind our proposal to design even more portable and self-contained architectures still remains a promising open line. Moreover, it would be interesting to evaluate the extension of our proposal to cover a broader spectrum of embedded and edge computing systems for heavy industry applications.

Acknowledgements. We are grateful and would like to thank the engineering team at Globant that helped us to design and implement the architecture introduced in this article. In particular, we would like to thank for their invaluable collaboration Agustín Huerta, Alejandro Galeano, Ana Maloberti, Diego Medina, Esteban Lussich, Fabiana Tamburrini, Haldo Tabaré Sponton, Ilan Rosenfeld, Javier Minhondo, Marcela Rodríguez and Matías Boix.

References

1. Amershi, S., et al.: Software engineering for machine learning: a case study. In: Proceedings of the 41st International Conference on Software Engineering: Software Engineering in Practice, ICSE (SEIP) 2019, Montreal, QC, Canada, May 25–31, 2019, pp. 291–300. IEEE/ACM (2019). https://doi.org/10.1109/ICSE-SEIP.2019.00042

2. Apache Software Foundation: Hadoop. http://hadoop.apache.org/. Accessed Mar 2020
3. Bailis, P., et al.: Infrastructure for usable machine learning: the Stanford DAWN project (2017). http://arxiv.org/abs/1705.07538
4. Baylor, D., et al.: TFX: a TensorFlow-based production-scale machine learning platform. In: Proceedings of the 23rd ACM SIGKDD International Conference on Knowledge Discovery and Data Mining, Halifax, NS, Canada, August 13–17, 2017, pp. 1387–1395. ACM (2017). https://doi.org/10.1145/3097983.3098021
5. Burke, J., et al.: Participatory sensing. In: Workshop on World-Sensor-Web (WSW 2006): Mobile Device Centric Sensor Networks and Applications (2006)
6. Dean, J., Ghemawat, S.: MapReduce: simplified data processing on large clusters. In: Proceedings of the 6th Conference on Symposium on Operating Systems Design & Implementation, OSDI 2004, vol. 6. USENIX Association (2004). http://dl.acm.org/citation.cfm?id=1251254.1251264
7. Dunn, J.: Introducing FBLearner flow: Facebook's AI backbone (May 2016). https://engineering.fb.com/core-data/introducing-fblearner-flow-facebooks-ai-backbone/. Accessed Mar 2020
8. Esteva, A., et al.: Dermatologist-level classification of skin cancer with deep neural networks. Nature **542**(7639), 115–118 (2017). https://doi.org/10.1038/nature21056
9. Ford, N., et al.: Building Evolutionary Architectures. O'Reilly UK Ltd., UK (2017)
10. Foster, I.: Designing and Building Parallel Programs: Concepts and Tools for Parallel Software Engineering. Addison-Wesley, Reading (1995)
11. Ghemawat, S., et al.: The Google file system. In: ACM SIGOPS Operating Systems Review, vol. 37, pp. 29–43. ACM (2003)
12. Goodhope, K., et al.: Building LinkedIn's real-time activity data pipeline. IEEE Data Eng. Bull. **35**(2), 33–45 (2012). http://sites.computer.org/debull/A12june/pipeline.pdf
13. Hermann, J., Balso, M.D.: Meet Michelangelo: Uber's machine learning platform (September 2017). https://eng.uber.com/michelangelo-machine-learning-platform/. Accessed Mar 2020
14. Lopez Murphy, J., Zarza, G.: La ingeniería del Big Data, Cómo trabajar con datos. Editorial UOC, Barcelona (October 2017). http://www.editorialuoc.cat/la-ingenieria-del-big-data
15. Mattson, P., et al.: MLPerf training benchmark. CoRR abs/1910.01500 (2019). http://arxiv.org/abs/1910.01500
16. Reddi, V.J., et al.: MLPerf inference benchmark. CoRR abs/1911.02549 (2019). http://arxiv.org/abs/1911.02549
17. Sculley, D., et al.: Hidden technical debt in machine learning systems. In: Proceedings of the 28th International Conference on Neural Information Processing Systems, NIPS 2015, vol. 2, pp. 2503–2511. MIT Press (2015)
18. Silva, Thiago H., de Melo, Pedro O.S.Vaz., Viana, Aline Carneiro., Almeida, Jussara M., Salles, Juliana, Loureiro, Antonio A.F.: Traffic condition is more than colored lines on a map: characterization of Waze alerts. In: Jatowt, A., et al. (eds.) SocInfo 2013. LNCS, vol. 8238, pp. 309–318. Springer, Cham (2013). https://doi.org/10.1007/978-3-319-03260-3_27
19. Lakshmanan, V.: All your data leads to machine learning. In: Conference Keynote, Converge Buenos Aires 2018 (March 2018). https://converge.globant.com/events/converge-ba-MAR-2018

20. Vavilapalli, V.K., et al.: Apache Hadoop YARN: yet another resource negotiator. In: Proceedings of the 4th Annual Symposium on Cloud Computing, SOCC 2013. ACM (2013). https://doi.org/10.1145/2523616.2523633
21. Wang, D., et al.: Deep learning for identifying metastatic breast cancer. CoRR abs/1606.05718 (2016). http://arxiv.org/abs/1606.05718
22. Wang, L., Wong, A.: COVID-Net: a tailored deep convolutional neural network design for detection of COVID-19 cases from chest radiography images. [open-access preprint] (2020). https://arxiv.org/abs/2003.09871
23. Wang, Y., et al.: Benchmarking TPU, GPU, and CPU Platforms for Deep Learning (2019). http://arxiv.org/abs/1907.10701
24. Zaharia, M., et al.: Accelerating the machine learning lifecycle with MLflow. IEEE Data Eng. Bull. **41**(4), 39–45 (2018)

Big Data

Harmonizing Big Data with a Knowledge Graph: *OceanGraph KG* Uses Case

Marcos Zárate[1,2]([✉]) [ID], Carlos Buckle[2] [ID], Renato Mazzanti[2,3] [ID],
Mirtha Lewis[1] [ID], Pablo Fillottrani[4,5] [ID], and Claudio Delrieux[6] [ID]

[1] Centre for the Study of Marine Systems,
Patagonian National Research Centre (CENPAT-CONICET),
Puerto Madryn, Argentina
{zarate,mirtha}@cenpat-conicet.gob.ar
[2] Laboratorio de Investigaciones en Informática (LINVI) - Facultad de Ingeniería,
Universidad Nacional de la Patagonia San Juan Bosco (UNPSJB),
Puerto Madryn, Argentina
[3] Unidad de Gestión de la Información, (UGI-CENPAT), Puerto Madryn, Argentina
renato@cenpat-conicet.gob.ar
[4] Computer Science and Engineering Department,
Universidad Nacional del Sur, (DCIC-UNS), Bahía Blanca, Argentina
prf@cs.uns.edu.ar
[5] Comisión de Investigaciones Científicas, Provincia de Buenos Aires (CICPBA),
Buenos Aires, Argentina
[6] Electric and Computer Engineering Department,
Universidad Nacional del Sur (DIEC-UNS), Bahía Blanca, Argentina
cad@uns.edu.ar

Abstract. In this paper we introduce recent efforts carried out by the *OceanGraph KG* project to integrate semi-structured or unstructured content. We present some of the practical applications of *OceanGraph* through use cases, and finally summarize the lessons learned during the development process.

Keywords: Big data integration · Knowledge graph · Linked open data · OceanGraph KG

1 Introduction and Motivation

The management of data generated in several disciplines, including Oceanography and Meteorology, is currently facing great challenges. Among other facts, this is triggered by the recent exponential increase in its volume and diversity of sources, due to the growth of technology and advances in remote ocean observatories [1]. In addition, there is a great diversity in data types that must be handled together. This includes physicochemical, geological, meteorological and biological data, which must be integrated, and the analysis/information products for scientific, governmental, and productive purposes must be based on

© Springer Nature Switzerland AG 2020
E. Rucci et al. (Eds.): JCC-BD&ET 2020, CCIS 1291, pp. 81–92, 2020.
https://doi.org/10.1007/978-3-030-61218-4_6

integrating all of them to be meaningful [2]. Taking into account the definition of Big Data (BD) [3], both ocean observation and weather data fit within
the "5V" characterization of BD (volume, velocity, value, veracity, and variety).
Therefore, data management in this context can be considered as a typical Big
Data case [4]. In scientific activities, this situation presents both challenges and
opportunities regarding the access and integration of data they need to conduct
novel research activities that may trigger new discoveries enabled by the integration of multidisciplinary information sources [5,6]. In the context of the *Horizon
2020 program (H2020)*[1] of the European Union, and at the National level in the
strategic plan *Argentina Innovadora 2020*, established by the Ministry of Science, Technology and Innovation (MINCyT) of Argentina, BD and data science
are considered fundamental disciplines to address the complexity and scope of
the issues that require an interdisciplinary approach and a broad projection in
the use of information. In the research activities focused on the South Atlantic,
data collection campaigns are scarce, and an adequate information management
system is not readily available. Therefore, it is necessary to develop systems
capable of managing data integration and delivery, both for the direct and indi-
rect use by the participating research groups and institutions, and for external
users that require information (*f.e.*, governmental, third parties, etc.).

One of the advantageous features of BD is its ability to manage information in schema-free formats that are both agnostic with respect to technological
aspects, and that allow further schema-evolution that will be typically be the
case in Natural Sciences. This allows the use of practical internal representations that facilitate specific purposes, for instance the management of datasets
in graph form. The Semantic Web (SW) [7] provides solutions to these needs by
enabling the Linked Data (LD) Web [8] where data objects are uniquely identified and the relationships between them are defined explicitly. LD is a powerful
and compelling approach to store, disseminate and consume scientific data from
various disciplines [6,9,10]. LD enables the publication, exchange and connection of data on the Web and offers a new way of integration and interoperability.
Recently the term *knowledge graph* (KG) emerged [11], which has been used
in research and business, generally in close association with SW technologies,
LD, large-scale data analysis and cloud computing. The popularity of KGs is
related to the launch of Google Knowledge Graph in 2012[2], and through the
introduction of other large databases by major technology companies, such as
Yahoo, Microsoft, AirBnB and Facebook, which have created their own KGs to
enhance semantic searches [12]. Not only in the industry there are successful uses
of KGs, in the oceanographic domain and in the Life sciences in general there is
a growing recognition of the advantages of SW technologies [13–18].

Related to these problems, two previous works were developed for the creation of an Oceanographic linked dataset, both were developed jointly with the
Centro de investigación y transferencia Golfo San Jorge, (CIT-GSJ-CONICET):

---

[1] https://eshorizonte2020.es/.

[2] https://googleblog.blogspot.com/2012/05/introducing-knowledge-graph-things-
not.html.

the proposal of publication of oceanographic campaign metadata [19], and the definition of initial steps for the development of an oceanographic KG called *OceanGraph KG* [20]. Based on the experience gained in this previous work, a series of recommendations related to interoperability and information integration of The Integrated Ocean Observing System (IOOS) [21] was proposed.

This paper describes in a general way the *OceanGraph KG* and its recent efforts focused on the integration of heterogeneous oceanographic and meteorological data. In Sect. 2 we present the underlying idea of *OceanGraph KG* and its main features. In Sect. 3 we discuss its usefulness through case studies. Finally, in Sect. 4 lessons learned and future guidelines are presented.

2   OceanGraph KG Overview

The first version developed to integrate heterogeneous data taking advantage of a KG was described in [20]. *OceanGraph* bases its main structure on the relationships established between the selected datasets. The main classes that we define and reuse are: *campaigns, occurrences, papers, researchers, environmental variables and positions.* If a researcher consults *OceanGraph*, the expected results could recover one or more oceanographic campaigns in which she/he was involved from *National Marine Data System (NMDS)*[3], datasets they collected (from *Global Biodiversity Information Facility* (GBIF)[4] and *Ocean Biogeographic Information System* (OBIS)[5], and papers written by themself (from Springer Nature SciGraph)[6]. In the same way, the user could query data related to the occurrence of a species and the KG must retrieve in which campaigns it was observed, the information of the person who collected it, the exact place and date and associated variables that may be of importance (*e.g.*, weather or other environmental conditions during the collection).

2.1   Ontologies and Vocabularies Used

To ensure that our data will be available to multiple scientific communities, the resource description should adopt well-known standards. Next, we will describe the main resources related to the oceanographic domain and we will see the selected standards to model information on agents and organizations. Different data providers use their own ontologies and reuse existing ones.

- National Environmental Research Council's (NERC) Vocabulary Server (NVS) [14] provides access to standardized lists of terms which are used to facilitate data mark-up, interoperability and discovery in the marine science domain. NVS is published as Linked Data on the web using the data model of the Simple Knowledge Organization System (SKOS)[7].

---

[3] http://www.datosdelmar.mincyt.gob.ar/index.php.
[4] https://www.gbif.org/.
[5] http://www.iobis.org/.
[6] https://www.springernature.com/gp/researchers/scigraph.
[7] https://www.w3.org/2004/02/skos/.

- GeoSPARQL [22] defines an ontology that supports geospatial semantics, developed by the Open Geospatial Consortium (OGC)[8]. The definition of this ontology (based on well-known OGC standards) is intended to provide a basis for the standardized exchange of RDF geospatial data that can offer query capabilities and qualitative spatial reasoning using the W3C standard SPARQL [23].

- Darwin Core Standard [24] provides a stable, direct and flexible structure for compiling and sharing biodiversity data from different sources. *OceanGraph*, uses it to describe properties and concepts related to occurrences of marine species.

- Geolink [15] dataset includes diverse information, such as port stops made by oceanographic cruises, physical sample metadata, funding for research projects and staff. This dataset is based on an ontological design pattern (ODP). This ODP it is generic enough to adapt it to the modeling needs established by *Ocean-Graph*.

- BiGe-Onto [25] is an ontology designed to manage Biodiversity and Marine Biogeography data. *BiGe-Onto* uses the idea of *occurrence* (the observation of a species in a place at a given time), since the censuses are observations of SES at a specific time and place, we consider that *BiGe-Onto* fits to nature of our data. *BiGe-Onto* also reuses different appropriate vocabularies to represent information from these domains. In particular, Darwin Core (DwC) [24] is the most important thereof, and reuses several classes that will be considered here: *Occurrence*, *Event*, *Taxon* and *Organism*. *BiGe-Onto* also reuses *foaf:Person void:Dataset* and *dcterms:Location*. Our ontology models occurrences that are related to other concepts through the following relationships.

- *bigeonto:associated.* Each of the occurrences are described according to the existence of an organism, which was observed at a specific place and time. The organism and the taxon are related through *bigeonto:belongsTo* property.
- *bigeonto:has_event.* The occurrence has a location (since they are species observations) and they are given by the relation *bigeonto:has_location*, which belongs to a specific environment *bigeonto:caracterizes*. The Relations Ontology (RO).[9] defines the relationships between *bigeonto:Environment* and the classes of the Environment Ontology (EnvO) [26].
- *dwciri:recordedBy.* This property enables non-literal ranges in comparison to its analog *dwc:recordedBy*, so it allows to relate URIs that describe people, groups or organizations involved in the occurrence, *e.g.* relate a person to their ORCID.
- *dwciri:inDataset.* Allows the occurrences to be related to the data set to which they belong.

- SSN/SOSA [27] To describe the sensors and their oceanographic observations, we use the Semantic Sensor Network (SSN) ontology, and especially the Sensor, Observation, Sample and Actuator (SOSA) ontology that describes the elemental classes and properties, for example (depth, temperature, salinity, etc.).

---

[8] http://www.opengeospatial.org/.
[9] https://github.com/oborel/obo-relations.

Both vocabularies are suitable for a variety of applications, like large-scale scientific monitoring, satellite imagery, among others. The SSN ontology is an OWL vocabulary developed by the W3C, in collaboration with the Open Geospatial Consortium (OGC), so its adoption guarantees its reuse in many other applications.

2.2 Cross-linking

A challenge, in order to improve the discovery of information, is to generate links between the different URIs of the KG. The interlinking of *OceanGraph* data sets was carried out semi-automatically. It is common for people who participated in an oceanographic campaign, after it, to publish their results in scientific journals. Even more complex is the case of a person who publishes a *datapaper* (scientific paper that describes data), this is made up of the publication itself, plus the primary data that supports it in OBIS or GBIF. *OceanGraph* allows people or species to be linked in different repositories, thus ensuring semantic interoperability between data sets. To generate the links we use the SILK framework[10], which uses the declarative language Silk-LSL (Link Specification Language) with which the user can establish the type of RDF links that must be discovered between the different data sets and the conditions that must be met, *e.g.* to relate researchers who obtained data from a campaign with the results published in OBIS or GBIF, the *Levenshtein distance* is used to disambiguate entities by calculating the similarity between them.

This operator receives two inputs: `dwc:recordedBy`[11] and `foaf:name`, if there is enough match that the people are the same, SILK generates the link between them using the axiom `owl:sameAs`. Figure 1 shows the relationships used to integrate *OceanGraph* datasets.

2.3 Availability

One of the most important design decisions when developing a KG is the platform that supports it. After several performance comparisons, we decided to use GraphDB[12] since it allows a quick integration of new sources of information, analyzes structured data in CSV, XLS, JSON, XML or other formats, it allows to generate data in RDF and store it in a local or remote SPARQL endpoint, and last but not least, it allows to clean the input data with a generic script language. GraphDB allows users to explore the hierarchy of RDF classes and its instances (*Class hierarchy* menu). In the same way, we can check the relationships between the KG classes and visually explore how many links were created between different class instances (*Class relationship*). To access the OceanGraph dataset, the user must authenticate themselves on http://web.cenpat-conicet.gob.ar:7200/login, using the following credentials (user: **oceangraph** password:

---

[10] http://silkframework.org/.

[11] https://terms.tdwg.org/wiki/dwc:recordedBy.

[12] http://graphdb.ontotext.com/.

ocean.user). *OceanGraph KG* is also available for download in [28] under CC
BY 4.0 license. Table 1 summarizes the main links to explore the knowledge
graph in various ways.

Table 1. Main features of *OceanGraph KG*.

Feature	URL
Repository name	OceanGraph (user: `oceangraph` password: `ocean.user`)
Repository URL	http://web.cenpat-conicet.gob.ar:7200/login
SPARQL endpoint	http://web.cenpat-conicet.gob.ar:7200/OceanGraph
Visual SPARQL endpoint	http://web.cenpat-conicet.gob.ar:7200/sparql
Class hierarchy	http://web.cenpat-conicet.gob.ar:7200/sparql
Vocabularies	19
No. classes	23
No. properties	50
No. triplet	4.6 M

3   Big Data Use-Cases

As a result of the process described in the previous sections, a set of nodes
and links were created to connect references from the input data to entities and
relationships within the KG. We extended this generic approach to integrate
different functionality modes that are typical in BD contexts.

3.1   Complementing Information with SN SciGraph

As the development and adoption of novel research devices is growing exponen-
tially, it's getting harder to track all the documents related to a given scientific subject. SciGraph dataset integrates data sources from Springer Nature.
SciGraph collects information about research landscape: research projects, publications, conferences, funding agencies and others. This dataset [29] includes
around 35 million records and is refreshed on a monthly basis.

It is often necessary to connect researchers or other stakeholders that contribute to the same subject. This is specifically the case in the oceanographic
domain, in which is required to determine researchers who are part of an oceanographic campaign, and connect their subject with other researchers from another
part of the world who are working on the same subjects. In the particular case
study of this paper, the research subject is physical oceanography.

We will explore the instances of the *sg:Subject* class and their related subjects
using the *core#narrower* property. As can be seen in Fig. 2, there are five subjects
directly related to physical oceanography (*ocean science, marine biology, climate
sciences*, etc.)

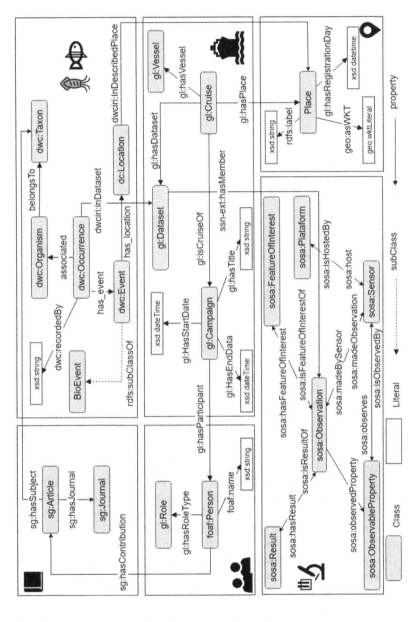

Fig. 1. Conceptual diagram of *OceanGraph KG*. For simplicity, only the main object properties are shown, which allow relationships between the classes of each data set to be established.

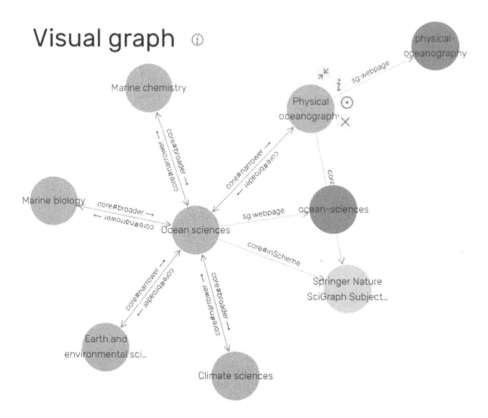

Fig. 2. Exploring terms related to the concept *physical oceanography* using the GraphDB visual interface.

3.2 Macroecological Analyzes

A very common requirement of macroecological analyzes, particularly those that consider the environmental drivers of species distributions, is to match occurrences of species' with environmental variables, and how distributions are expected to shift as the climate changes. This case study shows an example of how KG information can be exploited using the relationships between occurrences with environmental variables, for the example we will use the body of water temperature as a study variable. In particular, we need to associate the following variables: (i) the occurrence of a species under study, (ii) the region of interest, (in our case Golfo Nuevo), (iii) a specific time frame and (iv) the measurements of the water body temperature.

The first step is to define the region under study, to later and then recover the occurrences of the chosen species in a specific time frame. To handle temporal concepts, we use Time Ontology [30]. Since NERC provides URIs for each of the variables that we need to analyze, we only need to search for the URI of the body water temperature, which is defined as: SDN:P01::TEMPCU01. Table 2 shows an RDF fragment that includes the concepts involved in performing the analysis.

Table 2. RDF serialization of the concepts involved in macroecological analysis.

```
bigeonto:ExtendedMeasurementOrFact a owl:Class.

bigeonto:mesasurement1 rdf:type bigeonto:ExtendedMeasurementOrFact;
rdfs:label "Medicion de temperatura de la columna de agua";
dwc:MeasurementTypeID http://vocab.nerc.ac.uk/collection/P01/current/TEMPCU01/;
dwc:MeasurementValue 6^^xsd:integer;
dwc:MeasurementUnitID http://vocab.nerc.ac.uk/collection/P06/current/UPAA/;
bigeonto:has_event bigeonto:bioevent/urncatalogcenpat-conicet-peces-p-331
bigeonto:has_occurrence bigeonto:occurrence/urncatalogcenpat-conicet-peces-p-331.

bigeonto:occurrence/urncatalogcenpat-conicet-peces-p-331
rdf:type dwc:Occurrence
dwciri:recordedBy http://www.cenpat-conicet.gob.ar/resource/person/unknown;
dwc:basisOfRecord "HumanObservation"^^xsd:string;
dwc:catalogNumber "CNP-P-331"^^xsd:string;
dwc:collectionCode "CNP-PECES"^^xsd:string .

bigeonto:bioevent/urncatalogcenpat-conicet-peces-p-331
rdf:type bigeonto:BioEvent;
dwc:eventDate "08/02/1983"^^xsd:date;
bigeonto:has_location bigeonto:location/urncatalogcenpat-conicet-peces-p-331
```

In Listing 1.1, you can see the query that we implemented using SPARQL, it associates the occurrence of *Merluccius hubbsi* (a fish species of specific scientific and productive interest) with the temperature in a particular region. To do this, we define *Golfo Nuevo*, as an instance of (*geo:Polygon*), then look for observations of *Merluccius hubbsi*, which has its location associated and are instances of the class (*geo:point*). One of the advantages of adopting GeoSPARQL is that we can perform spatial operations, *e.g.* to determine if a point is contained within a polygon, for this we use the provided function (*geof:sfWithin*). As a last step, we must obtain the temperature (also georeferenced) and define it by NERC as *TEMPCU01*. To execute the query in GraphDB, see the following link[13]. This specific example shows how our proposed data integration effort around KGs, bridges the gap between the sometimes isolated existing data collection initiatives worldwide, and a centralized and uniform data access that may be automated. A standardization like the provided by our proposal further enables the next and more fruitful BD stages, including massive automated data analysis, online real-time actionable dashboards, and visual analytics.

---

[13] http://web.cenpat-conicet.gob.ar:7200/sparql?savedQueryName=OG-Q001.

Listing 1.1. Query required to associate observational occurences of a particular species within a given geographic region and with specific environmental conditions.

```
PREFIX dwc: <http://rs.tdwg.org/dwc/terms/>
PREFIX bigeonto: <http://www.w3id.org/cenpat-gilia/bigeonto/>
PREFIX gl: <http://schema.geolink.org/1.0/base/main#>
PREFIX geosparql: <http://www.opengis.net/ont/geosparql#>
PREFIx geof:<http://www.opengis.net/def/function/geosparql/>
PREFIX nerc:<http://vocab.nerc.ac.uk/collection/P01/current/>

SELECT ?occ ?measurement ?PointWKT
WHERE {
    ?occ a dwc:Occurrence.
    ?occ bigeonto:associated ?organism.
    ?organism bigeonto:belongsTo ?taxon.
    ?taxon dwc:scientificName ?sciname.
    ?occ bigeonto:memberOf ?dataset.
    ?dataset gl:hasMeasurementType ?measurement.
    ?occ bigeonto:has_event ?event.
    ?event dwc:eventDate ?date.
    ?event bigeonto:has_location ?location.
    ?location geosparql:hasGeometry ?point.
    ?point geosparql:asWKT ?PointWKT.
    bigeonto:polygon/golfo-san-matias-polygon geosparql:asWKT ?PWKT.
    FILTER (geof:sfWithin(?PointWKT, ?PWKT))
    FILTER(regex(str(?measurement), "TEMP" ) )
    FILTER regex(STR(?sciname), "Merluccius hubbsi")
    FILTER (?date >= xsd:date("date") && ?date < xsd:date("date"))
}
```

4   Conclusion

Based on the results of this experience, KGs proved to be powerful and flexible enough to integrate diverse data sets. However, the integration process required to correctly map input data into a KG can be exhausting, since automated techniques have so far been unable to fully understand the semantics of input data. Through the *OceanGraph* development process, we learned a few lessons on how LD can contribute to addressing important BD challenges, especially within the area of oceanographic data.

First, the amount of linked datasets grows every year and is interrelated over a growing entanglement of scientific information. This presents new challenges, which require considering scalability and performance as crucial aspects for any future facility [31]. Around this issue is where LD needs to incorporate BD techniques and methodologies, specifically in the data management aspects.

Second, from the BD perspective, it is also a priority to start incorporating linked data results. Currently only a few large companies are able to take advantage of BD [32], which is unfortunate since individual scientists, small research groups, nongovernmental agencies, and other stakeholders that are engaged in potentially relevant activities are in a disadvantageous situation among the large commercial interest groups. In this foreseeable scenario, some questions that arose in other contexts begin to be visible. Among others we can mention [33]: *How can particular users delve into BD in a fruitful manner?* Having found useful data, *How to make it understandable to laypersons with little or no prior data science knowledge? How to handle data in a way that grants no privacy or licensing breaches? How can data generated from different cultures and over different languages (or even charsets) be rendered useful? What standards for data and metadata are necessary? How to link data from different repositories?*

What governance standards should be supported or even enforced to grant privacy, traceability, auditing, and other technical, ethical and legal features that systems like this must implement?.

BD is doomed to arrive into the realms of worldwide scientific enterprises, but its value will increase, and all the community will be able to take advantage of it, only when it becomes transparent and often usable by the largest number of users [34]. From this perspective, it is necessary to consider that BD, at least in the context of scientific enterprises, requires multi- and interdisciplinary integration, and, within such a decentralized scenario, the new challenges are also associated with meaning.

Acknowledgments. This work is partially funded by project *Linked Open Data Platform for Management and Visualization of Primary Data in Marine Science.* Supported by Secretariat of Science and Technology of the National University of Patagonia San Juan Bosco (UNPSJB). Some of the data used were provided by the *Golfo San Jorge Research and Transfer Center* (CIT-GSJ-CONICET).

References

1. Malik, T., Foster, I.: Addressing data access needs of the long-tail distribution of geoscientists. In: 2012 IEEE International Geoscience and Remote Sensing Symposium (IGARSS), pp. 5348–5351. IEEE (2012)
2. Hardisty, A., Roberts, D.: A decadal view of biodiversity informatics: challenges and priorities. BMC Ecol. **13**(1), 16 (2013). https://doi.org/10.1186/1472-6785-13-16
3. Beyer, M.A., Laney, D.: The importance of "big data": a definition, pp. 2014–2018. Gartner, Stamford, CT (2012)
4. Liu, Y., Qiu, M., Liu, C., Guo, Z.: Big data in ocean observation: opportunities and challenges. In: Wang, Y., Yu, G., Zhang, Y., Han, Z., Wang, G. (eds.) BigCom 2016. LNCS, vol. 9784, pp. 212–222. Springer, Cham (2016). https://doi.org/10.1007/978-3-319-42553-5_18
5. Campbell, P.: Data's shameful neglect. Nature **461**(7261), 145 (2009)
6. Lomotey, R.K., Deters, R.: Terms extraction from unstructured data silos. In: 2013 8th International Conference on System of Systems Engineering (SoSE), pp. 19–24. IEEE (2013)
7. Berners-Lee, T., Hendler, J., Lassila, O., et al.: The semantic web. Sci. Am. **284**(5), 28–37 (2001)
8. Bizer, C., Heath, T., Berners-Lee, T.: Linked data: the story so far. In: Semantic Services, Interoperability and Web Applications: Emerging Concepts, pp. 205–227. IGI Global (2011)
9. Bukhari, S.A.C., Nagy, M.L., Ciccarese, P., Krauthammer, M., Baker, C.J.: iCyrus: a semantic framework for biomedical image discovery. In: SWAT4LS, pp. 13–22 (2015)
10. Bukhari, S.A.C.: Semantic enrichment and similarity approximation for biomedical sequence images. Ph.D. thesis, University of New Brunswick (Canada) (2017)
11. Ehrlinger, L.,Wöß, W.: Towards a definition of knowledge graphs. In: SEMANTiCS (Posters, Demos, SuCCESS), vol. 48 (2016)
12. Ceravolo, P., et al.: Big data semantics. J. Data Semant. **7**(2), 65–85 (2018). https://doi.org/10.1007/s13740-018-0086-2

13. Leadbetter, A., Arko, R., Chandler, C., Shepherd, A., Lowry, R.: Linked data an oceanographic perspective. J. Ocean Technol. **8**(3), 7–12 (2013)
14. Leadbetter, A., Lowry, R., Clements, D.O.: The NERC vocabulary server: version 2.0. In: Geophysical Research Abstracts, vol. 14 (2012)
15. Krisnadhi, A., et al.: An ontology pattern for oceanographic cruises: towards an oceanographer's dream of integrated knowledge discovery (2014)
16. Cheatham, M., et al.: The GeoLink knowledge graph. Big Earth Data **2**(2), 131–143 (2018)
17. Page, R.D.M.: Ozymandias: a biodiversity knowledge graph. PeerJ **7**, e6739 (2019)
18. Springer Nature SciGraph (2018). http://www.springernature.com/gp/researchers/scigraph. Accessed 24 Jan 2019
19. Zárate, M., Rosales, P., Fillottrani, P., Delrieux, C., Lewis, M.:Oceanographic data management: towards the publishing of Pampa Azul oceanographic campaigns as linked data. In: Proceedings of the 12th Alberto Mendelzon International Workshop on Foundations of Data Management, AMW 2018 (2018)
20. Zárate, M., Rosales, P., Braun, G., Lewis, M., Fillottrani, P.R., Delrieux, C.: *Ocean-Graph*: some initial steps toward a oceanographic knowledge graph. In: Villazón-Terrazas, B., Hidalgo-Delgado, Y. (eds.) KGSWC 2019. CCIS, vol. 1029, pp. 33–40. Springer, Cham (2019). https://doi.org/10.1007/978-3-030-21395-4_3
21. The Integrated Ocean Observing System (IOOS) (2013). https://ioos.noaa.gov/. Accessed 19 July 2019
22. Battle, R., Kolas, D.: Enabling the geospatial semantic web with parliament and GeoSPARQL. Semant. Web **3**(4), 355–370 (2012)
23. SPARQL query language for RDF (2008). https://www.w3.org/TR/rdf-sparql-protocol/. Accessed 10 Mar 2019
24. Wieczorek, J., et al.: Darwin Core: an evolving community-developed biodiversity data standard. PLoS One **7**(1), e29715 (2012)
25. Zárate, M., Braun, G., Fillottrani, P.R., Delrieux, C., Lewis, M.: BiGe-Onto: an ontology-based system for managing biodiversity and biogeography data. Appl. Ontol. J. (2019, accepted paper)
26. Buttigieg, P.L., Pafilis, E., Lewis, S.E., Schildhauer, M.P., Walls, R.L., Mungall, C.J.: The environment ontology in 2016: bridging domains with increased scope, semantic density, and interoperation. J. Biomed. Semant. **7**, 57 (2016). https://doi.org/10.1186/s13326-016-0097-6
27. W3C: Semantic Sensor Network Ontology (SSN) W3C Recommendation (2017)
28. Zárate, M., Buckle, C., Mazzanti, R., Fillottrani, P., Delrieux, C., Lewis, M.: OceanGraph RDF dataset (2020). https://doi.org/10.17632/9t5xkt9wwk.1. Accessed 18 Mar 2019
29. Michele Pasin and FigShare Admin SN SciGraph. Dataset: Persons, April 2019
30. Time Ontology in OWL W3C Recommendation 19 October 2017 (2017). https://www.w3.org/TR/owl-time/. Accessed 27 Jan 2020
31. Bikakis, N., Sellis, T.: Exploration and visualization in the web of big linked data: a survey of the state of the art. arXiv preprint arXiv:1601.08059 (2016)
32. Hernández-Pérez, T.: In the age of the web of data: first open data, then big data. El profesional de la información (EPI) **25**(4), 517–525 (2016)
33. Hendler, J.: Broad data: exploring the emerging web of data. Big Data **1**(1), 18–20 (2013)
34. Manyika, J.: Big data: the next frontier for innovation, competition, and productivity (2011). http://www.mckinsey.com/Insights/MGI/Research/Technology_and_Innovation/Big_data_The_next_frontier_for_innovation. Accessed 29 Jan 2020

Data Management Optimization in a Real-Time Big Data Analysis System for Intensive Care

Rodrigo Cañibano[1], Claudia Rozas[1], Cristina Orlandi[2], and Javier Balladini[1][(✉)]

[1] Universidad Nacional del Comahue,Neuquén, Argentina
{rcanibano,claudia.rozas,javier.balladini}@fi.uncoma.edu.ar
[2] Hospital Francisco López Lima, Río Negro, Argentina
cristina.orlandi@gmail.com

Abstract. Vital signs monitors in intensive and intermediate care units generate large amounts of data, most of which are not recorded nor taken advantage of. We propose a computer system that allows the automatic and early detection of the deterioration of critical patients, through the real-time processing and analysis of digital health data, including physiological waveform data generated by the medical monitors. Our system tries to emulate the behavior of an expert intensivist physician, giving recommendations for clinical decision making to reduce the uncertainty on diagnosis, treatment options and prognosis. In our previous works, we presented an real-time Big Data infrastructure built using free software technologies. In this paper we improve its data management. We present and evaluate three different data representation models in Apache Kafka. One of this models outperforms the other two in storage space use and delivery time of both real-time and historical data. Our results show that Kafka can be used for historical data storage. This in turn allows us to eliminate the NoSQL database of our previous system. Unlike other works, ours attempts to reduce the number of components to lower system overhead and administration complexity.

Keywords: Intensive care unit · Clinical decision support system · Medical rules processing · Big data

1 Introduction

In Intensive Care Units (ICU), patients' data are composed of low frequency clinical data, and high frequency physiological data streams generated by the medical equipment (from sources such as vital signs monitor). On a typical ICU, clinical and physiological data are manually recorded through forms by the nurses. Physiological data are gathered by observing the medical equipment screens (placed next to the beds) at regular intervals (hourly or a fraction of an hour) defined by the physician for each patient [18]. The medical equipment

ⓒ Springer Nature Switzerland AG 2020
E. Rucci et al. (Eds.): JCC-BD&ET 2020, CCIS 1291, pp. 93–107, 2020.
https://doi.org/10.1007/978-3-030-61218-4_7

emits an alert if it detects that the patient's health is at risk, based on its own measurements captured via sensors. Physicians will later thoroughly analyze the data recorded on the forms and will specify the treatment for the patient to the nurses.

This methodology gives rise to many problems. One of them is that the management of the information is prone to human errors. The source of this is related to the errors made by the nurses during the manual gathering of the data, and the huge quantities of data that physicians must analyze for each patient (physiological data, x-rays, laboratory data analysis, patient's clinical data, etc.) [21]. This can lead to misdiagnosis or inconsistent information that requires additional staff effort to detect its origin. This methodology also presents loss of data between nursing records (taken at intervals of several minutes), which can decrease the accuracy of diagnosis [20,24]. Furthermore, the unavailability of a complete historical data record does not permit new knowledge extraction wich would benefit the critical care research [23,25].

Another problem this methodology can be affected by is the late detection of the patient's health deterioration. A long time may pass between the recording of the data by the nurses and the physician's analysis of them. This situation may be aggravated by the shortage of intensive care specialists [3,10,22]. Because of this, most ICUs in Argentina don't have an intensive care specialist during the 24 hours of the day. This context (caused by a deficient methodology and lack of intensive care specialists) is prone to late detections of the deterioration of the patient's health. This negatively affects their health, increases the risk of death [9], increases the economic costs of the treatments, and results in longer stays and therefore less patients treated.

The ICUs can substantially improve its throughput with the capture, automatic analysis, and visualization of vast quantities of data in real time [6]. This problem, beyond the scope of traditional data collection and analysis methods, is a Big Data challenge [12]. With the adoption of increasingly affordable technologies of parallel and distributed computing, and the new advances in data science and artificial intelligence, it is possible to radically transform the working methodology of the ICUs.

We propose a computer system that allows the automatic and early detection of the deterioration of critical patients, through the real-time processing and analysis of digital health data, including physiological waveform data streams. Our system strives to emulate the behavior of an expert intensivist physician, giving recommendations for clinical decision making. Therefore it is possible to reduce the uncertainty on diagnosis, treatment options and prognosis [14].

Our clinical decision support system (CDSS) can also be used in lower complexity units, like intermediate care units. In these units, patients are monitored via a vital signs monitor, with permanent nursing staff, meanwhile physician are present only on demand. Our system can alert the nursing personnel at the increase of the severity of a patient, reducing the number of unexpected deaths [19].

In this paper, we propose a implemented solution using high performance free software frameworks: Apache Kafka and Apache Flink. This system allows the emission of early alerts based on the real time processing of medical rules and telemedicine to allow the query of the patient's real-time and historical data. The main contribution of this work is a simplified architecture of a real-time big data infrastructure. Compared to our previous original proposal [5,7], we eliminated the need of Cassandra (a NoSQL database) for the query of historical data. In its place, we use Kafka's historical storage.

Experiments are presented to show that Apache Kafka can perform the reading of historical data in a satisfactory way. An evaluation of performance and required storage space was made for different data representations in Kafka, both for historical and real-time data access. For the evaluation, we use the most resource-demanding data streams: physiological waveforms.

The rest of this paper is organized as follows. Section 2 details related works. Section 3 presents the system overview. Section 4 shows the simplified real-time big data infrastructure. Section 5 discusses the alternatives for the representation of physiological waveforms and the design of experiment for its evaluation in terms of required storage space and performance, and defines the experimental platform. Section 6 exposes the obtained results. Section 7 shows an analysis of results. Finally, Sect. 8 presents the conclusions and future works.

2   Related Works

In [12] a high performance waveform storage and retrieval system is proposed, and the importance of storing the waveforms beyond storing its derived variables is mentioned. The solution is efficient, but currently does not allow the visualization of real time data, nor the integration with real-time predictive models. It also does not provide fault tolerance, a characteristic necessary for critical computer health systems. Similarly, in [18] a system is proposed for the storage and retrieval of ICU signals, based on an adaptation of a computer system by McLaren used to continually monitor and analyse the data from F1 racing cars in real-time. The system can be connected to an analytics software (MATLAB 8.5), although it is not described what type of analysis it would perform. [11] presents a big data cluster based on the Hadoop ecosystem technology coupled with ElasticSearch technology that can replace the existing RDBMS-based technology. This platform was designed to support data from different applications of big data on the Mayo Clinic, although no CDSS is described. In [8] successful cases on signal analytics using big data are presented. In [1] a system is presented for patient monitoring and disease detection in mobile environments using cloud computing.

Specifically on CDSS in critical care, both concrete systems and infrastructure frameworks have been presented. In [13], an early framework (designed before developing the system) for an infrastructure of stream data management, mining and fusion for monitored patients is proposed. Artemis [4,16] is a CDSS for neonatal intensive care units that uses InfoSphere Streams middleware system of IBM; Artemis might be the most detailed system of all literature. In [2], a system with a pipeline architecture is presented, which is implemented with free software technologies: Apache Kafka (streaming stage), Apache Spark (process stage) and Apache Hive - HDFS (storage stage). In [15], a framework is described that follows a pipeline architecture with multiple stages: Data Source, Collect Data, Process Data, Store Data, Serve Data. The various free software technologies available for use at each stage are mentioned, but no concrete solution is presented (a system with specific details on the integration and configuration of the components). In [17], a system is presented that utilizes Microsoft Azure services (lambda architecture) to support real-time and batch analytics. Other systems are commercial and there is no scientific publications about them, like ehCOS SmartICU[1] and Excel Medical[2].

Unlike other alternatives, our objective is oriented to the construction of a multi hospital system (in order to increase the volume of data and consequent extraction of knowledge) with telemedicine support. Our aim is for the final system to integrate mature free software components, be efficient in its use of computing resources, secure, fault tolerant and resilient, and to allow integration with other health systems.

3   System Overview

Our expert system is based on clinical rules associated with a diagnosis, or with a prognosis or probability of developing a certain condition. The rules consist of two parts: an antecedent and a consequent. The antecedent defines the conditions, relating parameters and values, which must be met to generate an alert (the consequent of the rule) indicating possible risk, current or future, in the patient's health. Each patient can be associated with a specific set of rules. Rules are continuously evaluated in real time, considering: the most current values of a parameter, values of a parameter that occur in a time window, or events that happen in a certain order.

Rules are initially created from experts' knowledge or clinical guidelines. Then, once enough data has been collected, it is possible to extract knowledge to generate new rules.

Our system records the complete physiological waveforms (raw data at 500 Hz or 1 KHz) so that clinicians or nurses can observe, in real time, the waveforms (for telemedicine), and for historical storage useful for future research. Each waveform is processed to obtain derived variables, for example heart rate derived from electrocardiogram (ECG). Typically, these derived variables are of relatively low frequency (no more than 1 Hz). These streams of derived variables, along with non-contiguous data such as clinical, laboratory, radiologic data, and others, are used by the clinical rules (that is, rules do not use high-frequency stream data).

3.1   High-Level System Architecture

Figure 1 describes the system architecture, divided into two subsystems. A global subsystem, shared by all hospitals, and a local subsystem to each hospital. The

---

[1] https://www.ehcos.com.
[2] http://excel-medical.com.

global subsystem is a centralized database for storing **historical data**. This database can be explored for **knowledge extraction** to generate new clinical rules. The local subsystem implements the detection and early warning system. The separation of these two subsystems allow the system to be implemented in institutions with unreliable Internet access.

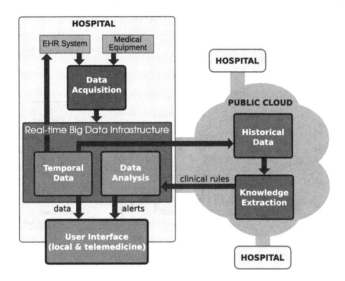

Fig. 1. High-level system architecture

The local subsystem includes the following components:

Data Acquisition: this component retrieves data generated by medical equipment and the Health Record (EHR) System, and delivers it to the Real-time Big Data Infrastructure.

Real-time Big Data Infrastructure: it is responsible for the temporary storage of patient data, which is deleted once they leave the unit. Before deleting the data, they are copied to the cloud storage. In addition, this component performs data analysis, which involves signal processing and clinical rules processing. This component demands the largest computational resources of the entire system in order to be able to process the large volume of messages in real time. In case of a fault, the system must recover quickly without losing information.

User Interface: it allows nurses and physicians to receive alerts, and to visualize current and retrospective data of patients as raw data (signals, vital signs, etc.) or statistical processed data (tables, charts, etc.).

4   Real-Time Big Data Infrastructure: Simplified Architecture

Figure 2 shows the architecture of the Real-time Big Data Infrastructure. Data are organized in a central platform, the Streaming Data Platform, which receives data streams and makes them available to other components to be consumed in real time. It works as a messaging system or message queue, under the publication-subscription pattern. This organization of the data allows to simplify the flow of communications between the different components, producing a low coupling between them.

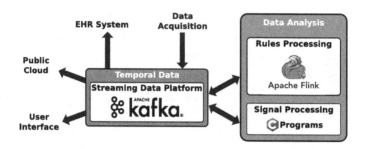

Fig. 2. Architecture of the real-time big data infrastructure

4.1   Apache Kafka

Kafka [26] is a distributed platform designed for handling large data streams, generated and consumed by multiple agents. It provides low latency, high availability, message order unification, and allows scaling to multiple nodes in a cluster.

Communication between consumers and producers is done through subscription to topics and consumer groups. Each producer subscribes to a topic to write messages, while consumers subscribe to a group and topic to read messages.

To increase availability, the message flow is partitioned. Each message is sent only to one partition, and each partition is assigned to a single consumer in the group. All partitions are distributed among the consumers in the group (a consumer can read multiple partitions). If there are more consumers than partitions, they will be idle consumers. Each message written by a producer on the topic will be delivered to only one consumer of each group subscribed to the topic. Since different consumer groups can retrieve messages at different rates, each "group, partition" pair maintains a pointer to the next message to be read. This pointer is called "offset", and the framework provides functions to change it, if necessary. The number of partitions must be configured before starting the Kafka cluster.

Each message has four main components:

Topic: name of the specific Kafka stream.

Key: used to determine to which partition the message should be sent. Multiple messages can have the same key. If the key is "Null" then the partition will be chosen at random.

Value: contains the data of the message.

Timestamp: indicates the message creation time.

Kafka implements fault tolerance through partition replication. The number of replicas is configured before starting the Kafka cluster, and they are distributed among the cluster nodes.

Although the main function of this framework is to communicate producers and consumers, it allows the retrieval of historical data and is capable of storing the data volume equivalent to several days of messages. The initial design of our system included a NoSQL database for temporary historical data storage (maintained during the patient's stay). However, the experimentation presented in this work shows that Apache Kafka can store and retrieve historical data in a satisfactory way. Thus, we have eliminated the NoSQL database, reducing the number of components and the complexity of the system.

4.2 Apache Flink

Apache Flink is a distributed processing platform for fault-tolerant and low-latency data streams processing. The framework was developed to use Apache Kafka for reading and writing streams, therefore its integration is easy. The main loop of a program written in Apache Flink consists of reading data from one or more "data sources", analyzing the data along with its internal state (this stage is called transformation), and writing the results to a "data sink".

Flink works with data in main memory (does not use secondary storage). It is possible to expand memory capacity by using multiple nodes in a cluster. Furthermore, Flink has an automatic load balancer to improve its performance in the parallel computing system.

The framework natively supports failure recovery through a checkpoint-restart mechanism.

5 Data Representation in Kafka: Impact on Storage and Performance

5.1 Alternatives for the Representation of Physiological Waveforms

The representation of high frequency physiological data streams is critical because, in addition to affecting the space required for data storage, it significantly affects the performance achieved by the system.

A waveform sample is identified by the following data: patient, parameter, creation time and sample value. The latter two data are specific to each sample (they could even be grouped into small sample groups to store a single time for a group of uniformly spaced samples). In contrast, the first two data could be deduced from the context, for example if they are implicitly determined by the topic.

A topic could be associated with a single patient. Thus, the deletion of a patient's data (when he leaves the unit) can be done through the removal of the topic (or topics); a simple operation with no cost in performance.

If there is only one topic per patient, then each message should contain explicit information to identify the parameter. In this case, each consumer must filter the messages on the topic according to the required parameters. However, if the topic is associated with a « Patient, Parameter » pair, the parameter is also implicit, and each consumer will be able to directly access the messages of the required parameters.

Contemplating these variants, we proposed three data representation models of physiological waveforms in Kafka, shown in Table 1.

Table 1. Data representation models of physiological waveforms in Kafka

	Model A	Model B	Model C
Topic	patientID_parameter	patientID	patientID
Key	Null	parameter	Null
Value	Sample	Sample	Parameter, sample
Timestamp	Sample creation time (microseconds)	Sample creation time (microseconds)	Sample creation time (microseconds)

5.2 Design of Experiments

Experiments were designed to determine which of the three proposed waveforms representation models is most appropriate for information storage and processing, and to verify the feasibility of using Apache Kafka for historical data storage. Three performance measures are used to evaluate the models: storage space per message, delivery delay of real-time data and delivery delay of historical data.

Storage Space per Message. This metric measures the number of bytes each message occupies in secondary storage. For each model, an ECG waveform of 1 KHz is produced for 48 h (the system is stopped every hour and disk usage is measured). Each sample is represented by a single-precision floating-point number (4 bytes). The average number of bytes per message is calculated from the total storage space used for the entire waveform. The long duration of the experiment tries to avoid fluctuations in storage space that could be caused by temporary management structures created by Kafka.

Delivery Delay of Real-Time Data. It is the time elapsed between the creation of a sample and its reading by a consumer. For each model, two scenarios are analyzed. Scenario 1 has ten patients and a single 1 KHz waveform per patient with a duration of one hour. Scenario 2 has a single patient with ten 1 KHz waveforms. Each sample is represented by a single-precision floating-point number (4 bytes).

In all experiments, each waveform is generated by a different producer (there are always 10 producers), and only one waveform is read by only one consumer. Note that, for scenario 2, model B and C, all 10 waveforms are stored in a single topic. Thus, the consumer must read the messages of all the parameters and discard those that do not belong to the searched parameter. In other cases, as each of the 10 waveforms are stored in a different topic, no filtering is required.

Delivery Delay of Historical Data. It is the time it takes to locate the newest sample with time equal to or less than the one indicated, plus the time to recover that sample. The experiment consists of the production of ten waveforms at 1 KHz for one hour. Later ten thousand searches and retrievals will be performed, uniformly distributed over the interval. This is done twice, the first starting from the oldest to the most current sample and then from the most current to the oldest sample.

The consumer calculates the time from the moment the message search is started until their data are retrieved. The delivery delay of contiguous data is not evaluated because, as data are available for reading, this time should be equal to or less than the delivery delay of real-time data.

To locate a message from a timestamp, the *offsets_for_times* and *seek* functions are used. The function *offsets_for_times* returns, for each partition, the earliest offset whose timestamp is greater than or equal to the given timestamp. However, our system needs to fetch the message with the latest offset whose timestamp is less than or equal to the given timestamp. The following strategy is applied: given a timestamp, the lowest offset whose timestamp is $timestamp+1$ is searched in each partition. Then, for each partition, the *seek* function is applied to locate the message at position $offset - 1$. Finally, the topic is ready to start reading the messages sequentially (the data are delivered in order).

In the case of models B and C, consumers should discard messages that do not belong to the target parameter, going through the message flow in a decreasing offset direction.

5.3 Experimental Platform

The experiments are conducted on three nodes of a cluster, each with two 10-core Intel Xeon E5-2650 processors with hyperthreading disabled, and 62 GiB of main memory. Each node has access to a shared folder via NSF and a local disk (HDD). The connection network is gigabit Ethernet. The operating system of the nodes is CentOS 7, running the kernel v3.10.0. The Kafka version is 2.12, running on Java SE Runtime Environment 1.8.0_211. The consumers and producers were built using Python-Kafka.

Two nodes run the Kafka cluster, while the third runs the producers and consumers. The consumers and producers are located on the same node in order to measure the difference between creation and reading time more accurately. Two partitions per topic are used, with two replicas each, the Kafka logs are stored on the local disk. Data compression is disabled.

6   Experimental Results

6.1   Storage Space per Message

The Fig. 3 shows the average storage required per message at hourly intervals. On all the three proposed models, the storage space required for the messages is stabilized after a certain time. Model A's messages are the smallest, requiring an average of 154.85 bytes each. Model C's messages use 166.90 bytes each (about 7,8% more than model A), and Model B's messages are the largest, using 170.93 bytes each (about 10,4% more than model A).

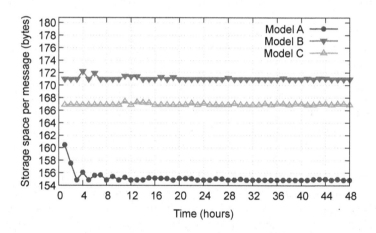

Fig. 3. Storage space per message

6.2   Delivery Delay of Real-Time Data

Table 2 summarizes the maximum and average delivery delay of real-time data for scenario 1 (ten patients and one waveform per patient) and scenario 2 (one patient with ten waveforms). Figure 4 shows the creation and reading time of each message for scenario 1 (subfigure a) and 2 (subfigure b).

Table 2. Maximum and average delivery delay (seconds) of real-time data

	Model A		Model B		Model C	
	Max	Avg	Max	Avg	Max	Avg
Scenario 1	0.202	0.023	0.149	0.018	0.16	0.019
Scenario 2	0.2	0.06	2297.32	1424.96	1739.60	924.07

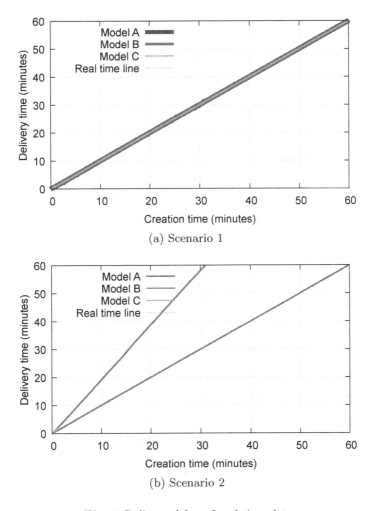

Fig. 4. Delivery delay of real-time data

6.3 Delivery Delay of Historical Data

Table 3 summarizes the maximum and average delivery delay of historical data for each model. Figure 5 shows the maximum delivery delay (solid lines) and average delay (dashed lines) for each message proportions. For example, 55.39% of model A's messages achieved a delivery delay of less than 1 s. The table and figure only consider the reading of the first message (one sample of the waveform). However, once the first message has been retrieved, the reading of the following 9,999 messages takes less than 2 ms.

Table 3. Maximum and average delivery delay (seconds) of historical data

	Model A	Model B	Model C
Max	1.37	4.37	1.71
Avg	0.95	2.59	1.2

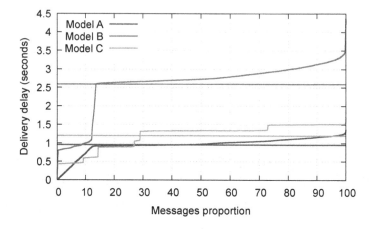

Fig. 5. Delivery delay of historical data

7   Analysis of Results

Model A's messages use the least amount of storage space per message, using about 155 bytes each (12 bytes of useful data, and 143 of overhead).

The delivery delay of real-time data was evaluated for two scenarios. In the first scenario (ten patients and a single waveform per patient), all three models performed well, with non-significant differences. In the second scenario (a single patient with ten waveforms), model A achieved good performance. However, the B and C models are unsuitable for use because of their low performance. From the Fig. 5 it can be seen that, at the beginning of the execution, the delivery delay is not high, but it grows linearly. This is produced because the time required to filter the messages of the parameter of interest by the consumer is bigger than the time of generation of the messages.

Regarding the delivery delay of historical data, the best performance was obtained with model A, with a maximum time of 1.37 s, and an average of 0.95 s. It was observed that once the first message of interest is located, the contiguous messages can be quickly accessed. Due to historical data searches are sporadic, we consider these results as acceptable.

In all the experiments that involved reading messages from a topic, it was observed that the filtering of the messages by parameter performed by the consumer, considerably increases the delivery delay of real-time and historical data. Therefore, it is necessary that consumers only read the messages of the parameter they need. This occurs naturally in the case of model A, but by making some changes to the system, it can also be achieved with model B. For this, it is necessary to modify the hash function, which is applied to the keys of the messages to determine the target partition. Thus, it is possible to store messages of different parameters on different partitions. Then consumers can subscribe only to the partition of interest. But the amount of partitions and the hash function must be changed every time the number of parameters changes.

Model A presented the best overall performance of the three data representation models, and does not require the system modifications that the model B need in order to achieve similar performance.

8   Conclusions and Future Works

We propose a real-time Big Data infrastructure solution which is implemented using high performance free software frameworks: Apache Kafka and Apache Flink. This system allows the emission of early alerts based on the real time processing of medical rules and telemedicine to allow the query of the real-time and historical patient's data. The proposed infrastructure is part of a clinical decision support system for intensive and intermediate care units.

In this article, we describe the system in general, and in more detail the proposed infrastructure. The two most complex components that make up the infrastructure were presented: Apache Flink and Apache Kafka. Emphasis was placed on the management of the system's data, which we implemented using Kafka. We evaluated three different data representation models in Kafka, contemplating the most resource-demanding data streams: physiological waveforms. One of this models outperforms the other two in storage space use and delivery time of both real-time and historical data. The results show that Kafka can be used for historical data storage, allowing us to eliminate the NoSQL database of our previous system. Simplifying the system by reducing the number of components is key to lower system overhead and administration complexity.

In future work, we will evaluate the performance of the system using data compression in Kafka using real waveforms. We are also going to evaluate the simultaneous reading of the total waveforms (which is required to transmit the data to the public cloud for permanent storage), and increase the number of samples per message. Once the system has a real and complete workload, the number of partitions that achieve the best system performance will be determined.

References

1. Agbo, C.C., Mahmoud, Q.H., Eklund, J.M.: An architecture for cloud-assisted clinical support system for patient monitoring and disease detection in mobile environments. In: Proceedings of the 12th EAI International Conference on Pervasive Computing Technologies for Healthcare, pp. 245–250, PervasiveHealth 2018, Association for Computing Machinery, New York, NY, USA (2018). https://doi.org/10.1145/3240925.3240944

2. Akhtar, U., Khattak, A.M., Lee, S.: Challenges in managing real-time data in health information system (HIS). In: Chang, C.K., Chiari, L., Cao, Y., Jin, H., Mokhtari, M., Aloulou, H. (eds.) ICOST 2016. LNCS, vol. 9677, pp. 305–313. Springer, Cham (2016). https://doi.org/10.1007/978-3-319-39601-9_27

3. Alconada Magliano, J.P., García, E.F.: La situación de la terapia intensiva y su contexto. Rev. Argent. de Terapia Intensiva **32**(1) (2015). https://revista.sati.org.ar/index.php/MI/article/view/418

4. Balaji, S., Patil, M., McGregor, C.: A cloud based big data based online health analytics for rural NICUs and PICUs in India: opportunities and challenges. In: 2017 IEEE 30th International Symposium on Computer-Based Medical Systems (CBMS), pp. 385–390. IEEE (2017)

5. Balladini, J., Bruno, P., Zurita, R., Orlandi, C.: An automatic and early detection of the deterioration of patients in intensive and intermediate care units: technological challenges and solutions. J. Comput. Sci. Technol. **18**(03), 218–227 (2018). https://journal.info.unlp.edu.ar/JCST/article/view/1139

6. Balladini, J., et al.: A tool for improving the delivery of integrated intensive health care performance. Int. J. Integr. Care **19**(4), 222 (2019)

7. Balladini, J., Rozas, C., Frati, F.E., Vicente, N., Orlandi, C.: Big data analytics in intensive care units: challenges and applicability in an Argentinian hospital. J. Comput. Sci. Technol. **15**(2), 61–67 (2015)

8. Belle, A., Thiagarajan, R., Soroushmehr, S., Navidi, F., Beard, D.A., Najarian, K.: Big data analytics in healthcare. BioMed Res. Int. **2015** (2015)

9. Blunt, M.C., Burchett, K.R.: Out-of-hours consultant cover and case-mix-adjusted mortality in intensive care. The Lancet **356**(9231), 735–736 (2000)

10. Buchman, T.G., et al.: Innovative interdisciplinary strategies to address the intensivist shortage. Crit. Care Med. **45**(2), 298–304 (2017)

11. Chen, D., et al.: Real-time or near real-time persisting daily healthcare data into HDFS and elasticsearch index inside a big data platform. IEEE Trans. Industr. Inf. **13**(2), 595–606 (2017)

12. Goodwin, A.J., et al.: A practical approach to storage and retrieval of high-frequency physiological signals. Physiol. Meas. **41**(3), 035008 (2020)

13. Han, H., Ryoo, H.C., Patrick, H.: An infrastructure of stream data mining, fusion and management for monitored patients. In: 19th IEEE Symposium on Computer-Based Medical Systems (CBMS 2006), pp. 461–468. IEEE (2006)

14. Herasevich, V., Keegan, M.T., Pickering, B.W.: The future of ICU prediction scores in the era of big data. J. ICU Manage. Pract. **16**(2), 112–113 (2016)

15. Kaur, J., Mann, D.K.S.: AI based HealthCare platform for real time, predictive and prescriptive analytics using reactive programming. In: Journal of Physics: Conference Series 933, p. 012010, January 2018. https://doi.org/10.1088%2F1742-6596%2F933%2F1%2F012010

16. Khazaei, H., McGregor, C., Eklund, M., El-Khatib, K., Thommandram, A.: Toward a big data healthcare analytics system: a mathematical modeling perspective. In: 2014 IEEE World Congress on Services, pp. 208–215 (2014)

17. López-Martínez, F., Núñez-Valdez, E.R., García-Díaz, V., Bursac, Z.: A case study for a big data and machine learning platform to improve medical decision support in population health management. Algorithms **13**(4), 102 (2020)

18. Matam, B.R., Duncan, H.: Technical challenges related to implementation of a formula one real time data acquisition and analysis system in a paediatric intensive care unit. J. Clin. Monit. Comput. **32**(3), 559–569 (2017). https://doi.org/10.1007/s10877-017-0047-6

19. Mathukia, C., Fan, W., Vadyak, K., Biege, C., Krishnamurthy, M.: Modified early warning system improves patient safety and clinical outcomes in an academic community hospital. J. Community Hosp. Intern. Med. Perspect. **5**(2), 26716 (2015)
20. Nemati, S., Holder, A., Razmi, F., Stanley, M.D., Clifford, G.D., Buchman, T.G.: An interpretable machine learning model for accurate prediction of sepsis in the ICU. Crit. Care Med. **46**(4), 547–553 (2018)
21. Reiz, A.N., de la Hoz, M.A., García, M.S.: Big data analysis and machine learning in intensive care units. Medicina Intensiva (English Edition) **43**(7), 416–426 (2019)
22. Salomon, G.: The intensivist shortage: is there a way around it? Healthcare. https://www.healthcareglobal.com/public-health/intensivist-shortage-there-way-around-it
23. Sanchez-Pinto, L.N., Luo, Y., Churpek, M.M.: Big data and data science in critical care. Chest **154**(5), 1239–1248 (2018)
24. Tegtmeyer, K.: The pediatric intensive care unit of the future: technological advances in pediatric critical care medicine. In: Wheeler, D., Wong, H., Shanley, T. (eds.) Science and Practice of Pediatric Critical Care Medicine, pp. 1–7. Springer, London, London (2009). https://doi.org/10.1007/978-1-84800-921-9_14
25. Topol, E.J.: High-performance medicine: the convergence of human and artificial intelligence. Nat. Med. **25**(1), 44–56 (2019). https://doi.org/10.1038/s41591-018-0300-7
26. Wang, G., et al.: Building a replicated logging system with Apache Kafka. Proc. VLDB Endow. **8**(12), 1654–1655 (2015). https://doi.org/10.14778/2824032.2824063

Machine and Deep Learning

Reddening-Free Q Indices to Identify Be Star Candidates

Yael Aidelman[1,2] (iD), Carlos Escudero[2] (iD), Franco Ronchetti[3,4] (iD),
Facundo Quiroga[3(✉)] (iD), and Laura Lanzarini[3] (iD)

[1] Departamento de Espectroscopía, Facultad de Ciencias Astronómicas Y Geofísicas,
Universidad Nacional de La Plata (UNLP), Paseo Del Bosque S/N,
B1900FWA La Plata, Argentina
[2] Instituto de Astrofísica La Plata, CCT La Plata, CONICET-UNLP, Paseo Del
Bosque S/N, B1900FWA La Plata, Argentina
[3] Instituto de Investigación en Informática LIDI, Facultad de Informática,
Universidad Nacional de La Plata, La Plata, Argentina
fquiroga@lidi.info.unlp.edu.ar
[4] Comisión de Investigaciones Científicas de la Pcia. De Bs. As. (CIC-PBA),
La Plata, Argentina

Abstract. Astronomical databases currently provide high-volume spectroscopic and photometric data. While spectroscopic data is better suited to the analysis of many astronomical objects, photometric data is relatively easier to obtain due to shorter telescope usage time. Therefore, there is a growing need to use photometric information to automatically identify objects for further detailed studies, specially Hα emission line stars such as Be stars. Photometric color-color diagrams (CCDs) are commonly used to identify this kind of objects. However, their identification in CCDs is further complicated by the reddening effect caused by both the circumstellar and interstellar gas. This effect prevents the generalization of candidate identification systems. Therefore, in this work we evaluate the use of neural networks to identify Be star candidates from a set of OB-type stars. The networks are trained using a labeled subset of the VPHAS+ and 2MASS databases, with filters u, g, r, Hα, i, J, H, and K. In order to avoid the reddening effect, we propose and evaluate the use of reddening-free Q indices to enhance the generalization of the model to other databases and objects. To test the validity of the approach, we manually labeled a subset of the database, and use it to evaluate candidate identification models. We also labeled an independent dataset for cross dataset evaluation. We evaluate the recall of the models at a 99% precision level on both test sets. Our results show that the proposed features provide a significant improvement over the original filter magnitudes.

Keywords: Stellar classification · Ob-type stars · Be stars ·
VPHAS+ · 2MASS · IPHAS · SDSS · LAMOST

© Springer Nature Switzerland AG 2020
E. Rucci et al. (Eds.): JCC-BD&ET 2020, CCIS 1291, pp. 111–123, 2020.
https://doi.org/10.1007/978-3-030-61218-4_8

1   Introduction

In the big data era, free access to databases in different wavelength ranges, from gamma-rays to radio waves, together with machine-learning methods, has drastically incremented the possibility to study and identify different types of peculiar line-emission stars using photometric information (e.g., Vioque et al., 2019 [30]; Akras et al., 2019 [2]; Pérez-Ortiz et al., 2017 [21]).

While spectroscopic techniques are excellent to perform accurate stellar classification and deepen into the study of various spectral features, the telescope time required to obtain such information is longer compared to obtaining photometric data.

The goal of this work is then to use the potential of photometric data to search for emission-line star candidates. These can be later observed and be confirmed spectroscopically as such. Particularly, we are interested in detecting Be star candidates.

Be stars are emission-line objects that rotate at high speed (Jaschek et al., 1981 [15]; Struve, O., 1931 [28]) and constitute unique astrophysical laboratories. They are of interest in various branches of stellar physics dedicated to the study of mechanisms of mass loss, angular momentum distribution, astroseismology, among others.

The rest of this section describes Be stars in detail, classical techniques to detect plausible candidates as well as previous star candidate proposals based on machine-learning methods.

1.1   Be Stars

Be stars are defined as non-supergiant spectral B-type stars that exhibit, or have exhibited, one or more hydrogen lines in emission (Jaschek et al., 1981 [15]; Collins, II, G., 1987 [7]), particularly the Hα line. In some cases, it is also possible to observe the presence of once-ionized helium and metal lines in emission. Thus, this definition not only applies to B-type stars but also to late O- and early A-type stars.

The analysis of spectrophotometric observations of Be stars at different wavelengths, combined with interferometric and polarimetric data (Gies et al., 2007 [11]; Meilland et al., 2007 [18], among others), indicate that the different properties shown by these stars could be interpreted by the existence of an optically-thin gaseous circumstellar equatorial disk in Keplerian motion (see Rivinius et al., 2013 [25]). This suggests that the high rotation speed would play a significant role in the development of the equatorial disk (e.g., Struve, O., 1931 [28]; Huang, S., 1972 [14]; Quirrenbach, A., 1993 [23]; Quirrenbach et al., 1994 [24]; Hirata, R., 1995 [13]). However, despite the increasing observational evidence that Be stars do not rotate at their critical rotational speed (Zorec et al. 2016 [31], Zorec et al. 2017 [32], Aidelman et al. 2018 [1], Cochetti et al., 2019 [6]), there is still no consensus on disk formation mechanism(s).

Other observed effects induced by stellar rotation during the main sequence phase of hot stars, are the development of axi-symmetric winds, the modification in pulsation modes, changes in metallicity or the presence of magnetic fields (see Peters et al., 2020 [22]; Rivinius et al., 2013 [25]). These properties make Be stars perfect stellar laboratories, of interest in different astrophysical topics, as mentioned above.

In this context, the discovery, classification and analysis of a considerable sample of Be stars in different environments are necessary to understand their nature.

1.2   Related Work

To the best of our knowledge, there are no previous works focused on Be stars that use the reddening-free Q indices as we propose in this work (see Sect. 2.2). Therefore we briefly summarize work similar to ours.

Pérez-Ortiz et al. (2017 [21]) select Be star candidates using light curves of the I band obtained from OGLE-IV data (Udalski et al., 2015 [29]). They train classification trees, random forest, gradient boosted trees, support vector machines (SVM) and K-nearest neighbours on OGLE-III data. To evaluate the models, they compare the average f-score from 10-fold cross validation. While random forests achieve the best scores, most models behave similarly. To improve the cross-dataset robustness of their models, they employ a custom feature based on fourier coefficients of the data. They propose 50 new Be star candidates selected from OGLE-IV data.

Vioque et al., (2019 [30]) use photometric data similar to ours which includes a passband filter for the Hα wavelength. However, their sources include many other filters, resulting in 48 variables for each sample. In order to avoid problems caused by interstellar extinction, they select objects for which the effect of this phenomena is negligible. They apply Principal Component Analysis (PCA) to reduce the features to a 12 latent dimensions which contain 99.99% of variability. Afterwards, they employ a neural network composed of three linear layers to classify candidates.

Akras et al., (2019 [2]) identify symbiotic stars from other objects. Their data includes various photometric filters that can detect Hα. They perform a thorough manual evaluation of color-color[1] diagrams (CCDs) to identify feature combinations which can separate these stars from other kinds of similar objects. Afterwards, they repeat this approach to classify symbiotic stars into subsets. Their approach can identify a small subset of previously labeled symbiotic stars and also proposes 125 new candidates. They employ a combination of k-nearest neighbours, linear discriminant analysis, and classification trees as models.

---

[1] A color index is defined as the difference of two magnitudes at different wavelengths $(m_{\lambda_1} - m_{\lambda_2})$. Magnitude is a unitless measure of the brightness of an object on a logarithmic scale in a defined passband. The brighter an object, the more negative the value of its magnitude.

1.3 Proposed Work

One technique commonly used to identify classical Be star candidates relies on photometric color-color diagrams. These diagrams use differences of apparent magnitudes between narrow-band filters, such as Hα passband, and broad-band filters centered at other given wavelengths, such as the filters r or i. However, these colors are affected by interstellar extinction. Therefore, in this work we propose to use the reddening-free Q photometric indices, as described in Sect. 2.2.

The construction of the Q indices from different apparent magnitudes opens up the potential of broad-band and narrow-band photometric data together with machine-learning techniques to quickly obtain a significant number of Be star candidates observed in any direction in the sky. Subsequently, this method will allow us to carry out a rapid and accurate spectroscopic follow-up of these stars to confirm their classification and properties.

2 Datasets and Features

2.1 Datasets

We use the data published by Mohr-Smith et al. (2017 [20]) on the Carina Arm region ($282° \leq l \leq 293°$). These authors used data from the VST Photometric Hα Survey of the Southern Galactic Plane and Bulge (VPHAS+; Drew et al., 2014 [10]) in u, g, r, Hα, i filters (see Fig. 1 bottom panel) combined with J, H, K magnitudes from the Two Micron All Sky Survey (2MASS; Skrutskie et al., 2006 [27]). Performing fittings to the spectral energy distribution, Mohr-Smith et al. grouped the sample of OB-type stars in four groups: emission-line stars (EM), sub- and over-luminous stars, and normal stars. The features of the dataset consist of the fluxes at the 8 filters mentioned above. The dataset contains a sample of 5877 OB-type stars labeled with four classes. Since we are only interested in detecting emission-line stars from the other classes, we group all non-EM stars into a single set called *Normal OB*. The resulting class distribution is shown in Table 1.

To test the inter-database accuracy of the model, we manually labeled a subset of OB-type stars classified spectroscopically by Liu et al. (2019 [17]). The photometric data of this subset was obtained from VPHAS+ dr2 (for the southern hemisphere). Data in filters r, Hα, i were from the INT Photometric Hα Survey of the Northern Galactic Plane (IPHAS dr2; Barentsen et al., 2014 [4]) while the data in filters u, g were obtained from the Sloan Digital Sky Survey (SDSS dr12; Alam et a., 2015 [3]), for the northern hemisphere. Additionally, the data in filters J, H, K for both hemispheres were obtained from the 2MASS. Spectroscopic data is available from the Large Sky Area Multi-Object Fiber Spectroscopic Telescope (LAMOST dr5; Cui et al., 2012 [8]).

We selected stars which have both photometric and spectroscopic data. Among the 22901 OB-stars classified by Liu, only 1113 have measurements for the same set of 8 filters used by Mohr-Smith et al.

Via visual inspection of the spectra, we were able to label 283 stars (among 1113 OB-stars with photometry). We identified OB-stars that present the Hα line in emission (see Fig. 1 middle and upper panel). As shown in Table 1, we identify 98 objects as EM stars.

Table 1. Class distribution of samples.

Dataset	Normal OB	EM	Total
Mohr-Smith et al. (2017 [20])	5629	248	5877
Liu et al. (2019 [17])	185	98	283

2.2 Features

As mentioned in Sect. 2.1, the data used corresponds to magnitudes (hereinafter original features) obtained in seven different broad-band filters: u, g, r, i, J, H, and K, and in one narrow-band filter, Hα. However, the intrinsic magnitude of an object can be affected by several factors, such as the distance to the star and the interstellar extinction. Particularly, in the latter, the interstellar material (dust and gas) located between the observer and the object absorbs part of its radiation (mainly ultraviolet light). A priori, neither the amount of interstellar material in the visual direction nor the distance to the star are known. For these reasons, the use of magnitudes (available in the databases) as a tool to try to classify objects of different morphology or characteristics is not enough.

On the other hand, although the color index is independent of distance, it is still affected by interstellar reddening, as shown in Fig. 2. The left panel shows the CCD done by Mohr-Smith et al. (2015 [19]) with the stars detected in the Carina Arm region (gray dots). The blue crosses represent B-type stars whose location in the diagram is affected by the interstellar extinction.

In particular, as previously mentioned, one technique commonly used to identify classical Be star candidates is to use CCDs that combine a narrow-band filter centered at the Hα line and a filter that samples the nearby continuum region. Figure 2 (right panel) shows $(r - H\alpha)$ versus $(r - i)$ diagram with the location of stars with different characteristics (Mohr-Smith et al., 2015 [19]). As seen in this figure, Be stars (red crosses) are separated from other objects because they show an excess emission in Hα. However, the presence of other astrophysical sources, such as Wolf Rayet (WR) and Herbig AeBe (HAeBe) stars, in the same region can still be observed.

For all the aforementioned, in order to avoid the effects of interstellar extinction and distance, we propose the use of the reddening-free Q indices (hereinafter Q features). This index was introduced by Johnson & Morgan, (1955 [16]) and it is defined as:

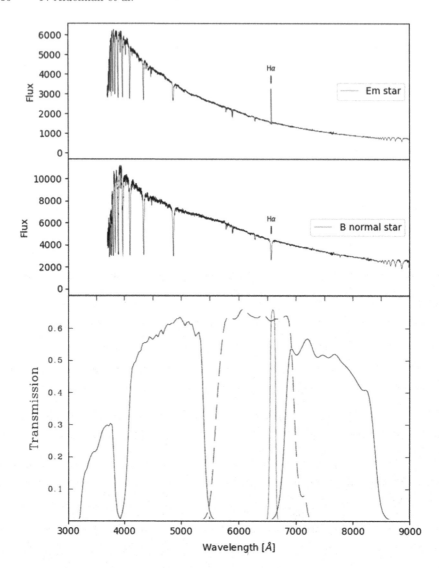

Fig. 1. Upper and middle panel show two B-type star spectra from LAMOST (Cui et al., 2012 [8]). The upper panel corresponds to a Be star, while the middle panel to a typical B-type star. Bottom panel shows the transmission profiles of the filters used by VPHAS+ (Drew et al., 2014 [10]). The Hα narrow-band filter is shown in red. (Color figure online)

$$Q_{1234} = (m_{\lambda_1} - m_{\lambda_2}) - \frac{r_{\lambda_1} - r_{\lambda_2}}{r_{\lambda_3} - r_{\lambda_4}} (m_{\lambda_3} - m_{\lambda_4})$$

$$= (m_{\lambda_1}^0 - m_{\lambda_2}^0) - \frac{r_{\lambda_1} - r_{\lambda_2}}{r_{\lambda_3} - r_{\lambda_4}} (m_{\lambda_3}^0 - m_{\lambda_4}^0) \qquad (1)$$

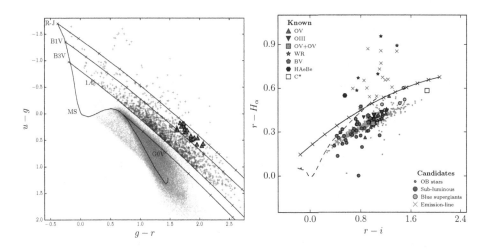

Fig. 2. Color-color diagrams taken from Mohr-Smith et al. (2015 [19]). Left: Location of B-type stars using u, g, r apparent magnitudes (blue crosses), and their corresponding location in the main sequence (MS) if they were not affected by interstellar extinction (black crosses). Right: location of the brightest stars in the Hα passband. (Color figure online)

where m_{λ_i} is the apparent (observed) magnitude and $m_{\lambda_i}^0$ is the apparent magnitude corrected by interstellar extinction effect in four (in some cases three) different filters centered at given wavelength λ_i, $r_{\lambda_i} = A_{m_{\lambda_i}}/A_V$, were $A_{m_{\lambda_i}}$ and A_V are the extinction coefficient for λ_i and for the V^2 filter, respectively. The r_{λ_i} values adopted in this work were those calculated by Schlafly et al. (2011 [26]) for a selective absorption coefficient[3] $R_V = 3.1$.

3   Experiments

3.1   Metodology

In order to test the suitability of the Q features, we trained and evaluated models with the original magnitudes and the features, separately. Additionally, we use Neighborhood Components Analysis (NCA; Goldberg et al., 2005 [12]) to perform dimensionality reduction to 2 components from the 56 variables of the Q features (built with the combinations of the 8 original magnitudes taken from 3) and generate another set of features (see Table 2). The 2-dimensional projection obtained by NCA can provide diagrams similar to the CCD commonly used in astronomy, albeit using latent variables (see Section 3.2).

We also compare different models in terms of their relative performances. We use a simple logistic regression as a baseline, and compare it against Support

---

[2] Filter V corresponds to Johnson's photometric system.

[3] The selective absorption coefficient relates the absorption coefficient in the visual, A_v, with the excess color $E(B-V)$, through the ratio $A_v = R_v E(B-V)$.

Table 2. Features and their dimensionalities.

Features	Description	Dimensionality
Originals	Magnitudes in $u,g,r,H\alpha,i,J,H,K$ filters	8
Q	Reddening-free index (Sect. 2.2)	56
NCA	Neighborhood Components Analysis[a] over Q features	2

[a] Goldberg et al., 2005 [12]

Vector Machines (SVM) with Linear and Gaussian kernels, with $C = 10$ in both cases. We also compare Neural Networks with 1 hidden layer with 8 linear units and $tanh$ activation function.

Given that candidate selection is essentially a binary classification task, the most natural overall performance metric is the F-score. However, since the goal of our work is to avoid manual verification of stars with a low probability of being Be stars, we focus on reducing the number of selected candidates. Therefore, we prefer to evaluate models in terms of their recall at a 99% level of precision[4]. That is, for each model we set a threshold so that its precision is around 99% and measure the resulting recall.

All models are trained on the Mohr-Smith dataset (see Sect. 2.1). Given the small sample size of the datasets, we use random subsampling cross validation with 20 random splits to obtain average values of each measure. We perform a 90/10 split, obtaining train/test sizes of approximately 5000 and 500 samples. For each split, a model is trained on Mohr-Smith, and evaluated on its test set. Afterwards, the same model is evaluated on the Liu dataset, using all samples as a test set. The same threshold used to obtain 99% precision for Mohr-Smith is also employed when evaluating the Liu dataset.

3.2   Results

Table 3 shows the recall rate for various model and feature combinations. The best result on the Liu dataset was obtained with Neural Network using Q features, obtaining a 25% recall rate. For the Mohr-Smith dataset, all models perform similarly.

Linear models, however, don't generalize as well as non-linear models for Liu. Nonetheless, a simple linear model with a non-linear dimensionality reduction such as NCA (Fig. 4) can obtain almost 14% recall in Liu. This indicates that the classes are not linearly separable even in the 56 dimensional space of the Q features.

In the case of SVM, results are somewhat erratic (Fig. 3). This may be due to the fact that calibrating a SVM to output probabilities is usually difficult, given that the probability estimation model must be fitted on top of the SVM after the model is trained.

---

[4] We note that *Purity* and *Completeness* are commonly used as synonyms for *Precision* and *Recall*, respectively. These terms are more prevalent in astronomy.

Given the recall increment when using Q features ($+11.9\%$) from the best model using magnitudes (Gaussian SVM) to the best model using Q features (Neural Network), we can conclude that these features indeed help with the identification of Hα emitting stars.

Table 3. Recall of models on the Mohr-Smith and Liu datasets, with a threshold set for 99% precision.

Model	Features	Mohr-Smith (Recall)	Liu (Recall)
Log. Regression	Magnitudes	84.2 (±7)%	5.7 (±0.1)%
Log. Regression	Q	81.3 (±12)%	5.5 (±10)%
Log. Regression	NCA	74.6(±11)%	13.9 (±9)%
SVM (Linear)	Magnitudes	82.4(±14)%	0(±0)%
SVM (Linear)	Q	85.2(±9)%	9.2 (±11)%
SVM (Gaussian)	Magnitudes	85.2(±11)%	13.1 (±2)%
SVM (Gaussian)	Q	37.2(±3)%	4.7 (±3)%
Neural Network	Magnitudes	84.8(±8)%	9.5(±4)%
Neural Network	Q	85.2(±14)%	**25** (±8)%

Figure 3 shows precision-recall curves evaluated in Liu dataset for a Neural Network model using the Q features. As listed in Table 3, the model achieves a 25% recall rate with 100% precision. For larger values of recall, precision rates drop in an approximately linear fashion, which indicates a good balance between these two metrics.

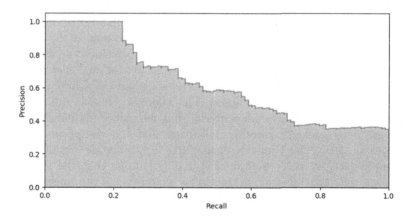

Fig. 3. Precision-Recall curves in Liu dataset for a Neural Network trained with Q features.

3.3   Recall Rate Analysis

We plot the 2-dimensional NCA features for both test set of Mohr-Smith and Liu (Fig. 4). As can be seen in the figure, a significant number of EM stars fall in the region of normal OB stars, and vice versa. For this reason, we decided to visually inspect the spectra of some objects in which this situation occurred.

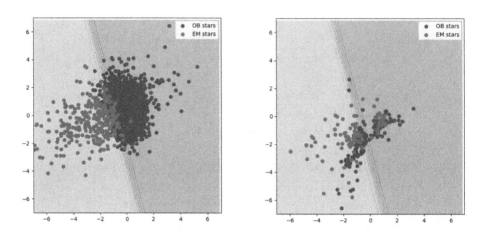

Fig. 4. NCA features for the Mohr-Smith (left) and Liu (right) datasets. The decision lines corresponds to a Sigmoid function from a Logistic Regression classifier trained on Mohr-Smith.

The high number of false-negative cases (reflected in the low recall rate) may be due to the detection limits existing in each observation technique. In most of the objects classified as false negatives, the Hα line profile is observed with the wings in emission (absorption) and the nucleus in absorption (emission) (Catanzaro, G., 2013 [5]; Dimitrov et al., 2018 [9]). However, if the emission is not intense enough, it is not reflected in the photometry since the values of the color indices and Q parameters correspond to that of a normal star.

On the other hand, false-negative and false-positive cases may also be due to the variability of the Be phenomenon. This effect is probably due to a significant increase in the circumstellar material that intensifies the emission in Hα. Subsequently, this intensity decreases with time and may disappear completely (Rivinius et al., 2013 [25]; Dimitrov et al., 2018 [9]). Since the photometric and spectroscopic data are not simultaneous, it may happen that the photometric data does not reflect an emission in the Hα passband even if the emission Hα line in the spectrum is observed. Therefore, for a correct photometric classification of these stars, it is necessary to carry out spectroscopic follow-up close in time between both observation modes.

4 Conclusions and Future Work

In this work, we have compared different classification models to distinguish objects with emission in the Hα line from normal OB stars. The models are trained with photometric data collected from various sources. Afterward, these models can be employed to identify Be star candidates, a type of Hα emitting OB stars.

We also propose the use of the reddening-free Q indices to remove unwanted variations caused by interstellar extinction effects. Experiments show these features improve the cross-dataset performance of the classification models, obtaining up to 25% recall for 99% precision on an unseen dataset. Meanwhile, the best model trained with the original features obtains at most 13.1% recall at the same precision level.

In order to test the cross-dataset performance of the models, we manually labeled samples obtained from different sources to form a new test set. Posterior analysis shows that there is significant variability in the cross-dataset test samples, which the model cannot learn given the original training data.

The presented models can detect Hα emitting stars, which are good candidates for Be stars. However, confirmation requires spectroscopic follow up. We plan on expanding the pipeline and train classification models to also identify different classes of Hα emitting objects, including Be stars, with a higher degree of automation. We will also focus on expanding the data sources used, in order to both train a more robust model and test with more variable sets of objects.

Acknowledgements. This work is based on data obtained as part of the INT Hα photometric study of the northern galactic plane (IPHAS; https://www.iphas.org), VST Photometric Hα Survey of the Southern Galactic Plane and Bulge (VPHAS+; https://www.vphasplus.org), Two Micron All Sky Survey (2MASS, https://irsa.ipac.caltech.edu/Missions/2mass.html), Sloan Digital Sky Survey (SDSS; https://www.sdss.org) and The Large Sky Area Multi-Object Fibre Spectroscopic Telescope (LAMOST; http://www.lamost.org).

YA is grateful to L. Cidale, G. Baume and A. Smith Castelli for their helpful comments and suggestions.

References

1. Aidelman, Y., Cidale, L.S., Zorec, J., Panei, J.A.: Open clusters. III. Fundamental parameters of B stars in NGC 6087, NGC 6250, NGC 6383, and NGC 6530 B-type stars with circumstellar envelopes. A&A 610, A30F(February 2018). https://doi.org/10.1051/0004-6361/201730995
2. Akras, S., Leal-Ferreira, M.L., Guzman-Ramirez, L., Ramos-Larios, G.: A machine learning approach for identification and classification of symbiotic stars using 2MASS and WISE. MNRAS **483**(4), 5077–5104 (2019). https://doi.org/10.1093/mnras/sty3359
3. Alam, S., et al.: The eleventh and twelfth data releases of the Sloan digital sky survey: final data from SDSS-iii. Astrophys. J. Suppl. Ser. **219**(1), 12 (2015)

4. Barentsen, G., et al.: The second data release of the INT photometric hα survey of the northern galactic plane (IPHAS DR2). Mon. Not. R. Astron. Soc. **444**(4), 3230–3257 (2014)

5. Catanzaro, G.: Spectroscopic atlas of Hα and Hβ in a sample of northern Be stars. A&A **550**, A79 (2013). https://doi.org/10.1051/0004-6361/201220357

6. Cochetti, Y.R., Arcos, C., Kanaan, S., Meilland, A., Cidale, L.S., Curé, M.: Spectro-interferometric observations of a sample of Be stars. Setting limits to the geometry and kinematics of stable Be disks. A&A **621**, A123 (2019). https://doi.org/10.1051/0004-6361/201833551

7. Collins, II, G.W.: The use of terms and definitions in the study of Be stars. In: Slettebak, A., Snow, T.P. (eds.) IAU Colloq. 92: Physics of Be Stars, pp. 3–19 (1987)

8. Cui, X.Q., et al.: The large sky area multi-object fiber spectroscopic telescope (LAMOST). Res. Astron. Astrophys. **12**(9), 1197–1242 (2012). https://doi.org/10.1088/1674-4527/12/9/003

9. Dimitrov, D.P., Kjurkchieva, D.P., Ivanov, E.I.: A study of the Hα variability of Be stars. AJ **156**(2), 61 (2018). https://doi.org/10.3847/1538-3881/aacbd8

10. Drew, J.E., et al.: The VST photometric Hα survey of the southern galactic plane and bulge (VPHAS+). MNRAS **440**(3), 2036–2058 (2014). https://doi.org/10.1093/mnras/stu394

11. Gies, D.R., et al.: CHARA array K'-band measurements of the angular dimensions of Be star disks. ApJ **654**, 527–543 (2007). https://doi.org/10.1086/509144

12. Goldberger, J., Hinton, G.E., Roweis, S.T., Salakhutdinov, R.R.: Neighbourhood components analysis. In: Advances in Neural Information Processing Systems, pp. 513–520 (2005)

13. Hirata, R.: Interpretation of the long-term variation in late-type active Be stars. PASJ **47**, 195–218 (1995)

14. Huang, S.S.: Profiles of emission lines in Be stars. ApJ **171**, 549 (1972). https://doi.org/10.1086/151309

15. Jaschek, M., Slettebak, A., Jaschek, C.: Be star terminology. Be Star Newsl. **4**, 9–11 (1981)

16. Johnson, H.L., Morgan, W.W.: Some evidence for a regional variation in the law of interstellar reddening. ApJ **122**, 142 (1955). https://doi.org/10.1086/146063

17. Liu, Z., Cui, W., Liu, C., Huang, Y., Zhao, G., Zhang, B.: A catalog of OB stars from LAMOST spectroscopic survey. ApJs **241**(2), 32 (2019). https://doi.org/10.3847/1538-4365/ab0a0d

18. Meilland, A., et al.: First direct detection of a Keplerian rotating disk around the Be star α Arae using AMBER/VLTI. A&A **464**, 59–71 (2007). https://doi.org/10.1051/0004-6361:20064848

19. Mohr-Smith, M., et al.: New OB star candidates in the Carina Arm around Westerlund 2 from VPHAS+. MNRAS **450**(4), 3855–3873 (2015). https://doi.org/10.1093/mnras/stv843

20. Mohr-Smith, M., et al.: The deep OB star population in Carina from the VST photometric Hα survey (VPHAS+). MNRAS **465**(2), 1807–1830 (2017). https://doi.org/10.1093/mnras/stw2751

21. Pérez-Ortiz, M.F., García-Varela, A., Quiroz, A.J., Sabogal, B.E., Hernández, J.: Machine learning techniques to select Be star candidates. An application in the OGLE-IV Gaia south ecliptic pole field. A&A **605**, A123 (2017). https://doi.org/10.1051/0004-6361/201628937

22. Peters, M., et al.: The hubble space telescope advanced camera for surveys emission line survey of andromeda. I. classical Be stars. AJ **159**(3), 119 (2020). https://doi.org/10.3847/1538-3881/ab6d74

23. Quirrenbach, A.: Seven Be stars resolved by optical interferometry. In: American Astronomical Society Meeting Abstracts #182. Bulletin of the American Astronomical Society, vol. 25, p. 916 (May 1993)

24. Quirrenbach, A., Buscher, D.F., Mozurkewich, D., Hummel, C.A., Armstrong, J.T.: Maximum-entropy maps of the Be shell star zeta Tauri from optical long-baseline interferometry. A&A **283**, L13–L16 (1994)

25. Rivinius, T., Carciofi, A.C., Martayan, C.: Classical Be stars. Astron. Astrophys. Rev. **21**(1), 1–86 (2013). https://doi.org/10.1007/s00159-013-0069-0

26. Schlafly, E.F., Finkbeiner, D.P.: Measuring reddening with Sloan digital sky survey stellar spectra and recalibrating SFD. ApJ **737**(2), 103 (2011). https://doi.org/10.1088/0004-637X/737/2/103

27. Skrutskie, M.F., et al.: The two micron all sky survey (2MASS). AJ **131**(2), 1163–1183 (2006). https://doi.org/10.1086/498708

28. Struve, O.: On the origin of bright lines in spectra of stars of class B. ApJ **73**, 94 (1931). https://doi.org/10.1086/143298

29. Udalski, A., Szymański, M., Szymański, G.: Ogle-iv: fourth phase of the optical gravitational lensing experiment (2015). arXiv preprint arXiv:1504.05966

30. Vioque, M., Oudmaijer, R., Baines, D., Pérez-Martínez, R.: New catalogue of intermediate mass Pre-main sequence objects in Gaia DR2 using machine learning. In: The Gaia Universe, p. 52 (April 2019). https://doi.org/10.5281/zenodo.3237084

31. Zorec, J., et al.: Critical study of the distribution of rotational velocities of Be stars. I. Deconvolution methods, effects due to gravity darkening, macroturbulence and binarity. A&A **595**, A132 (2016). https://doi.org/10.1051/0004-6361/201628760

32. Zorec, J., et al.: Critical study of the distribution of rotational velocities of Be stars. II: Differential rotation and some hidden effects interfering with the interpretation of the V sin I parameter. A&A **602**, A83 (2017). https://doi.org/10.1051/0004-6361/201628761

A Web System Based on *Spotify* for the automatic generation of affective playlists

Pedro Álvarez$^{(\boxtimes)}$ ⓘ, Jorge García de Quirós, and Sandra Baldassarri ⓘ

Computer Science and Systems Engineering Department, Zaragoza University
of Zaragoza, María de Luna, 1, Ada Byron Building, Zaragoza, Spain
{alvaper,jgarciaqg,sandra}@unizar.es

Abstract. The online music streaming providers offer powerful person-alization tools for recommending songs to their registered users. These tools are usually based on users' listening histories and tastes, but ignore other contextual variables that affect users while listening to music, for example, the user's mood. In this paper, a Web-based system for generating affective playlists that regulate the user's mood is presented. The system has been implemented integrating resources and data offered by *Spotify* through its service platform, and the playlists generated are directly published in the user's *Spotify* account. Internally, the emotions play a relevant role in the processes of cataloguing songs and making personalized music recommendations. Novel affective computing solutions are combined with traditional information retrieval and artificial intelligence techniques in order to solve these complex engineering problems. Besides, these solutions consider users' collaboration as a first-class element in an attempt to improve affective recommendations.

Keywords: Affective playlists · Music recommendations · Web-based systems · Spotify · Emotions

1 Introduction

The popularization of online music streaming services has promoted a new way of accessing and listening to songs. Users have at their disposal a wide variety of songs which makes difficult the process of choosing the music to be consumed at each moment. Music streaming providers offer their clients different services and tools for solving this problem, specially, solutions for discovering songs of interest, creating personalized playlists from these songs and sharing the resulting playlist with friends and followers. Therefore, playlists become a relevant element in the field on the online music consumption.

Although users use to manually create their playlists, nowadays, the goal is the development of technological solutions that automate this task, releasing the user from the effort involved in the process. The resulting playlist must consider the user's musical preferences, convey an emotion and serve for being used during an activity (such as a travel, a study session or a sport training) or in an event

E. Rucci et al. (Eds.): JCC-BD&ET 2020, CCIS 1291, pp. 124–137, 2020.
https://doi.org/10.1007/978-3-030-61218-4_9

(a party or a wedding, for instance), as it was discussed in [10]. Besides, these playlists must fulfill a set of desirable properties that guarantee the quality of the result from the perspective of user perception. [11] summarizes the conclusions of different studies in order to understand and determine the properties of a good playlist. Although the automatic generation of these high-quality playlists is still a complex task, the advances in the fields of Music Information Retrieval and Music Recommendation Systems have solved some of the challenges involved.

With the intention of creating more personalized playlists, physiological constructs have been integrated into the playlist generation systems [26], in particular, the user's emotions. These emotions have a strong impact on her/his short-time music preferences; and, vice-versa, music can produce different effects on the user's mood. This influence has promoted a new model of emotion-aware playlists, called affective playlists [16]. In recent years, some systems able to generate automatically affective playlists have been developed, as we will review in Sect. 2. These solutions require to infer the user's emotional state, to understand the emotional responses that the songs can produce on the listeners, and to correlate these two issues for generating the final playlists. Audio extraction libraries and a wide variety of artificial intelligence techniques have been combined for fulfilling these requirements. Nevertheless, some important challenges still need to be addressed, such as the scalability of systems in order to use large-sized collections of emotionally-annotated songs, the inclusion of the real user's feedback in personalization algorithms, the integration of emotional devices that monitor the evolution of the listener's mood for improving the future recommendations, or the definition of benchmarks for evaluating the playlist's quality, among others. The solutions to these challenges will make easier the integration of the emotional perspective into the online music streaming providers' services.

In this paper, we propose an Affective Playlist Generation (APG) system based on *Spotify*. The system works with the complete catalog of songs published by the music streaming provider (more than 30 million of songs), unlike the existing solutions. As part of the proposal has been needed to develop a music emotion recognition system able to annotate emotionally all the *Spotify* songs. These annotations represent the emotions that the users feel when listening to the songs. This user-based point of view is a contribution with respect the existing proposals and requires to combine the knowledge of *Spotify* users with machine-learning techniques. The APG system's goal is to regulate the user's mood by applying a *cascade hybrid method* as strategy for generating playlists (in accordance to the classification proposed in [11]). The method takes advantage of the different techniques employed for improving the listener's experience. These techniques include a emotion-aware music recommendation system, a set of content-based and collaborative filters that considers users' feedback and tastes, and, finally, a procedure for fulfilling the desirable properties of playlist. This combination guarantees the personalization and the quality of affective playlists proposed.

The rest of the paper is structured as follows. Section 2 reviews the existing techniques for generating affective playlists paying attention in those solutions that do not require user intervention. Section 3 describes the proposal for generating playlists, and Sect. 4 presents the software system that implements this proposal. The most relevant components involved in the generation process are also detailed. Finally, Sect. 5 discusses the main conclusions obtained and the future work.

2 State of the Art

Several surveys [7, 26, 27] present the existing techniques for the automatic generation of playlists and provide an overview of the most important open challenges. As it is discussed in these papers, the great challenge is to create more personalized recommendations, which requires to combine the user's preferences with different contextual and psychological constructs. In this paper, we are specially interested in the user's mood and in the emotional effects of music as part of the generation of playlists. For this reason, the most relevant proposals in the domain of the affective playlist generation are reviewed in this section.

First of all, we would like to distinguish emotion-based music players from automatic systems for generating playlists. The former integrates music recommendation systems for determining the next song to be played at each moment. Although playlists are not explicitly created, the process of selecting the next song is based on the same techniques as used in the automatic playlist generation. Besides, in some cases these players take also in account the listener's preferences and emotions [2, 15, 20]. Despite these similarities, the interest of the paper focuses on the second type of systems.

Most of these systems use audio-based similarity for the automatic generation of affective playlists [6, 8, 9, 12, 16, 17]. These proposals begin extracting songs' audio features and, then, use these features for recognizing the emotion that a song can produce in the listeners. This recognition can be based on the use of an intelligent system [17], clustering techniques [6, 8, 12], or users' manual annotations [9]. The recognized emotion is mapped to a point in the two-dimensional space defined by an emotional model (the two most popular dimensional models are the *Russell* circumflex model [25] and the Thayer's mood model [28]). Once all the songs have been emotionally annotated, the user introduces her/his mood [12, 16, 17] or a seed song [6, 8] which can be also mapped to an emotion. In both cases, similarity algorithms are subsequently applied for determining the nearest songs to the input emotion on the dimensional space, and, then, these songs are directly used for generating the output playlist. In general, these similarity-based proposals present some relevant drawbacks: the songs' audio is necessary and, therefore, the solutions are usually applied to small-sized music collections; the resulting playlists may not vary widely because they are composed of similar songs; the user's feedback is not considered for improving and personalising the resulting playlists; and none of the proposals evaluate whether the desirable properties of playlists are fulfilled.

Other approaches gather data from social networks [14, 22] or from listeners' opinions [3] for classifying songs from an emotional perspective, as an alternative to the solutions based on the audio extraction. In these cases, the songs are usually emotionally classified using some categorical model, such as the musical genres [14] or the user's personal perception of music [3,22]. The process of generating the final playlist is also based on the use of similarity algorithms and, therefore, these solutions present the same drawbacks as the audio-based ones.

Unlike the proposals based on similarity techniques, other works have the goal of modifying the user's mood through the music and explicitly consider as input parameter the target emotion. [21] presents a system that shifts the listener's state towards a positive mood. At the beginning, each song is manually tagged with a label that defines its (positive/negative) impact in the listener's mood (the impression of a song). Then, the authors define abstract patterns of playlists that consist basically of a ordered list of impression values. The automatic generation of affective playlists consists of replacing these values for concrete songs with a similar impact. On the other hand, [18] defines a probabilistic model for understanding the physiological effects of music on the user. Every time the user listens to a song, the model learns from her/his responses. This learning takes also into account the users' musical preferences and activity. Authors discuss the possibility of applying the model for generating playlists that change the user's mood, but a concrete solution is not published. And, finally, [4,19] represent a line in the two-dimensional space of an emotional model, from the start emotion to the desired emotion. Then, they calculate the distance of each song contained in an emotionally annotated database to the line, and go through the line selecting the songs closest to it for creating an ordered playlist.

3   Description of the Proposal

Nowadays, *Spotify* offers more than 30 million of songs and provides different data services that allow easy access these songs' metadata and the playlists created by registered users. These services have been published for encouraging the development of new *Spotify*-based applications. The proposal presented in this paper consists of using these services for creating a large-size music catalog in which all *Spotify* songs are emotionally annotated, and combining recommendation algorithms and content-based and collaborative filtering techniques for generating affective playlists from these songs. Besides, these playlists will have to fulfil a set of desirable properties that guarantee their quality.

Figure 1 shows the tasks involved in the generation of affective playlists. The red rectangles represent interactions with the user; whereas, the white ones represent internal tasks carried out automatically by the software system that will implement the process of generation.

At the beginning, the user introduces the mood wanted to be induced through music. The list of recommended songs will be created from a seed that describes the characteristics of songs to be included into the playlist. The *Generation of the seed information* task is responsible for creating this characterization from the mood introduced by the user. Then, the *Recommendation of candidate songs* task searches a set of songs that fulfills the target characteristics in the best

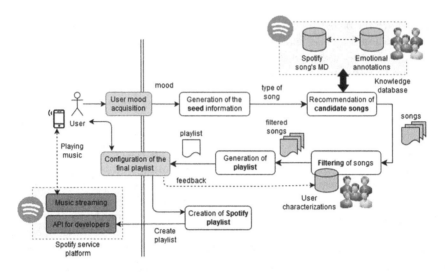

Fig. 1. Process of generating a playlist

possible way, using a knowledge database that contains the *Spotify* songs and their emotional annotations. These annotations describe the emotions that each song produces in the users when listen to it, and were previously created from the *Spotify* data services (specifically, from the playlists published by registered users). The result is a list of candidate songs to be included in the final playlist.

Different filtering techniques are subsequently applied for refining the list of candidate songs. Firstly, the users' musical preferences, listening histories and explicit feedback are considered for personalising the results; and, then, the behaviour similarity between users is analyzed for improving these results. Before generating the playlist from the filtered list of songs, some extra filters are used to guarantee the quality of the final playlist. These actions are completed by the *Filtering of songs* and the *Generation of playlists* tasks.

Finally, the *Configuration of the final playlist* task presents the resulting playlist to the user. She/he can discard those songs that are not interesting to her/him. Afterwards, on the one hand, these user decisions (dislikes) are sent as feedback to the system for improving the future filtering decisions; and, on the other hand, the final playlist is created and submitted to the *Spotify* service platform. This action is carried out by the *Creation of the Spotify playlist* task. From this moment the user can play the new playlist in her/his mobile phone.

Once the tasks have been described, some relevant issues involved into the generation of playlists are discussed in more detail:

– *Emotions induced by Spotify songs*: Most of the solutions for generating affective playlists work with a small-size catalogs of songs, as it was previously commented. In [23] we built a set of machine learning models for annotating emotionally *Spotify* songs. These models have been used for creating a large-size music database that contains the metadata (artist, musical genre, audio features, etc.) and the emotional labels of all *Spotify* songs (more than 30 million of songs). The emotion that the users feel when listening to a song is represented by a vector of four values, one per each of the Russell quadrants [25]. These values are the probability that the emotion felt belongs to the corresponding quadrant. For example, the "I want to hold your hand" song by "The Beatles" has the following emotional annotation [0.174, 0.765, 0.155, 0.006] which represents that is a *happy* song with a 0.765 probability (the sad, angry and relaxed probabilities are 0.174, 0.155 and 0.006, respectively).

– *The collaborative role of users*: In the proposal the users play a relevant role. On the one hand, we are using the playlists published by *Spotify* registered users for creating the music emotion recognition system that annotates songs. When an user creates a new playlist, fills some textual metadata (such as the name and the description of the playlist) that have helped us to understand the emotions that can produce in the listener and the purpose for which it was created. On the other hand, users also provide explicit feedback (specifically, the dislikes) to the system before submitting the final playlists to the streaming provider. This feedback is stored jointly with the user's listening histories and her/his musical preferences, allowing us to characterise to each particular user. Then, similarity algorithms are applied to find users with similar listening habits and tastes, and to improve the playlist generated by the system in the future.

– *Criteria for the selection of songs*: The main purpose of our playlists is the *mood regulation*, which is one of the most important reasons why people listen to music. User emotions change rapidly, but mood changes happen gradually [24]. As consequence, multiple songs are usually needed for producing these changes. Traditionally, this type of playlists comprise a sequence of songs that are as similar as possible in order to guarantee the *playlist continuity* (or the ability of reducing the effects between the transitions of songs) [26]. Obviously, this criteria is compatible with applying different strategies for improving the user's experience. In view of these issues, we propose a *cascade hybrid method* that combines similarity algorithms and collaborative filtering methods, and refines successively the recommendations of the different recommenders. Additionally, we have considered as part of the method some of the most relevant properties that a good playlist must fulfill [11], specifically, the user's satisfaction, the popularity and freshness of songs, the homogeneity and diversity, and the coherence.

4   The System Architecture

Figure 2 shows the different systems programmed for supporting the automatic generation of affective playlists. At the bottom of the figure are represented the *Music Information Retrieval* system (MIR) and the *Music Emotion Recognition* system (MER) developed for annotating songs' emotions. These two systems interact with the *Spotify* data services for creating a knowledge database that contains the metadata and the emotional labels of the songs available in the music streaming provider. These songs are subsequently used for the service-oriented APG system for creating the playlists.

On the other hand, as it is shown at the top of Fig. 2, the APG system consists of a Web-based application and a Web service. The application allows users to register their personal profile and to create new affective playlists. When a user signs up, she/he must specify her/his musical preferences and the Spotify credentials needed to access to the provider's services. Once the registration has been completed, she/he can request a new playlist specifying as input parameter the target mood. The web application will show the ordered list of recommended songs and allow the requester to play each song during 30 s. Before generating the final playlist, the user can remove those songs that are not to her/his liking. These actions are an interesting feedback for improving future recommendations and, therefore, are submitted to the service. Finally, the user can accept the final version of the playlist and, in that case, it will be automatically published in her/him *Spotify* account using the corresponding user credential.

The Web service offers all the functionality needed for generating affective playlists. Internally, it integrates the four components that implement the process described in Sect. 3. The *Manager of requests* creates an internal workflow for each user request. The workflow controls the sequence of tasks needed to generate a new playlist and invokes the components responsible for executing these tasks, specifically, the *Analysis of mood* component, the *Decision maker*, and the *Spotify integrator* component. The first generates the seed needed for making the music recommendations. The service's core is the decision maker. It processes the seed for creating a list of candidate songs, applies a set of filters for personalizing the recommendations and, finally, elaborates a proposal of playlist. This playlist is returned to the user for being improved and, once has been accepted, the Spotify integrator interacts with the *Spotify* service platform for publishing it in the user's account.

In the following subsections we will explain in detail some of the most relevant components of the system.

4.1 Music Information Retrieval System

Before starting the system, the database of songs must be created. These songs have to be annotated by the music emotion recognition system. It is responsible for determining the emotions that the users feel when listening a song. As it will be explained in the next subsection, we have built a set of machine learning models for making the emotional recognition of songs. Nevertheless, a dataset of emotionally-annotated songs is previously needed for building, training and validating these models. A *Spotify*-based MIR system has been programmed for creating this dataset. Internally, it is composed of two data acquisition processes that gather the information necessary from the music streaming provider's data services.

The music provider offers two Web data services that play a relevant role in the solution: the *Spotify Web API for developers* and the *Spotify Playlist miner API*. The former allows to access the music database of the provider (list of

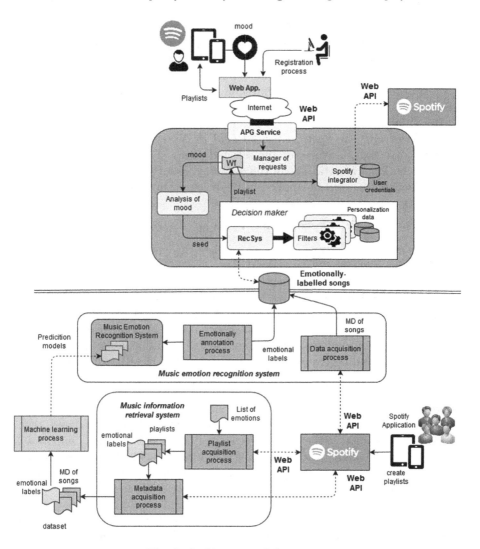

Fig. 2. Architecture of the system

songs) and to get the metadata (author, album, musical genre, etc.) and audio features of each song; whereas the second aggregates the top songs from the most popular playlists created by the *Spotify*'s users. These aggregations are created from search criteria based on keywords which are matched with names and descriptions of published playlists.

Spotify's users create their playlists using the *Spotify* applications. We have assumed that a song contained into a playlist called "Motivating music for running" is likely that conveys positive energy and emotions. Therefore, that song could be annotated as *happy* or *excited*. With this in mind, a list of emotions of interest has been defined to be used as search keywords. The *Playlist acquisition process* interacts with the *Spotify miner* and uses these keywords for creating the dataset of annotated songs. In more detail, the acquisition process determines a search criteria for each input emotion and searches for aggregations that contain songs that could match with that criteria. Then, the results are ranked and filtered in order to select the songs to be emotionally annotated. Specifically, 10,000 *Spotify* songs were labelled from the text descriptions created by users and stored into the intermediate repository. Then, the *Metadata acquisition process* interacts with the *Spotify Web API for developers* for getting the general attributes and audio features of the selected songs. These are stored together with the emotional annotations in the dataset created for building the machine learning models that will be applied in the recognition process.

4.2 Music Emotion Recognition System

The Music emotion recognition system predicts the emotions that the users feel when listening the songs. These predictions are made from the songs' audio features and the result is represented as an emotional label, particularly, as a vector of four probabilistic values, as was explained in Sect. 3. Internally, the system consists of a set of machine learning models responsible for making the emotional predictions. In [23] we applied a complete machine-learning process for creating, training and evaluating these models from the dataset generated by the MIR system. A different model was built for each of the Russell's dimensional quadrants (for *happy*, *sad*, *angry* and *relaxed* quadrants), and validated using the *AcousticBrainz* database [1]. The resulting models are the core of the MER system which has been used for the large-scale annotation of *Spotify* songs.

Specifically, 3 million of *Spotify* songs were emotionally annotated and, then, stored in the database of the APG system. At first, the *Emotionally annotation process* gets songs' audio features from the *Spotify Web API for developers*, and invokes the MER system for creating the emotional labels. Internally, this process has been implemented as a master-slave system for facilitating the parallelism of annotations. This type of distributed architecture is suitable for this problem since the recognition of each song is an independent task. Besides, it has been programmed to be deployed in a private cluster of computer or in a cloud-based environment. In this particular case, we deployed the system in the *Amazon EC2 infrastructure* using a set of homogeneous virtual machines for executing the slaves nodes.

Once the recognition is completed, the *metadata acquisition process* interacts with the *Spotify Web API* for getting the metadata of interest of annotated songs. Finally, all these data are stored into the *MongoDB* database used by the APG system.

4.3 An Emotion-Aware Music Recommendation System

The music recommendation system (RecSys) is one of the most relevant components of the solution. Its implementation is based on a *Nearest Neighbor Search* algorithm (NNS). This class of algorithms solve the problem of finding the point in a given set that is closest (or most similar) to a given point. Formally, they are defined from a set of points in a *space M* and a *metric distance* that allows to determine the similarity (or dissimilarity) between these points. In our proposal, each *Spotify* song has been translated to a point of the *space M*. Therefore, the search space of our problem is complex (more than 3 million of songs were selected and a point is defined for each of these songs). When working with large size spaces in the field of multimedia recommendation, it is not necessary to retrieve an exact search result [5]. Therefore, we have decided to use the *Annoy* algorithm [13], an *approximate NNS* algorithm that has provided good results in this kind of domains. These algorithms are able to retrieve approximate nearest neighbors much faster than NNS algorithms. Besides, our implementation of *Annoy* was internally configured for using the *angular distance* as similarity measurement between the points.

Figure 3 shows the internal components of the decision maker. Before starting the recommendation system, the emotionally-annotated songs have been translated to points in the search space. The translation function is based on songs' audio features (loudness, energy, tempo, acousticness, valence, liveness, speechiness, instrumentalness, danceability, key, duration, and mode) and emotional annotations (the vector of probabilities). Then, the analysis mood component applies a set of rules for determining the seed corresponding to each playlist generation request. This seed is a *search point* (in red color) that characterises the songs to be included into the playlist. The *Annoy* algorithm processes this point and returns a list of candidate songs applying similarity criteria. It is important to remark that, in our approach, these criteria are based on the songs' audio feature and the emotions that can produce in the listeners. The number of returned songs can be easily configured.

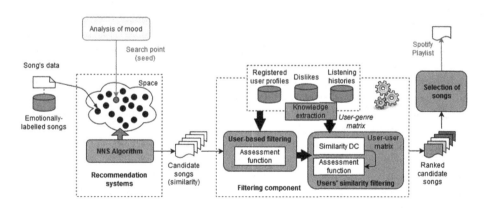

Fig. 3. Components of the decision maker (Color figure online)

4.4   Filtering of the Recommendations

The aim of the filtering components is to personalise the recommendations for improving the listener's experience. As shown in Fig. 3, the list of recommended songs is processed by two different kind of filters: the user-based filter and the similarity-based filter. The former scores with a value of interest each of the recommended songs in accordance the target user's musical preferences, listening habits and tastes. The second searches users that are similar to the target user based on similarity of preferences and musical tastes, and, applies collaborative filtering techniques for refining the songs' values of interest. Finally, the songs are ranked in accordance with their values of interest which will be used for deciding what songs are included into the playlist generated by the decision maker.

The user-based filter uses the knowledge that the system has stored of the user for making a first assessment of the recommendations. This knowledge includes the user's listening habits and explicit feedback provided during the process of generating playlists. Specifically, the assessment function considers three factors: the music preferences defined into the user's profile, the music genres that the user usually listens to (these are determined from her/his listening histories by considering the list of genres available in *Spotify*), and the characteristics of songs (genre and audio features, mainly) that were disliked by the user in the past.

On the other hand, the similarity-based filter has been programmed using collaborative-filtering techniques. This filter work with the user-genre matrix, that describes the users' taste ratings according to music genres. These ratings are calculated from the user's listening histories (implicit feedback) and dislikes (explicit feedback) and provide a measure of the type of music preferred by users. The filter computes the cosine distance for measuring the similarity between users, and a nearest neighbour search for finding the most similar users to the target user. The ratings of these users are subsequently used for refining the songs' values of interest. Currently, we are applying matrix factorization for discovering latent features between the users' profiles and the songs' audio features listened to them. This factorization reuses the similarity matrix for making predictions that improve recommendations, and it is a powerful alternative to the ratings based on music genres.

The result is a ranked list of recommended songs, as shown on the right side of the figure. Finally, the *selection of songs* component processes this list for generating the playlist that will be proposed to the user. It has to fulfill a set of desirable properties. Following, we explain briefly how the fulfillment of these properties has been addressed. Firstly, the popularity and freshness of songs were taken in account when the database of annotated songs was created. It contains 3 million of songs that were selected using certain information provided by the *Spotify* data services, specifically, the top artists and songs in accordance to users' latest listening histories. Secondly, the playlist coherence (or continuity) has been guaranteed by applying a similarity-based recommendation. Besides, the similarity criteria is not only based on songs' audio features, but it also considers the emotions produced in the listeners by these songs. Thirdly, the playlist generated by the selection component consists mainly of songs with a high value of interest, but it also includes some songs with medium/low values (for instance, songs that do not fit the user's preferences or that she/he has not listened to them at any time). This selection criteria introduces the requirement of diversity into the resulting playlists. Finally, once the generation of a playlist is completed, the user can accept/discard the recommended songs before publishing the final version in *Spotify*. These actions are aimed to improve the user's satisfaction before playing the final playlist (as future work, we are interesting in collecting users' opinions after playing the playlists and using this feedback for improving future recommendations).

5   Conclusions and Future Work

In this paper, a Web-accessible system for generating affective playlists has been presented. The playlists are created for regulating the listener's mood by considering the emotions that the users feel when listening the songs. Internally, the system is based on different resources (songs, playlists, users' listening data, etc.) provided by *Spotify* through its platform for developers. These resources have been used for developing a music emotion recognition system able to annotate emotionally a large-size music database. These annotations play a relevant role in the process of selecting candidate songs to be included in playlists. This selection is based on similarity algorithms and takes in account users' explicit and implicit feedback for the improvement of recommendations. The final result is directly published in the user's *Spotify* account. From an implementation point of view, the systems involved have been mainly programmed combining the Java technology (the Spring framework) and the Scipy ecosystem.

Currently, we are organizing a set of experiments with real users for evaluating the suitability and quality of affective playlists generated. The results of these experiments will help us to improve the filtering and personalization strategies and to decide which new techniques could be included in the future (for example, the combination of clustering and matrix factorization applied to songs' audio features and users' profiles). Additionally, as future work, we are also interested in extending the system to a product that is accessible to any *Spotify* user, but some legal issues must be still reviewed by experts. Finally, we would like to include other contextual variables (such as, the user's context or activity) as input parameters in order to introduce new constructs in recommendations.

Acknowledges. This work has been supported by the TIN2017-84796-C2-2-R and RTI2018-096986-B-C31 projects, granted by the Spanish Ministerio de Economía y Competitividad, and the DisCo-T21-20R and Affective-Lab-T60-20R projects, granted by the Aragonese Government.

References

1. AcousticBrainz (2015). http://acousticbrainz.org/
2. Interactive music recommendation based on artists' mood similarity: moodplay. Int. J. Hum. Comput. Stud. **121**, 142–159 (2019). https://doi.org/10.1016/j.ijhcs. 2018.04.004. advances in Computer-Human Interaction for Recommender Systems
3. Abderrazik, H., et al.: Tagging playlist vibes with colors. In: The 6th Joint Workshop on Interfaces and Human Decision Making for Recommender Systems, Co-located with 13th ACM Conference on Recommender Systems (RecSys) (2019)
4. de Assunção, W.G., de Almeida Neris, V.P.: M-motion: A mobile application for music recommendation that considers the desired emotion of the user. In: Proceedings of the 18th Brazilian Symposium on Human Factors in Computing Systems, IHC 2019, Association for Computing Machinery, New York, NY, USA (2019). https://doi.org/10.1145/3357155.3358459
5. Aumüller, M., Bernhardsson, E., Faithfull, A.: Ann-benchmarks: a benchmarking tool for approximate nearest neighbor algorithms. Inf. Syst. **87**, 101374 (2020). https://doi.org/10.1016/j.is.2019.02.006
6. Bakhshizadeh, M., Moeini, A., Latifi, M., Mahmoudi, M.T.: Automated mood based music playlist generation by clustering the audio features. In: 2019 9th International Conference on Computer and Knowledge Engineering (ICCKE), pp. 231–237 (2019). https://doi.org/10.1109/ICCKE48569.2019.8965190
7. Bonnin, G., Jannach, D.: Automated generation of music playlists: survey and experiments. ACM Comput. Surv. **47**(2), 1–35 (2014). https://doi.org/10.1145/2652481
8. Cardoso, L., Panda, R., Paiva, R.P.: Moodetector: a prototype software tool for mood-based playlist generation. In: INForum 2011, Simpósio de Informática. Coimbra, Portugal (2011)
9. Chi, C., Tsai, R.T., Lai, J., Hsu, J.Y.: A reinforcement learning approach to emotion-based automatic playlist generation. In: 2010 International Conference on Technologies and Applications of Artificial Intelligence, pp. 60–65 (2010). https://doi.org/10.1109/TAAI.2010.21
10. Cunningham, S.J., Bainbridge, D., Falconer, A.: More of an art than a science: supporting the creation of playlists and mixes. In: Proceedings of the 7th International Conference on Music Information Retrieval, pp. 240–245. Victoria (2006)
11. Dias, R., Gonçalves, D., Fonseca, M.J.: From manual to assisted playlist creation: a survey. Multimedia Tools and Appl. **76**(12), 14375–14403 (2016). https://doi.org/10.1007/s11042-016-3836-x
12. Dittenbach, M., Neumayer, R., Rauber, A.: Playsom : An Alternative Approach to Track Selection and Playlist Generation in Large Music Collections (2005)
13. Erik Bernhardsson: Annoy (2013). https://github.com/spotify/annoy
14. Gajjar, K., Shah, S.: Mood based playlist generation for Hindi popular music: a proposed model. Int. J. Comput. Appl. **127**, 11–14 (2015). https://doi.org/10.5120/ijca2015906505
15. Gilda, S., Zafar, H., Soni, C., Waghurdekar, K.: Smart music player integrating facial emotion recognition and music mood recommendation, pp. 154–158 (2017). https://doi.org/10.1109/WiSPNET.2017.8299738
16. Griffiths, D., Cunningham, S., Weinel, J.: Automatic music playlist generation using affective computing technologies (2013)
17. Griffiths, D., Cunningham, S., Weinel, J.: An interactive music playlist generator that responds to user emotion and context, pp. 275–276 (2016). https://doi.org/10.14236/ewic/EVA2016.53

18. Janssen, J.H., van den Broek, E.L., Westerink, J.H.D.M.: Personalized affective music player. In: 2009 3rd International Conference on Affective Computing and Intelligent Interaction and Workshops, pp. 1–6 (2009). https://doi.org/10.1109/ACII.2009.5349376

19. Janssen, J., van den Broek, E.L., Westerink, J.: Tune in to your emotions: A robust personalized affective music player. User Model. User-Adap. Inter. **22**, 255–279 (2012). https://doi.org/10.1007/s11257-011-9107-7

20. Nathan, K., Arun, M., Kannan, M.: Emosic - an emotion based music player for android, pp. 371–276 (2017). https://doi.org/10.1109/ISSPIT.2017.8388671

21. Ogino, A., Uenoyama, Y.: Music playlist generation system for changing a listener's mood to a positive state. In: International Symposium on Affective Science and Engineering, ISASE 2019, pp. 1–4 (2019). https://doi.org/10.5057/isase.2019-C000020

22. Pichl, M., Zangerle, E., Specht, G.: Understanding playlist creation on music streaming platforms. In: 2016 IEEE International Symposium on Multimedia (ISM), pp. 475–480 (2016). https://doi.org/10.1109/ISM.2016.0107

23. de Quirós, J.G., Baldassarri, S., Beltrán, J.R., Guiu, A., Álvarez, P.: An automatic emotion recognition system for annotating *Spotify*'s songs. In: Panetto, H., Debruyne, C., Hepp, M., Lewis, D., Ardagna, C.A., Meersman, R. (eds.) OTM 2019. LNCS, vol. 11877, pp. 345–362. Springer, Cham (2019). https://doi.org/10.1007/978-3-030-33246-4_23

24. Russell, J.: Core affect and the psychological construction of emotion. Psychol. Rev. **110**, 145–72 (2003). https://doi.org/10.1037//0033-295X.110.1.145

25. Russell, J.A.: A circumplex model of affect. J. Pers. Soc. Psychol. **39**(6), 1161 (1980)

26. Schedl, M., Zamani, H., Chen, C.-W., Deldjoo, Y., Elahi, M.: Current challenges and visions in music recommender systems research. Int. J. Multimedia Inf. Retrieval **7**(2), 95–116 (2018). https://doi.org/10.1007/s13735-018-0154-2

27. Sneha, A., Jayarajan, J.: Survey on playlist generation techniques. Int. J. Adv. Res. Comput. Eng. Technol. **3**(2), 437–439 (2014)

28. Thayer, R.: The Biopsychology of Mood and Arousal. Oxford University Press, New York (1989)

Classification of Summer Crops Using Active Learning Techniques on Landsat Images in the Northwest of the Province of Buenos Aires

Lucas Benjamin Cicerchia[1,3](✉) (iD), María José Abasolo[2,4] (iD), and Claudia Cecilia Russo[1,2] (iD)

[1] Institute of Research and Transfer of Technology (ITT), National University of Norwest of Buenos Aires Province (UNNOBA), Sarmiento 1169, 6000 Junín, Buenos Aires, Argentina
{lucas.cicerchia,claudia.russo}@itt.unnoba.edu.ar
[2] Commission of Scientific Research of the Buenos Aires Province (CICPBA), Buenos Aires, Argentina
[3] Consejo Nacional de Investigaciones Científicas Y Técnicas (CONICET), Buenos Aires, Argentina
[4] III-LIDI, Faculty of Informatics, National University of La Plata (UNLP), 50 and 120 Street, 2nd Floor, 1900 La Plata, Buenos Aires, Argentina
mjabasolo@lidi.info.unlp.edu.ar

Abstract. The present work aims to obtain a classifier for summer crops in the northwest of Buenos Aires province from Landsat satellite images. Active Learning (AL) was used as the classification technique since it obtains satisfactory results using a small set of labeled samples to train the algorithm. The construction of the training set is iteratively performed by means of a heuristic for the selection of the unlabeled samples to be classified by an expert. The following heuristics were used for comparison: Breaking Ties, Multiclass Level Uncertainty, Margin Sampling, and Random Sampling. The algorithm was also compared with the supervised technique Support Vector Machine (SVM). The experiments were tested on three Landsat 8 images from different dates using 6 bands per image and various vegetation indices. The results obtained using AL in combination with the different heuristics do not differ substantially from SVM.

Keywords: Active learning · Cropland classification · Land cover classification · Remote sensing · Multispectral image · Big data

1 Introduction

The advance of technology in recent years has covered different disciplines, including agriculture. The identification of land cover has become an important aspect of monitoring, providing information for resource management and decision support. Precision Agriculture (PA) has begun to apply information and communication technology to all farming techniques [1]. In this way, it has become a fundamental tool to achieve an adequate management of the soil and its crops, taking into account their variability

© Springer Nature Switzerland AG 2020
E. Rucci et al. (Eds.): JCC-BD&ET 2020, CCIS 1291, pp. 138–152, 2020.
https://doi.org/10.1007/978-3-030-61218-4_10

within a lot [2]. It allows adapting to the demands of modern agriculture in the optimal management of large areas [3].

Remote Sensing (RS) [4], which includes satellite images, generates a great amount of data (Big Data) for PA. The use of Machine Learning (ML) techniques may be applied to all kinds of data, including that generated by RS to obtain information [5, 6].

As can be seen in Lary et al. [4] the application of ML techniques to RS is relatively new and limited, covering different fields of application and examples [7]. Also, in D. Marcos et al., it can find the contribution that digital image processing can give to these two previous one kind of works [8]. Based on ML techniques in RS it can obtain classification, prediction, selection, and feature extraction maps, among other things [9–11]. Also, as mentioned by A. Gonzalez-Sanchez et al. [12] and S. Veenadhari et al. [13], soil, crop, and climate monitoring could be implemented to provide a decision support system. It may also be able to learn, among other things, how to predict crop yields or, as indicated by S. Dimitriadis et al. [14] determine crop-specific treatments such as irrigation, fertilizer, or pesticide application for different parts of the soil.

In Supervised Learning (SL) techniques, such as Support Vector Machine (SVM) all the samples have to be labeled. Deep Learning (DL) is used in remote agriculture and remote sensing [15, 16]. The large amount of data generated by remote sensors nowadays, given the high spatial and spectral resolution, makes data labeling for Supervised Learning algorithms a hard task and time-consuming. Besides, in the specific case of agriculture, it is required that such labeling be performed by experts in the field. DL as mentioned by Kamilaris & Prenafeta-Boldú [15] in many cases requires large sets of labeled data or hundreds of images. This problem often means that these algorithms can be applied to a small data set. Meanwhile, Active Learning (AL) [17] is a Semi-Supervised Learning (SSL) technique that aims to obtain a satisfactory classification performance with a smaller number of labeled samples and exploits the continuous interaction with the classifier [7, 18]. It builds efficient training sets, improving iteratively the performance of the model. This allows for constant retraining of the algorithm and enables the exploitation of the data and reduces the cost of labeling. The samples to be labeled are selected by a heuristic selection to be representative enough to improve the model and then they will be labeled by an expert [17].

The present work aims to explore different AL techniques applied to RS in comparison with SVM to achieve a classifier of different summer crops in the Northwest of Buenos Aires province, Argentina. More specifically, the study was carried out on fields in the districts of Junín, Rojas, and Chacabuco, which are part of the so-called "Humid Pampa", one of the most relevant regions in agricultural production and less studied with this type of techniques. Most of the work found in the literature was performed on hyperspectral images or multi-temporal images [19, 20]. In our work, it will be performed on a single Landsat multispectral image. Also, the classification will be done on two types of maize crops and two types of soybean crops.

The rest of the article is organized as follows: Sect. 2 presents the problem and the proposed solution; Sect. 3 presents the results of the tests, and Sect. 4 presents the conclusion and future work.

2 Problem and Proposed Solution

2.1 Problem Description

The aim of the present work is the application of AL algorithms to classify summer crops in the northwest of the province of Buenos Aires by using Landsat 8 images. The crops cultivated in the region include Maize, Soybean, and Sorghum, where the first two are the main and most widely planted. The region also has large lakes and rivers that cross it, which means that some plots are adjacent to these large concentrations of water and many of them contain lowlands.

The particularity of this development lies in three fundamental aspects; first of all, it works with Landsat images when many works are done with hyperspectral, multi-temporal, or multi-source images [21]. When working with Landsat images, there are fewer data available than in other cases, for example, in [22] it uses hyperspectral images, where it has about 200 spectral bands that provide information. In contrast to Landsat 8, which only has 6 bands to provide information. In this work, 4 more bands with vegetation indices were added to these 6 bands. Another aspect to highlight is that it will be applied to a region where this type of algorithm has not been studied much yet. There are some works about coverage in our country, but they are applied in other regions of the country, to different coverage, using multi-temporal images and with different vegetation indices [23]. And finally, among the crops to be classified, there are varieties of two of the above-mentioned crops. That is to say that the intention is to classify maize in three classes: Maize, Late Maize, and Double Crop Maize, and soybean in two classes: Soybean and Double Crop Soybean, in addition to Sorghum and Water. The main challenge is that they are variants of the same crops and they have the same spectral signature.

It is important to note that, in the case of maize, the only difference between Maize and Late Maize is the planting date, where Late Maize is planted later than the first. In the case of the Double Crop Maize, it is maize that, like the Late Crop Maize, was planted at a later date than the Maize and it was also planted after a winter crop. That is, previously in the same lot there was a winter crop, in contrast to the Maize and Late Maize, where during the winter crop date there was bare soil. Concerning soybeans, Soybean, and Double Crop Soybean just like maize, the planting dates differ, the Double Crop Soybean was planted at a later date than the Soybean and it was also planted after a winter crop.

During the first tests, it was detected the difficulty to distinguish the Late Maize from the Double Crop Maize. Because they are the same crop and can be planted on the same dates. And, the companies that sell grains carry out genetic modifications in their seeds (hybrids), which causes that the same type of crop planted on the same date responds, grows, and develops differently. In the Fig. 1 using false color, where the RGB color bands are represented by R = B and 4, G = B and 5 and B = B and 3, it can be seen, inside the yellow box, that a lot with two different Double Crop Maize hybrids planted on the same date are reflected differently.

From the preliminary tests using an SVM classifier with an RBF kernel, the confusion matrix in Fig. 2 was obtained, which shows the difficulty in differentiating both classes,

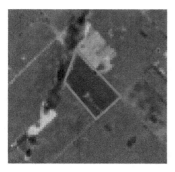

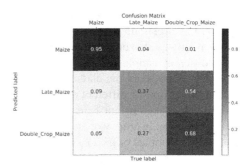

Fig. 1. Lot planted on the same date with two hybrids of Double Crop Maize

Fig. 2. Classification Confusion Matrix for Maize, Late Maize, and Double Crop Maize using SVM with an RBF kernel

Late Maize and Double Crop Maize. Because of this difficulty to separate both classes, it has been decided that these crops should appear unified as a single land cover type.

For the classification tests a single date image was used but within a particular range of dates. The decision of not using multi-temporal images is to prove that a good classifier can be obtained for these crops with a single image and to try to simplify the subsequent use of the classifier by the end-user. The optimal range of dates for the detection of summer crops in this region is from mid-January to the end of February, because of those dates some crops are going from flowering to senescence. Within this range of dates, it found 3 Landsat images on which the tests were carried out to observe what variations exist in the classification.

2.2 Classifiers

Active Learning Algorithm. AL techniques require a 3 part dataset, the training set, the test set, and the candidate set, that after the application of a heuristic, some of them will become part of the training set [18].

It takes as a starting point a set of Labeled Data "L", which will be used to train the supervised Classifier "C", which generates Classified Data from that training. The technique then continues with the set of Unlabeled Candidates "U", which are the input data for the Selection Criteria "Q" (heuristic). Those who were selected by the heuristic must be labeled by the expert user to add to the Labeled Data set and start the process again. The unlabeled data set not selected will be considered as candidates for selection by the Selection Criteria in the new iteration, repeating the procedure until the expected results are achieved. In other words, AL exploits the interaction with the user while decreasing the error.

Several supervised classifiers can be used to train the model in each iteration. Based on the literature consulted, it was decided that SVM will be used because it is widely applied in land cover classification [24], has better results than other techniques [25], and does not require as much labeling as neural network techniques [26].

Support Vector Machines (SVM). The AL algorithms that have been implemented using SVM as a classifier, which was popularized by Vladimir Vapnik in 1992 [27]. They are mainly used to build classifiers, which through supervised learning, distinguish between different samples.

In order to carry out the classification, there are multiple decision boundaries that allow the separation of different samples. SVM seeks to find a separation (decision) boundary that is equidistant from the samples to be classified, in order to minimize classification error. In other words, it seeks the separation boundary, which is equidistant to the closest examples of the classes under study.

In cases where the data cannot be separated in a linear manner, it is necessary to use special functions called *kernels* [28].

Heuristics. Below are different Selection Criteria Q (heuristics) of candidates that were implemented. The determination of the heuristics was made based on the consulted literature [22].

Random Sampling (AL-RS). Random sampling (AL-RS). AL-RS, as its name suggests, selects candidates at random from the set of candidates. This criterion has been chosen to have a measure to compare the performance of the other selected AL heuristics.

Margin Sampling (AL-MS). Also called Most Ambiguous (AL-MA), it is a candidate heuristic selection belonging to the large margin based heuristics family [22], which tries to incorporate into the training set the samples most susceptible to classification errors by a trained SVM.

To establish which elements should be incorporated into the training set, the distance between all samples in the candidate set and the SVM hyperplanes is measured. The samples that are closest to the decision boundaries (hyperplanes) of the SVM will be the most likely to be misclassified. And for that reason, the heuristics will select them to be classified by an expert and become part of the training set.

Multi-Class Level Uncertainty (AL-MCLU). MCLU also belongs to the large margin based heuristics family [22] and uses the two most probable classes. It makes the difference between the distances to the margin for the two most probable classes.

To establish the elements to be incorporated into the training set, it measures the distance between all samples in the candidate set and the SVM hyper-planes. For each sample it calculates the difference between the distances of the two most likely classes, these are the two greater distances, taking those with the least difference to incorporate to the training set. When the distance between these two classes is lower, the uncertainty is higher and therefore you are more likely to have classification errors.

Breaking Ties (BT). BT belongs to the Posterior Probability-Based family of algorithms [22] which uses posterior probability estimation to select a new candidate. Since the posterior probability gives a reference to the confidence of the class assignment. It intends to use the conditional probability to predict a certain class for each candidate. In the literature [22] Platt's estimate is proposed [29] but in the present development, Wo's estimate will be used [30]. Then to establish which elements should be incorporated into the training set, it calculates, for all samples of the candidate set, the probability of belonging to each of the classes. For every sample, it calculates the difference between the two largest probabilities and then it takes those where the difference is smaller. A smaller difference indicates that the uncertainty of classification is greater and that it is more prone to error (Fig. 2).

3 Tests and Results

3.1 Dataset and Ground Truth

The images were downloaded from the U.S. Geological Survey website [31] taken from the Landsat 8 sensor on path 226 and row 084, more specifically by the district of Junín, Rojas, and Chacabuco. The data set has two parts, the spectral image and an image of the same size, but with the ground truths (GT) or labels. The spectral image that covers part of the northwest of the province of Buenos Aires has 2615 by 2519 pixels and 6 bands of reflectance (blue, green, red, near-infrared, short-wave infrared 1, and short-wave infrared 2) with 30 m of spatial resolution. Then, some vegetation indices were analyzed to highlight aspects of the different coverage's taking into account the region [23]. The use of four vegetation indices was determined: Normalized Difference Vegetation Index (NDVI), Soil Adjusted Vegetation Index (SAVI), Enhanced Vegetation Index (EVI), and Normalized Difference Moisture Index (NDMI), which were added as bands to the Landsat image.

The study was based on the summer crops planted during the year 2019; this is cropped for the season 2019–2020. Since Landsat images have a frequency of 16 days between images of the same site, 3 images have been obtained in that period. One image is from January 25, 2020, the other is from February 10, 2020, and the last from February 26, 2020. For the ground truth, 6 local producers were consulted and a tour of the different fields was carried out taking note of the planted crop.

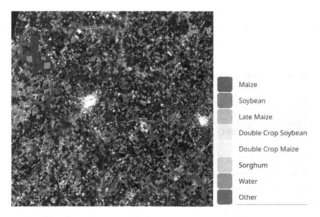

Fig. 3. Equalized RGB image with ground truths

The images contain different land cover, lagoons, lowlands, and buildings. In this first instance, these buildings were excluded from the classification and identified as background because it was composed of different elements, not responding to a specific pattern, making it difficult to classify.

Table 1 shows the 6 classes of land cover used on the ground truth and the number of samples of each of them. As can be seen in Table 1, the amount of Sorghum crop that was identified is lower than the rest of the land covers because Sorghum is less frequent than the rest of the crops in this region.

Table 1. Land cover, code and samples of the ground truth

Land Cover	Code	Number of Samples
Background	BG (Not Class)	6492999
Maize	MZ	10088
Soybean	SB	16731
Double Crop Soybean	DS	13187
Double Crop and Late Maize	DM	33108
Sorghum	SG	1758
Water	WT	19314

Since Landsat images have a frequency of 16 days between images of the same site, 3 images have been obtained in that period. And the images contain different land cover, lagoons, lowlands, and buildings. In this first instance, these buildings were excluded from the classification and identified as background.

Table 1 shows the 6 classes of land cover used on the ground truth and the number of samples of each of them. For the ground truth, local producers were consulted and a tour of different fields was carried out taking note of the planted crop. As can be seen in Table 1, the amount of Sorghum crop that was identified is lower than the rest of the land covers because Sorghum is less frequent than the rest of the crops in this region. And in the application of the algorithms, the background has been excluded, since it was composed of different elements, not responding to a specific pattern, making it difficult to classify.

3.2 Dataset Division and Tests

The spectral image is a cube of dimensions 2519 pixels (row) by 2615 pixels (column) by 10 bands which have been resized to a matrix of 6587185 pixels (row) by 10 bands (columns). Of the 6587185 pixels of the dataset, those that were labeled as the background were discarded, since they do not have a specific class of the object and therefore contain a spectral signature that can be very varied, making it very difficult to classify them. These were a total of 6492999 pixels belonging to the background, leaving a dataset of 94,186 pixels to be used.

For the construction of the initial training set, it was decided to take a certain amount of pixels from each of the classes to balance the initial classifier. The criterion for the selection of the initial training set has been to take a certain amount of pixels from each of the classes to balance the initial classifier. For this purpose, different tests were carried out, reaching a minimum of 5 pixels per class (about 30 training pixels) to build the training set. The amount was determined taking into account the objective of the technique which is to have to tag the least amount of pixels to obtain an optimal result. Afterward, it was determined that 30% of the total pixels of the dataset would be used in the training set and the remaining 70% of pixels for the training set and the candidates.

Throughout the work different tests were performed, where the different algorithms mentioned above, SVM and AL algorithms such as RS, MS, BT, and MCLU were used. All these were applied to Landsat images from 3 different dates. First, the size of the initial training set needed by the AL algorithms was defined and then it will be increased using any particular criteria (heuristics). After different tests, it was determined that a good starting classifier was obtained by using a minimum of 5 labeled pixels per class. In other words, with $n = 5$ it was obtained a classifier that on average has an Overall Accuracy (OA) of 76%.

When the performance of the algorithms was evaluated from this n, $i = 75$ iterations of the AL algorithm were executed, incorporating through the heuristics first 10 pixels in each iteration, and then, $i = 150$ iterations but with 20 pixels in each iteration. With each of these combinations, a total of 10 instances were executed for each AL algorithm with its different AL-RS, AL-MS, AL-BT, and AL-MCLU heuristics. All this makes a total of 50 executions, 10 for AL-RS, 10 for AL-MS, 10 for AL-BT, 10 for AL-MCLU, and 10 for SVM. But as the dataset had 3 images from different dates, a total of 150 runs were made.

Another aspect to determine was if a balanced dataset was used or not, that is, if the algorithms were trained with the same amount of labels for each class or if the classes were used with the number of labels that were obtained.

In the first test performed, because there were fewer labels from the sorghum crop, it was decided to balance the number of samples from each class of the dataset. When the division of the dataset was made, 30% of the test set had the same amount of labels for all classes. And the same was done with the 70% that included the training set and the set of possible candidates to be chosen by the heuristic. This reduced the total number of 94186 pixels labeled to 10548 pixels (1758 pixels, which is the number that Sorghum has, for the 6 classes), leaving 7383 pixels for the train and candidates, and about 3165 pixels for the test.

The code was written for Python 3 [32] and using libraries like Scikit-learn [33] for testing the machine learning algorithms.

3.3 Results

The result of the classification of each of the Landsat images of the three selected dates can be seen in Fig. 4. It shows the tests performed for each date with an initial training set of 5 pixels per class. Where on the x-axis it shows the amount of samples labeled in each iteration and on the y-axis the percentage of accuracy obtained for each of these sample amounts. It also all the tested variants, looking at what happened at the extremes of the number of iterations, is to say when $i = 75$ and when $i = 150$.

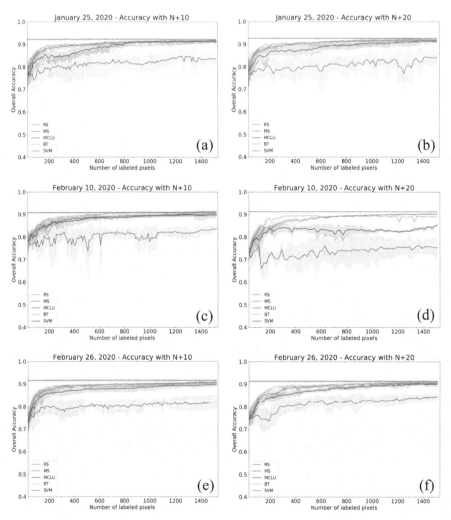

Fig. 4. Overall accuracy for each heuristic with (a) (c) (e) 150 iterations and 10 new pixels per iteration (b) (d) (f) 75 iterations and 20 new pixels per iteration

From the graphs can be seen that for these i values the result has converged. It can also be seen that AL-RS in two of the images works better than the rest of the heuristics, although the difference is not significant. Of the remaining heuristics in general, the AL-BT and AL-MCLU heuristics work well, and in the image of February 10, 2020, they are higher than AL-RS. It is also noted that AL-BT is the best performer at low i values. In general, when there are few labeled pixels, between 100 and 300 pixels, the performance of AL-BT is better than the rest and then it is matched with AL-RS.

The AL-MS heuristic, contrary to what was observed in the literature [23] is the worst performer for this dataset.

In addition to this, the matrices in Figs. 5, 6, and 7 shows the accuracy of the classifier for each of the classes, where the column shows the true label and the row the predicted labels. Although classifiers have an acceptable OA, here it can be observed that, depending on the date, the classifier works better in one class than in another or it is more difficult to classify certain classes.

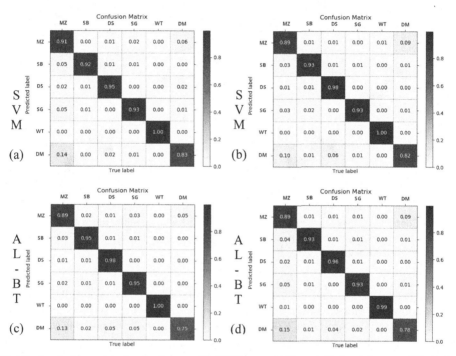

Fig. 5. Confusion matrix for the January 25, 2020 image with an initial training set of 5 pixels per class (30 pixels total). (a, c) 150 iterations and 10 new pixels per iteration (b, d) 75 iterations and 20 new pixels per iteration

Thus, it can be seen that in the image of January 25 it is more complicated to classify the unified class DM and that in the image of February 26 it is difficult to distinguish the SB from the DS. It is also observed that in the image of February 11 it classifies better the classes that had less performance in the previous images and although the accuracy of the classes is more homogeneous some of these are inferior to the accuracy of the other images.

Table 2 shows the OA for each classifier in the 3 images for the different dates. It can be seen that AL-RS and AL-BT show the best results. In addition, the results obtained from the confusion matrix by applying SVM, AL-RS, AL-BT, and AL-MCLU to each of the images are shown below. There it is possible to observe the accuracy for each of the classes and see how well the classifiers for these classes work.

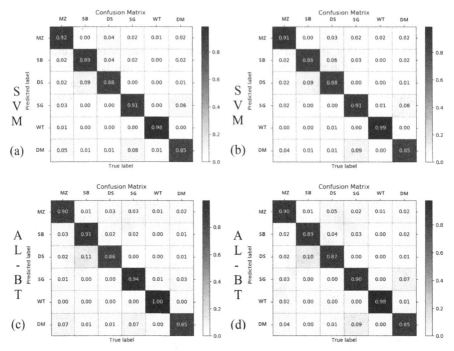

Fig. 6. Confusion matrix for the February 10, 2020 image with an initial training set of 5 pixels per class (30 pixels total). (a) 150 iterations and 10 new pixels per iteration (b) 75 iterations and 20 new pixels per iteration

The second test was performed without stratifying the samples, taking all the labeled pixels from all the classes. Thus, in the dataset division, 30% of the test set comprises 30% of each class and the same with 70% comprising the training set and possible candidates. In this case, the total of 94186 labeled pixels was used without any reduction, leaving 65930 pixels for the train and candidates, and about 28256 pixels for the test. This configuration was discarded because the results obtained do not differ from the previous ones with the stratified classes, moreover, in some cases, the results got worse with some heuristics. With this configuration, an SVM was trained with 65930 labeled pixels and the average OA was 91.12%. This result is similar to the stratified configuration with a training set of 7383 pixels which is significantly lower. It can be concluded then that for this dataset training the algorithm with more labeled pixels does not modify the result.

3.4 Discussion

Classification of land cover using remote sensing data requires the use of a large amount of labeled data. The challenge of finding a good classifier from a few labeled data that will facilitate the use of the expert was the reason for this work. Where AL techniques were used on 3 images from different dates to obtain a good classifier of summer crops in the Northwest region of the Province of Buenos Aires.

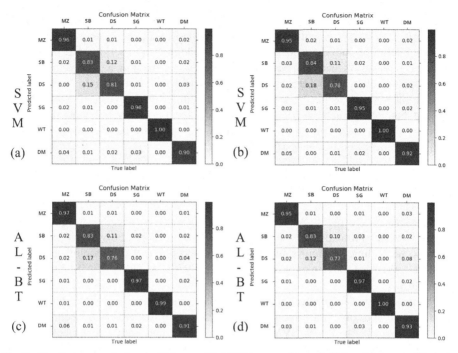

Fig. 7. Confusion matrix for the February 26, 2020 image with an initial training set of 5 pixels per class (30 pixels total). (a, c) 150 iterations and 10 new pixels per iteration (b, d) 75 iterations and 20 new pixels per iteration

Table 2. Mean OA for each date with each of the classifiers

Classifier	25 January 2020	10 February 2020	26 February 2020
SVM	92,61%	90,74%	91,29%
AL-RS	91,82%	89,91%	90,51%
AL-BT	91,53%	91,28%	90,45%
AL-MCLU	91,27%	89,91%	90,04%
AL-MS	84,21%	83,43%	84,38%

In the present work it was possible to verify the particularity that, for the used dataset, AL-RS had a better performance without too much difference with AL-BT in 2 of the 3 images, while in the remaining image AL-BT was which better performance had. In the case of AL-MS, contrary to the results found for other datasets in the literature, the performance was at all times worse than the rest of the heuristics. It is also noted that in the early stages of the algorithm, with few iterations or few labeled pixels, AL-BT has the best performance and then, as the size of the training set grows, the hit rate becomes similar to AL-RS or AL-MCLU.

Analyzing the results, it can be seen that with AL techniques a good performance is reached in comparison with SVM, observing that in all the cases the percentage difference between both does not exceed 1%. In addition to this, with AL, the cost of labeling is reduced since, as can be seen from the tests carried out, a total of 1530 pixels are needed to obtain good performance against SVM with 7383 pixels in the best of cases. In other words, with AL a classifier with similar performance to SVM can be achieved, but with a much lower cost, mainly in terms of the cost of labeling the classes by the expert. All these things make AL a good alternative for the classification of this kind of land cover in this region of the country.

4   Conclusions and Future Work

In the present work, different Active Learning algorithms were tested on Landsat images for land cover classification in the northwest of Buenos Aires province in Argentina. For these AL techniques, four sample heuristics selection that is, recommended in the literature for remote sensing applications were analyzed: AL-BT, AL-MS, AL-MCLU, and AL-RS.

The application of these techniques to Landsat satellite images with different dates made it possible to obtain a summer crop classifier for this region with accuracy comparable to that obtained with SVM. We can conclude that with a few labeled pixels similar results can be obtained as with the whole image labeled with the particularity that we were trying to classify varieties of the same crops. Moreover, this is applied to a single multi-spectral image, which makes it easier in comparison with other techniques that require multi-temporal images or hyperspectral images. The results obtained allow doing with less work a precise classifier, being able to become in the future a useful tool in the decision making for the experts of the sector.

The work performed until now is the beginning of the work in the subject, the initial kick to continue working on Machine Learning with Remote Sensing on own datasets with coverage of the region. The objective of future tests is to continue with the study of techniques and heuristics to achieve some modifications that will improve the results obtained until now.

In the future, it is expected to carry out tests with more datasets from other years to study how climate variations and changes in crop planting dates can affect the classification. And to study the possibility of incorporating more classes to the dataset, adding covers like bare soil, forests, constructions or roads.

References

1. Fernández-Quintanilla, C.: César: Agricultura de precisión. Segundas jornadas científicas sobre medio Ambient. del CCMA-CSIC. **2**, 187–194 (2002)
2. Wang, Y., Lee, K., Cui, S., Risch, E., Lian, J.: Agriculture robot and applications. In: Zheng, D. (ed.) Future Information Engineering and Manufacturing Science : Proceedings of the 2014 International Conference on Future Information Engineering and Manufacturing Science (FIEMS 2014), pp. 43–46, 26–27 June 2014. CRC Press, Taylor & Francis Group, Beijing (2015). https://doi.org/10.1201/b18167

3. Blackmore, S.: The role of yield maps in precision farming (2003)
4. Kiefe, T.M., Lillesand, R.W.: Remote Sensing and Image Interpretation. Wiley, New Jersey (2015)
5. Lary, D.J., Alavi, A.H., Gandomi, A.H., Walker, A.L.: Machine learning in geosciences and remote sensing. Geosci. Front. **7**, 3–10 (2016). https://doi.org/10.1016/j.gsf.2015.07.003
6. Camps-Valls, G.: Machine learning in remote sensing data processing. In: IEEE International Workshop on Machine Learning Signal Processing, pp. 1–6 (2009). https://doi.org/10.1109/MLSP.2009.5306233
7. Scheunders, P., Tuia, D., Moser, G.: Contributions of machine learning to remote sensing data analysis. In: Scheunders, P., Tuia, D., Moser, G. (eds.) Comprehensive Remote Sensing, pp. 199–243. Elsevier BV (2018)
8. Marcos, D., et al.: Learning deep structured active contours end-to-end. In: 2018 IEEE/CVF Conference on Computer Vision and Pattern Recognition, pp. 8877–8885. IEEE, Salt Lake City, UT (2018). https://doi.org/10.1109/CVPR.2018.00925
9. Maynard, J.J., Levi, M.R.: Hyper-temporal remote sensing for digital soil mapping: Characterizing soil-vegetation response to climatic variability. Geoderma **285** (2017). in press. https://doi.org/10.1016/j.geoderma.2016.09.024
10. Teluguntla, P., et al.: A 30-m landsat-derived cropland extent product of Australia and China using random forest machine learning algorithm on Google Earth Engine cloud computing platform. ISPRS J. Photogramm. Remote Sens. **144**, 325–340 (2018). https://doi.org/10.1016/j.isprsjprs.2018.07.017
11. Song, X., et al.: National-scale soybean mapping and area estimation in the United States using medium resolution satellite imagery and field survey. Remote Sens. Environ. **190**, 383–395 (2017). https://doi.org/10.1016/j.rse.2017.01.008
12. Gonzalez-Sanchez, A., Frausto-Solis, J., Ojeda-Bustamante, W.: Predictive ability of machine learning methods for massive crop yield prediction. Span. J. Agric. Res. **12**, 313–328 (2014). https://doi.org/10.5424/sjar/2014122-4439
13. Veenadhari, S., Misra, B., Singh, C.D.: Machine learning approach for forecasting crop yield based on climatic parameters. In: 2014 International Conference Computer Communication Informatics Ushering Technology, Tomorrow, Today, ICCCI 2014, pp. 1–5 (2014). https://doi.org/10.1109/ICCCI.2014.6921718
14. Dimitriadis, S., Goumopoulos, C.: Applying machine learning to extract new knowledge in precision agriculture applications. In: Proceedings of the 12th Pan-Hellenic Conference Informatics, PCI 2008, pp. 100–104 (2008). https://doi.org/10.1109/PCI.2008.30
15. Kamilaris, A., Prenafeta-Boldú, F.X.: Deep learning in agriculture: a survey. Comput. Electron. Agric. **147**, 70–90 (2018). https://doi.org/10.1016/j.compag.2018.02.016
16. Zhu, X.X., Tuia, D., Mou, L., Xia, G.-S., Zhang, L., Xu, F., Fraundorfer, F.: Deep learning in remote sensing: a comprehensive review and list of resources. IEEE Geosci. Remote Sens. Mag. Press. **60** (2017). https://doi.org/10.1109/MGRS.2017.2762307
17. Settles, B.: Active Learning Literature Survey. University of Wisconsin–Madison (2009)
18. Crawford, M.M., Tuia, D., Yang, H.L.: Active learning: Any value for classification of remotely sensed data? Proc. IEEE **101**, 593–608 (2013). https://doi.org/10.1109/JPROC.2012.2231951
19. Liu, P., Zhang, H., Eom, K.B.: Active deep learning for classification of hyperspectral images. IEEE J. Sel. Top. Appl. EARTH Obs. Remote Sens. **10**, 712–724 (2016). https://doi.org/10.1109/JSTARS.2016.2598859
20. Dallaqua, F.B.J.R., Faria, F.A., Fazenda, A.L.: Active learning approaches for deforested area classification. In: 2018 31st SIBGRAPI Conference Graphics Patterns Images, pp. 48–55 (2019). https://doi.org/10.1109/SIBGRAPI.2018.00013

21. Li, J., Huang, X., Chang, X.: A label-noise robust active learning sample collection method for multi-temporal urban land-cover classification and change analysis. ISPRS J. Photogramm. Remote Sens. **163**, 1–17 (2020). https://doi.org/10.1016/j.isprsjprs.2020.02.022
22. Tuia, D., Volpi, M., Copa, L., Kanevski, M., Munoz-Mari, J.: A survey of active learning algorithms for supervised remote sensing image classification. IEEE J. Sel. Top. Signal Process. **5**, 606–617 (2011). https://doi.org/10.1109/JSTSP.2011.2139193
23. Brendel, A.S., Ferrelli, F., Piccolo, M.C., Perillo, G.M.E.: Assessment of the effectiveness of supervised and unsupervised methods: maximizing land-cover classification accuracy with spectral indices data. J. Appl. Remote Sens. **13**, 1 (2019). https://doi.org/10.1117/1.jrs.13.014503
24. Rudrapal, D., Subhedar, M.: Land cover classification using support vector machine. Int. J. Eng. Res. **4**, 584–588 (2015). https://doi.org/10.17577/ijertv4is090611
25. Thanh Noi, P., Kappas, M.: Comparison of random forest, k-nearest neighbor, and support vector machine classifiers for land cover classification using sentinel-2 imagery. Sensors (Basel) **18**, 1–20 (2017). https://doi.org/10.3390/s18010018
26. Candade, N., Dixon, B.: Multispectral classification of Landsat images: a comparison of support vector machine and neural network classifiers. ASPRS Annu. Meet. Proc. **43**, 1882–1889 (2003)
27. Boser, B.E., Guyon, I.M., Vapnik, V.N.: A training algorithm for optimal margin classifiers. In: Proceedings of the Fifth Annual ACM Workshop on Computational Learning Theory, pp. 144–152. ACM Press, New York, USA (1992). https://doi.org/10.1145/130385.130401
28. Schölkopf, B., Smola, A.J.: Learning with Kernels: Support Vector Machines, Regularization, Optimization, and Beyond Adaptive Computation and Machine Learning. MIT Press, Cambridge (2002)
29. Platt, J.C., Platt, J.C.: Probabilistic outputs for support vector machines and comparisons to regularized likelihood methods. In: Advances in Large Margin Classifiers. pp. 61–74. MIT Press (1999)
30. Wu, T.-F., Lin, C.-J., Weng, R.C.: Probability estimates for multi-class classification by pairwise coupling. J. Mach. Learn. Res. **5**, 975–1005 (2004). https://doi.org/10.5555/1005332.1016791
31. U.S. Geological Survey (2020) 'Earth Explorer.' http://earthexplorer.usgs.gov. Accessed 28 Feb 2020
32. Van Rossum, G., Drake Jr., F.L.: Python Tutorial. Centrum voor Wiskunde en Informatica Amsterdam, The Netherlands (1995)
33. Pedregosa, F., et al.: Scikit-learn: machine learning in Python. JMLR **12**, 2825–2830 (2011)

Trainable Windowing Coefficients in DNN for Raw Audio Classification

Mario Alejandro García[1]([✉]) [iD], Eduardo Atilio Destéfanis[1], and Ana Lorena Rosset[2] [iD]

[1] Universidad Tecnológica Nacional, Facultar Regional Córdoba, Córdoba, Argentina
mgarcia@frc.utn.edu.ar
[2] Universidad Nacional de Córdoba, Córdoba, Argentina

Abstract. An artificial neural network for audio classification is proposed. This includes the windowing operation of raw audio and the calculation of the power spectrogram. A windowing layer is initialized with a hann window and its weights are adapted during training. The non-trainable weights of spectrogram calculation are initialized with the discrete Fourier transform coefficients. The tests are performed on the Speech Commands dataset. Results show that adapting the windowing coefficients produces a moderate accuracy improvement. It is concluded that the gradient of the error function can be propagated through the neural calculation of the power spectrum. It is also concluded that the training of the windowing layer improves the model's ability to generalize.

Keywords: Deep learning · Deep neural network · Speech recognition · Raw audio

1 Introduction

Audio pattern recognition is applied to a wide range of tasks, such as automatic speech recognition (ASR) [1–20], speaker recognition [21–25], emotion recognition [26,27], disease detection [28] and music information retrieval [29–32].

In traditional pattern recognition, building an appropriate feature representation and designing an appropriate classifier for these features have often been treated as separate problems. Audio processing is no exception. One drawback of this approach is that the designed features might not be optimal for the classification objective at hand. Deep neural networks (DNNs) can be thought of as performing feature extraction jointly with objective optimization such as classification. With the larger modeling capacity of deep learning models, there has been growing interest in building end-to-end trained systems that directly map the input audio signal to the target [33].

DNNs have also changed the way of extracting features from audio. In traditional acoustical models mel frequency cepstral coefficients (MFCCs) have been used as the dominant acoustic feature representation. MFCCs are commonly

ⓒ Springer Nature Switzerland AG 2020
E. Rucci et al. (Eds.): JCC-BD&ET 2020, CCIS 1291, pp. 153–166, 2020.
https://doi.org/10.1007/978-3-030-61218-4_11

derived as follows: the discrete Fourier transform (DFT) of the windowed signal is taken, the power of the obtained spectrum is filtered with mel filter banks, the log of the power spectrum is calculated for each mel frequency and finally the discrete cosine transform is calculated on the mel log powers. In the early days of deep learning in audio, researchers have found that DNNs work significantly bettter on filter bank outputs than on MFCCs [34,35].

As Nam et al. explained [36], the features in the first models were the outputs of the frequency-filter banks, then the output of the windowing and DFT, which is actually a short-time Fourier transform (STFT), and finally, some models began to take the raw audio as input. During this evolution, DNNs replace the operations of the traditional approach with transformations whose parameters can be learned. The STFT is usually replaced by trainable time-filter banks and mel filters are replaced by frequency-filter banks. Both filter banks are usually implemented with convolutional layers.

Although windowing is an important operation in the traditional approach, no scientific work has been found on the effect of windowing with adaptive coefficients on raw audio. As well as a designed filter bank is not always guaranteed to be the best in a statistical framework where the end goal is a particular problem [26], a designed window does not guarantee to be optimal in the same case.

1.1 Windowing

Windowing is the process of dividing long signals into short frames of N samples. A frame $\boldsymbol{x} = (x_0, x_1, \ldots, x_{N-1})$ is obtained by multiplying signal $s(n)$ with nonzero samples of window sequence $w(n)$.

$$x(n) = s(n)w(n), \qquad n = 0, \ldots, N - 1$$

The simplest window is rectangular window $\boldsymbol{w_r} = (1, 1, \ldots, 1)$. A rectangular window does not modify the data frame at all. It only multiplies by 1 inside the window and by 0 outside.

The DFT of a windowed signal develops non-zero values for nonexistent frequencies in the original signal. This (unwanted) effect is commonly called spectral leakage. The kind of information that can be extracted from the frequency spectrum depends mainly on the distribution of the lakage over the spectrum. In turn, the shape of the window function determines the lakage distribution, therefore the choice of the window depends on the objective of the classification.

Several windows have been designed, some are Hann, Hamming, flat top, Blackman and Tukey. A detailed description can be seen in [37].

Hann and Hamming windows are the most commonly used in audio pattern recognition [1,5,9,16–18,24,28,38,39], however some researchers have preferred to use others, such as Blackman-Harris window [31,32], or to propose new window functions. Morales-Cordovilla et al [40], Alam et al. [41] and Rozman et al. [42] proposed asymmetric windows and Sahidullah et al. [43] proposed a new windowing technique based on windowed DFT derivatives.

DNN models that take raw audio as features use rectangular windows. Learned filters are assumed to include multiplication by another (nonrectangular) window function, which implies a different window for each filter. There is no analysis on the improvement provided by the separate filters and windows.

1.2   Objectives

In this work, we study the behavior of a DNN for audio commands recognition. Our neural network is an end-to-end model, which receives raw audio as input and predicts the spoken word. The first layer of the model multiplies the inputs (raw audio) by a window whose shape adapts during training.

Research questions:

- Is it possible to adapt the windowing coefficients? To adapt the windowing weights it is necessary to propagate the gradient of the error function from the output layer to the windowing layer. As will be seen later, the proposed DNN calculates the power spectrum internally. So the gradient needs to be propagated correctly through the power spectrum calculation.
- Does the adaptation of the window function improve the recognition ability of the model?

In order to answer these questions we have experimented on the Speech Commands dataset.

1.3   Speech Commands

The Speech Commands dataset is a standard training and evaluation dataset for a class of simple speech recognition tasks. Its primary goal is to provide a way to build and test small models that detect when a single word is spoken, from a set of ten or fewer target words from background noise or unrelated speech. This task is often known as keyword spotting [44].

The dataset consisted of 105,829 utterances of 35 words ("Backward", "Bed", "Bird", "Cat", "Dog", "Down", "Eight", "Five", "Follow", "Forward", "Four", "Go", "Happy", "House", "Learn", "Left", "Marvin", "Nine", "No", "Off", "On", "One", "Right", "Seven", "Sheila", "Six", "Stop", "Three", "Tree", "Two", "Up", "Visual", "Wow", "Yes" and "Zero") spoken by 2,618 speakers and captured through phone or laptop microphones. Each utterance is stored as a one-second (or less) WAVE format file with a 16 KHz sample rate.

We chose this dataset in order to facilitate the reproducibility of the experiment. The dataset is freely available and a precise testing protocol is defined in [44]. We follow this protocol, which is explained in Sect. 4.1. In addition, the source code of a well-known project that uses Speech Commands dataset is also available[1]. This project, called Simple Audio Recognition (SAR), includes

---

[1] https://github.com/tensorflow/tensorflow/tree/master/tensorflow/examples/ speech_commands.

data preprocessing functions according to the protocol in Sect. 4.1 and a DNN model based on [45] to classify Speech Command data. We use these functions to pre-process the data and also use the neural model as a baseline. The model we propose is a modification of the baseline model, therefore it is easy for any researcher to reproduce the results.

2   Related Work

As mentioned before, neural audio classification models that take raw audio as input use rectangular windows [4, 7, 8, 10–13, 15, 19, 20, 23, 25–27, 29]. These windows are defined by the size of the convolution kernels. However, some researchers have found ways to include the effect of other windows functions in their models.

Tüske et al. [5] take raw audio as input and initialize the weights of the filter banks with gammatones. They compare the results with two other features, MFCC and STFT + Hann window. The best result is obtained with MFCC, but similar performance is obtained with STFT, whereas with raw audio they obtain poor results. In this case, the effect of windowing is given by the gamma distribution of weights amplitude.

In [3] Sainath et al. use gammatone impulse responses to initialize their time-convolutional layer (filter banks). They find that not training the time-convolutional layer is slightly worse than training this layer. This shows the benefit of adapting filters for the objective at hand, rather than using hand-designed filters.

Tripathi et al. [8] with a rectangular window, random initialization and raw audio as features got better domain-invariant representations than handcrafted representations like MFCC.

Guo et al. in [46] work on wake word detection. They use a rectangular window for a network that internally calculates a complex spectrum as a frequency representation. Weights are initialized randomly. Except for the window, this model can be compared with ours by the way of calculating the spectral representation. Although implemented with real numbers, our model calculates the STFT, which involves complex calculations.

Takeda et. al [14] train a complex valued network to speech recognition tasks. Weights are initialized with Fourier coefficients multiplied by a Hamming window.

Zeghidour et al. in [16] look for components that can be connected to the network as a replacement for classic filter banks without modifying the acoustic model in an ASR problem. They test convolutional layer weights initializing with random values, gammatones and Gabor filters. The output of the convolutional layer is multiplied by a square Hann window. In this article window coefficients are trained, but results are better when not trained. In [17] Zeghidour et al. presents a similar model with similar results. This is initialized with mel filter banks and improves reference results, but works better when windowing weights are not trained.

Ravanelli et al. in [21] propose an DNN for speaker recognition. Their network takes raw audio multiplied by a fixed Hamming window. Then, adapt the filter banks weights initialized with mel-scale cutoff frequencies.

Millet et al. [28] work on dysarthria detection. They apply a model whose first layer is initialized with mel filter banks multiplied by a fixed Hann window. This model has many similarities to ours because it also calculates the modulus and the square of the spectrogram.

3   Proposed Model

SAR offers different execution modes. The one chosen as baseline for the experiment is the largest model, with complete power spectrogram as input. We propose a neural network, called wSTFT, that calculates the power spectrogram from raw audio, also doing the windowing process. By replacing the inputs in the SAR model with the wSTFT network, the effect of coefficients adaptation on the windowing process can be analyzed (Fig. 1). In order to calculate the power spectrogram, wSTFT must multiply the raw audio by the window coefficients, calculate the STFT and calculate the squared STFT.

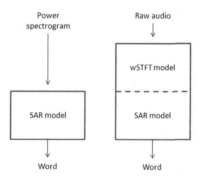

Fig. 1. Baseline model (left) vs proposed model (right).

3.1   Windowing with Neural Networks

For a signal s (raw audio) of length L and a window w of width N, the Hadamard product (or element-wise product) $x = w \odot s'$ must be calculated for each position of w on s, where s' is the segment of s under the w. Just like in a convolutional layer, the window moves a fixed number of elements (*strides*) at each step and the w_i coefficients are the same for each window location (shared weights). Unlike a convolutional layer, the result of each step is a vector, not a scalar. There are no standard layers of artificial neural networks with this behavior. We call it STHadamard layer. In Fig. 2 the operation of the model is shown highlighting the shared weights. Note that the output is a two-dimensional vector where each column is a windowed frame.

In the rest of the article, windowing coefficients will also be referred to as weights of windowing (STHadamard) layer.

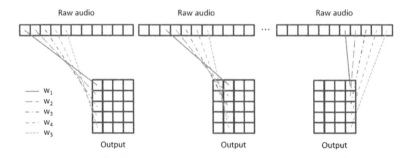

Fig. 2. STHadamard calculation for $L = 11$, $N = 5$ and *strides*= 2.

3.2 STFT with Neural Networks

As in [47], the STFT is calculated with a convolutional layer where the weights are the DFT coefficients. More specifically, the weight matrix is the concatenation of the $\boldsymbol{F_C}$ and $\boldsymbol{F_S}$ matrices.

$$
\boldsymbol{F_C} = \begin{bmatrix} 1 & 1 & 1 & \dots & 1 \\ 1 & \theta_1 & \theta_2 & \dots & \theta_{N-1} \\ 1 & \theta_2 & \theta_4 & \dots & \theta_{2(N-1)} \\ 1 & \vdots & \vdots & \ddots & \vdots \\ 1 & \theta_{N-1} & \theta_{2(N-1)} & \dots & \theta_{(N-1)^2} \end{bmatrix}
$$

$$
\boldsymbol{F_S} = \begin{bmatrix} 0 & 0 & 0 & \dots & 0 \\ 0 & \rho_1 & \rho_2 & \dots & \rho_{N-1} \\ 0 & \rho_2 & \rho_4 & \dots & \rho_{2(N-1)} \\ 0 & \vdots & \vdots & \ddots & \vdots \\ 0 & \rho_{N-1} & \rho_{2(N-1)} & \dots & \rho_{(N-1)^2} \end{bmatrix}
$$

for

$$
\theta_j = cos(-j\tfrac{i2\pi}{N})
$$

$$
\rho_j = sin(-j\tfrac{i2\pi}{N})
$$

DFT is a linear map with matrix representation $\boldsymbol{X} = \boldsymbol{Fx}$, where $\boldsymbol{x} = \begin{bmatrix} x_0 \ x_1 \ x_2 \dots x_{N-1} \end{bmatrix}^\mathsf{T}$, $\boldsymbol{X} = \begin{bmatrix} X_0 \ X_1 \ X_2 \dots X_{N-1} \end{bmatrix}^\mathsf{T}$ and $\boldsymbol{F} = \boldsymbol{F_C} + i\boldsymbol{F_S}$. Then, for each frequency k in spectrum $\boldsymbol{X}$, power spectrum is

$$|X_k|^2 = (\boldsymbol{F_C x})_k^2 + (\boldsymbol{F_S x})_k^2 \tag{1}$$

For a more detailed explanation of STFT and power spectrum calculation with neural networks see [47].

Figure 3 shows the complete model of wSTFT. The last two layers perform the sum and square of Eq. 1.

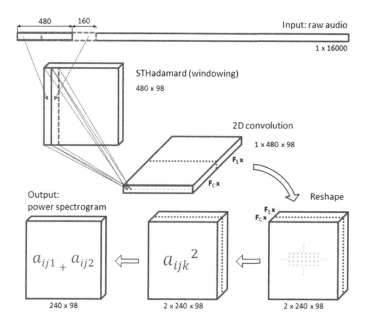

Fig. 3. Complete wSTFT model with output size of each layer.

4   Experiments

4.1   Data

As mentioned above, a test protocol was defined in [44]. The protocol specifies which audio files should be used to train, evaluate and test. Furthermore, it is defined that only the ten words "Yes", "No", "Up", "Down", "Left", "Right", "On", "Off", "Stop", and "Go" should be classified, and have one additional special label for "Unknown Word", and another for "Silence" (no speech detected). The testing is then done by providing equal numbers of examples for each of the twelve categories, which means each class accounts for approximately 8.3% of the total. The "Unknown Word" category contains words randomly sampled from classes that are part of the target set. The "Silence" category has one-second clips extracted randomly from the background noise audio files provided.

In this work the defined protocol has been followed. In addition, as in the SAR project, the audios corresponding to words have been mixed with background noise.

For all the audio files, the power spectrogram was calculated, after multiplying the audio by a Hann window, as in SAR. Spectrograms (size 240 × 98) are the inputs of the baseline model and raw audio (size 16,000) are the inputs of the proposed model.

4.2   Baseline

The baseline model layers are shown in Table 1. This is the same as SAR model, but there are two differences. The first difference is that in SAR model the third layer is a max pooling layer. The second difference is the value of the *padding* parameter in the pooling layers. In the SAR model *padding* = "SAME", while in the proposed model *padding* = "VALID". We noted that some columns of the spectrogram were not used in SAR model. With these changes all inputs are used and the accuracy was improved by approximately 3%.

Table 1. Layers of baseline model

Layer	Output shape	Parameters
Reshape	(1, 240, 98)	0
Dropout	(1, 240, 98)	0
Average pooling 2D	(1, 40, 98)	0
Convolution 2D	(64, 14, 98)	10304
Dropout	(64, 14, 98)	0
Max pooling 2D	(64, 7, 49)	0
Convolution 2D	(64, 7, 49)	41024
Dropout	(64, 7, 49)	0
Flatten	(21952)	0
Dense	(12)	263436

4.3   Proposed Model

The proposed model is formed by inserting the wSTFT layers to the beginning of the baseline model. Table 2 shows the wSTFT model.

The weights of convolutional layer in Table 2 are fixed, the only parameters to train in wSTFT are the STHadamard weights.

The behavior of the proposed model (*prop_model*) and two variants was analyzed. The variants are:

Table 2. Layers of wSTFT model

Layer	Output shape	Parameters
STHadamard	(480, 98)	480
Reshape	(1, 480, 98)	0
Convolution 2D	(480, 1, 98)	230400
Reshape	(2, 240, 98)	0
Square	(2, 240, 98)	0
Sum	(240, 98)	0

- *prop_model_smooth.* A penalty to high frequencies in window weights was added to the loss function.
- *prop_model_symm.* The window is forced to be symmetrical. In this case the STHadamard layer has $N/2$ parameters.

4.4 Set up

The weights of the STHadamard layer were initialized with the coefficients of a Hann window. The weights of the convolutional layer in wSTFT were initialized with the DFT coefficients. The rest of the weights were randomly initialized.

Adam (Adaptive Moment Estimation) [48] optimization method was used to train. The training ran for 150 epochs. The first 100 epochs with the parameters $\alpha = 0.001$, $\beta_1 = 0.9$ and $\beta_2 = 0.999$. In the last 50 epochs $\alpha = 0.0001$ was changed. Weights were updated in batchs sized 500.

The calculations were made on a GPU NVIDIA Titan Xp.

5 Results

The training of each model was repeated 30 times with different random seeds. Table 3 shows mean accuracies and mean relative improvements on test dataset. *Prop_model_smooth* and *Prop_model_symm* improvements are not significant. *Prop_model* improvement is small, but it is important to highlight that *Prop_model* was better than baseline model in all 30 trainings.

Table 3. Mean test accuracy and mean test relative improvement of 30 trainings.

Model	Accuracy	Rel. improvement
Baseline	0.9121	-
Prop_model	**0.9185**	**0.7%**
Prop_model_smooth	0.9130	0.1%
Prop_model_symm	0.9151	0.33%

With training dataset, proposed model and baseline model accuracies are almost the same (Fig. 4). With validation dataset the difference increases, it is similar to the difference obtained with test dataset. This means that the proposed model reduces the overfitting.

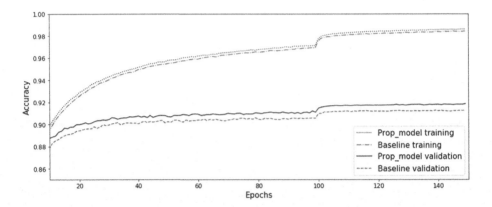

Fig. 4. Complete wSTFT model with output size of each layer.

Figure 5 shows the original and trained weights of the STHadamard layer for *prop_model*. Similar weights were obtained in all the trainings of this model. The bell becomes higher and some high and medium frequencies are added. *Prop_model_smooth* removes high frequencies from weights, but decreases accuracy. This suggests that the added frequency components are useful for classification.

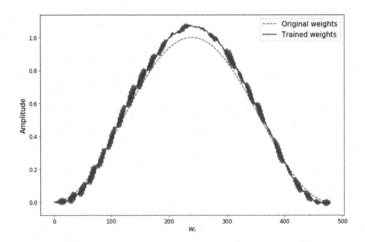

Fig. 5. Trained weights vs. original weights in STHadamard layer of *prop_model*.

6   Conclusions

First, it is concluded that it is possible to adapt the windowing coefficients with the proposed model, which implies that the gradient of the error function propagates correctly through neural calculation of the power spectrum. Second, it is concluded that the adaptation of the window function can improves the recognition performance, even in a moderate amount.

Medium and high frequencies appear added to the window in the adapted coefficients. It is unclear what role these frequencies play. It may be thought that they are adaptations to classify some particular inputs, but since the proposed model has improved the ability to generalize (reducing the overfit), it seems more possible that these added frequencies are really important in the classification task.

This approach could be applied directly to all models with power spectrum inputs. The training process is less efficient, but after training, the original model can be used changing the previous window for the trained window.

We plan to analyze in detail the changes that adaptation produces in the windowing coefficients and test this approach on other classification problems.

Acknowledgements. We gratefully acknowledge the support of NVIDIA Corporation through the NVIDIA GPU Grant Program.

References

1. Mohamed, A.R., Hinton, G., Penn, G.: Understanding how deep belief networks perform acoustic modelling. In: 2012 IEEE International Conference on Acoustics, Speech and Signal Processing (ICASSP), pp. 4273–4276. IEEE (2012)
2. Sainath, T.N., Kingsbury, B., Mohamed, A.R., Ramabhadran, B.: Learning filter banks within a deep neural network framework. In: 2013 IEEE Workshop on Automatic Speech Recognition and Understanding, pp. 297–302. IEEE (2013)
3. Sainath, T.N., Weiss, R.J., Senior, A., Wilson, K.W., Vinyals, O.: Learning the speech front-end with raw waveform CLDNNS. In: Sixteenth Annual Conference of the International Speech Communication Association (2015)
4. Hoshen, Y., Weiss, R.J., Wilson, K.W.: Speech acoustic modeling from raw multi-channel waveforms. In: 2015 IEEE International Conference on Acoustics, Speech and Signal Processing (ICASSP), pp. 4624–4628. IEEE (2015)
5. Tüske, Z., Golik, P., Schlüter, R., Ney, H.: Acoustic modeling with deep neural networks using raw time signal for LVCSR. In: Fifteenth Annual Conference of the International Speech Communication Association (2014)
6. Ghahremani, P., Hadian, H., Lv, H., Povey, D., Khudanpur, S.: Acoustic modeling from frequency domain representations of speech. In: Interspeech, pp. 1596–1600 (2018)
7. Palaz, D., Collobert, R., Doss, M.M.: Estimating phoneme class conditional probabilities from raw speech signal using convolutional neural networks. In: Interspeech, pp. 1766–1770 (2013)
8. Tripathi, A., Mohan, A., Anand, S., Singh, M.: Adversarial learning of raw speech features for domain invariant speech recognition. In: 2018 IEEE International Conference on Acoustics, Speech and Signal Processing (ICASSP), pp. 5959–5963. IEEE (2018)

9. Kim, Y., Kim, M., Goo, J., Kim, H.: Learning self-informed feature contribution for deep learning-based acoustic modeling. IEEE/ACM Trans. Audio, Speech, and Lang. Process. **26**(11), 2204–2214 (2018)
10. Guo, J., Xu, N., Chen, X., Shi, Y., Xu, K., Alwan, A.: Filter sampling and combination CNN (FSC-CNN): a compact CNN model for small-footprint ASR acoustic modeling using raw waveforms. In: Interspeech, pp. 3713–3717 (2018)
11. Menne, T., Tüske, Z., Schlüter, R., Ney, H.: Learning acoustic features from the raw waveform for automatic speech recognition. In: DEGA, pp. 1533–1536 (2018)
12. von Platen, P., Zhang, C., Woodland, P.: Multi-span acoustic modelling using raw waveform signals. In: Interspeech, pp. 1393–1397 (2019)
13. Alisamir, S., Ahadi, S.M., Seyedin, S.: An end-to-end deep learning model to recognize farsi speech from raw input. In: 2018 4th Iranian Conference on Signal Processing and Intelligent Systems (ICSPIS), pp. 1–5. IEEE (2018)
14. Takeda, R., Nakadai, K., Komatani, K.: Multi-timescale feature-extraction architecture of deep neural networks for acoustic model training from raw speech signal. In: 2018 IEEE/RSJ International Conference on Intelligent Robots and Systems (IROS), pp. 2503–2510. IEEE (2018)
15. Dubagunta, S.P., Kabil, S.H., Doss, M.M.: Improving children speech recognition through feature learning from raw speech signal. In: ICASSP 2019–2019 IEEE International Conference on Acoustics, Speech and Signal Processing (ICASSP), pp. 5736–5740. IEEE (2019)
16. Zeghidour, N., Usunier, N., Synnaeve, G., Collobert, R., Dupoux, E.: End-to-end speech recognition from the raw waveform. In: Interspeech, pp. 781–785 (2018)
17. Zeghidour, N., Usunier, N., Kokkinos, I., Schaiz, T., Synnaeve, G., Dupoux, E.: Learning filterbanks from raw speech for phone recognition. In: 2018 IEEE International Conference on Acoustics, Speech and Signal Processing (ICASSP), pp. 5509–5513. IEEE (2018)
18. Seki, H., Yamamoto, K., Nakagawa, S.: A deep neural network integrated with filterbank learning for speech recognition. In: 2017 IEEE International Conference on Acoustics, Speech and Signal Processing (ICASSP), pp. 5480–5484. IEEE (2017)
19. Sailor, H.B., Patil, H.A.: Novel unsupervised auditory filterbank learning using convolutional RBM for speech recognition. IEEE/ACM Trans. Audio, Speech, and Lang. Process. **24**(12), 2341–2353 (2016)
20. Zhu, Z., Engel, J.H., Hannun, A.: Learning multiscale features directly from waveforms. In: Interspeech, pp. 1305–1309 (2016)
21. Ravanelli, M., Bengio, Y.: Speaker recognition from raw waveform with sincnet. In: 2018 IEEE Spoken Language Technology Workshop (SLT), pp. 1021–1028. IEEE (2018)
22. Dinkel, H., Chen, N., Qian, Y., Yu, K.: End-to-end spoofing detection with raw waveform CLDNNS. In: 2017 IEEE International Conference on Acoustics, Speech and Signal Processing (ICASSP), pp. 4860–4864. IEEE (2017)
23. Muckenhirn, H., Magimai-Doss, M., Marcel, S.: End-to-end convolutional neural network-based voice presentation attack detection. In: 2017 IEEE International Joint Conference on Biometrics (IJCB), pp. 335–341. IEEE (2017)
24. Yu, H., Tan, Z.H., Zhang, Y., Ma, Z., Guo, J.: Dnn filter bank cepstral coefficients for spoofing detection. IEEE Access **5**, 4779–4787 (2017)
25. Muckenhirn, H., Magimai-Doss, M., Marcel, S.: On learning vocal tract system related speaker discriminative information from raw signal using CNNS. In: Interspeech, pp. 1116–1120 (2018)
26. Latif, S., Rana, R., Khalifa, S., Jurdak, R., Epps, J.: Direct modelling of speech emotion from raw speech. In: Interspeech, pp. 3920–3924 (2019)

27. Tzirakis, P., Zhang, J., Schuller, B.W.: End-to-end speech emotion recognition using deep neural networks. In: 2018 IEEE International Conference on Acoustics, Speech and Signal Processing (ICASSP), pp. 5089–5093. IEEE (2018)

28. Millet, J., Zeghidour, N.: Learning to detect dysarthria from raw speech. In: ICASSP 2019–2019 IEEE International Conference on Acoustics, Speech and Signal Processing (ICASSP), pp. 5831–5835. IEEE (2019)

29. Dieleman, S., Schrauwen, B.: End-to-end learning for music audio. In: 2014 IEEE International Conference on Acoustics, Speech and Signal Processing (ICASSP), pp. 6964–6968. IEEE (2014)

30. Pons Puig, J., Nieto Caballero, O., Prockup, M., Schmidt, E.M., Ehmann, A.F., Serra, X.: End-to-end learning for music audio tagging at scale. In: ISMIR, pp. 637–644. International Society for Music Information Retrieval (ISMIR) (2018)

31. Chen, N., Wang, S.: High-level music descriptor extraction algorithm based on combination of multi-channel cnns and LSTM. In: ISMIR, pp. 509–514 (2017)

32. Pons, J., Lidy, T., Serra, X.: Experimenting with musically motivated convolutional neural networks. In: 2016 14th International Workshop on Content-based Multimedia Indexing (CBMI), pp. 1–6. IEEE (2016)

33. Purwins, H., Li, B., Virtanen, T., Schlüter, J., Chang, S.Y., Sainath, T.: Deep learning for audio signal processing. IEEE J. Selected Top. Signal Process. **13**(2), 206–219 (2019)

34. Deng, L., Hinton, G., Kingsbury, B.: New types of deep neural network learning for speech recognition and related applications: an overview. In: 2013 IEEE International Conference on Acoustics, Speech and Signal Processing, pp. 8599–8603. IEEE (2013)

35. Deng, L., et al.: Recent advances in deep learning for speech research at microsoft. In: 2013 IEEE International Conference on Acoustics, Speech and Signal Processing, pp. 8604–8608. IEEE (2013)

36. Nam, J., Choi, K., Lee, J., Chou, S.Y., Yang, Y.H.: Deep learning for audio-based music classification and tagging: teaching computers to distinguish rock from bach. IEEE Signal Process. Magazine **36**(1), 41–51 (2018)

37. Harris, F.J.: On the use of windows for harmonic analysis with the discrete fourier transform. Proc. IEEE **66**(1), 51–83 (1978)

38. Phan, H., Hertel, L., Maass, M., Mertins, A.: Robust audio event recognition with 1-max pooling convolutional neural networks. In: Interspeech, pp. 3653–3657 (2016)

39. Takeda, R., Komatani, K.: Sound source localization based on deep neural networks with directional activate function exploiting phase information. In: 2016 IEEE International Conference on Acoustics, Speech and Signal Processing (ICASSP), pp. 405–409. IEEE (2016)

40. Morales-Cordovilla, J.A., Sánchez, V., Gómez, A.M., Peinado, A.M.: On the use of asymmetric windows for robust speech recognition. Circuits, Syst. and Signal Process. **31**(2), 727–736 (2012)

41. Alam, M.J., Kenny, P., O'Shaughnessy, D.: On the use of asymmetric-shaped tapers for speaker verification using i-vectors. In: Odyssey 2012-The Speaker and Language Recognition Workshop, pp. 256–262 (2012)

42. Rozman, R., Kodek, D.M.: Using asymmetric windows in automatic speech recognition. Speech Commun. **49**(4), 268–276 (2007)

43. Sahidullah, M., Saha, G.: A novel windowing technique for efficient computation of MFCC for speaker recognition. IEEE Signal Process. Lett. **20**(2), 149–152 (2012)

44. Warden, P.: Speech commands: A dataset for limited-vocabulary speech recognition. arXiv preprint arXiv:1804.03209 (2018)

45. Sainath, T.Ṅ., Parada, C.: Convolutional neural networks for small-footprint keyword spotting. In: Interspeech, pp. 1478–1482 (2015)
46. Guo, J., Kumatani, K., Sun, M., Wu, M., Raju, A., Ström, N., Mandal, A.: Time-delayed bottleneck highway networks using a dft feature for keyword spotting. In: 2018 IEEE International Conference on Acoustics, Speech and Signal Processing (ICASSP), pp. 5489–5493. IEEE (2018)
47. García, M.A., Destéfanis, E.A.: Power cepstrum calculation with convolutional neural networks. J. Comput. Sci. Technol. **19**, 132–142 (2019)
48. Kingma, D.P., Ba, J.: Adam: A method for stochastic optimization. arXiv preprint arXiv:1412.6980 (2014)

Correction to: Cloud Computing, Big Data & Emerging Topics

Enzo Rucci⬥, Marcelo Naiouf⬥, Franco Chichizola⬥,
and Laura De Giusti⬥

Correction to:
E. Rucci et al. (Eds.): *Cloud Computing, Big Data & Emerging Topics*, **CCIS 1291, https://doi.org/10.1007/978-3-030-61218-4**

Some errors were present in the originally published bookfrontmatter. The following modifications were made:

The affiliations for editors Enzo Rucci, Marcelo Naiouf, and Franco Chichizola have been corrected as "III-LIDI, Facultad de Informatica Universidad Nacional de La Plata, La Plata, Argentina".

The updated version of the book can be found at
https://doi.org/10.1007/978-3-030-61218-4

Author Index

Printed in the United States
By Bookmasters